A Reader's Guide to
Gerard Manley Hopkins

A Reader's Guide to
Gerard Manley Hopkins

Norman H. MacKenzie

CORNELL UNIVERSITY PRESS

Ithaca, New York

First published 1981 by Cornell University Press
First printing, Cornell Paperbacks, 1981

International Standard Book Number (cloth) 0–8014–1349–4
International Standard Book Number (paper) 0–8014–9221–1

Library of Congress Catalog Card Number 80–69275

Printed and bound in Great Britain

Contents

Preface

The 'Hopkins Country', famous for its unique organic inscapes, continues to attract numerous new readers every year. To enrich their experience many books of varying excellence have been written – theoretical analyses, organizing him into such regions as Ignatian and Scotist, or historical surveys, tracing the broad features of his syntax and concepts into areas before or after his own.

But to the man on foot, healthily determined to follow the poet's trail, such historical or linguistic 'geographies' seldom supply the mile-by-mile directions he needs. It is for him that *A Reader's Guide to Gerard Manley Hopkins* is intended, designed like its predecessors in this series to accompany the author through his poems in more or less chronological sequence. The territory, too rugged for the taste of his own contemporaries, is on that account all the more inviting to us today. Among the fully finished mature poems there are many still curiously underestimated and comparatively neglected. Others again offer an exhilarating challenge to the experienced and for them special aid has been here provided.

To keep this book within general reach (another objective of these *Reader's Guides*), the less frequented early and unfinished pieces have been mapped on a smaller scale. Yet by recommending little known ways of approach and drawing attention to aspects easily overlooked these more cursory notes should still serve a useful purpose. As the only full edition of the Poems (the Oxford Fourth edition) is published in an inexpensive paperback, this Guide, which refers to all Hopkins's original pieces, has been keyed to its numbering. Those with other collections of the major poems, however, should have no difficulty in using it.

Besides the textual commentary there is an introductory outline of Hopkins's life and interests, while in an alphabetical appendix a Reference Section provides brief sketches of people (the poet's main correspondents and Duns Scotus), along with compressed interpretations of his coinages or prosodic innovations (e.g., 'counterpoint', 'curtal sonnets', 'outrides', 'overreaving'), where the accepted definitions are re-examined in the light of actual practice revealed by the manuscripts. It also includes definitions of other terms relating to poetry.

Hopkins shares with the more sensitive of the Victorians many of that age's virtues. He contends for the preservation of the wilderness, the environment then being 'seared with trade' around him as England grew smokily rich. He shows genuine astonishment over the infinitely varied adaptations to be found among the distinctive species of plant and animal life (a wonder which we, with our greater though insufficient biological knowledge, can readily appreciate). The artist-naturalist alternates and co-exists with the priest throughout his poems in a balanced polarity. His sonnets often lead us from an octave of delight in nature to its corollary of reverence for the Maker, but he does not wing-clip his windhover into a merely symbolic theological bird.

These things we can spontaneously enjoy with him. More conscious but equally rewarding effort is required in matters where this Guide should assist – in recognizing the heritage of wisdom and literary grace from the Greek and Roman writers whom he studied and taught; the Biblical, liturgical, and devotional classics which shaped his phrases; the ideas, customs and even landscapes of Victorian Britain which echo in his works. If we ignore these in favour of some updated reassessment we may be substituting our own passing values for his in a sort of trans-cultural myopia. Yet where we ourselves most differ outwardly from our predecessors Hopkins often anticipates our recoil. He is not as impressed as his fellow-Victorians are by sheer bulk or surface decoration, in that period of three-volume novels and multi-volume poems, over-stuffed furniture and hooped petticoats. His phrases and verse-structures combine compactness with strength, concentrating upon weight-bearing words and avoiding loose grammatical fill. He can communicate mysteriously, sometimes through words drawn from a one-man dialect to which no complete glossary yet exists.

Because he prefers to suggest powerfully rather than to state in precise and delimiting terms, his lines may mean contrasting things to different people and arouse sharp controversies in an arena of imagery where no final umpire can issue rulings. I have seldom glanced at these disputes, except with a few poems written in Wales. Inevitably those of us whose first pleasure in Hopkins dates back many years will have established for ourselves or picked up from others particular readings of the text which tend now to seem canonical. While writing the *Reader's Guide*, however, to preserve my own zest and arouse it in others I attempted to relive freshly the events and statements of each poem, setting them in as total a context as length allowed. To have included all the explanations for every passage, each labelled with the name of its first propounder, besides being utterly impossible in the room allotted me would have turned the poems into dead monuments. One remembers the headmaster in a Samuel Butler novel, whose *Meditations upon the Epistle and Character of St. Jude* was so thorough that no one who read it ever wanted to meditate on them again.

Since comprehensiveness was precluded by space, it seemed better not to repeat what had already been well said in studies widely available. The bibliography of books on Hopkins, and the severely restricted cross-references to other treatments which could be included in the body of this work, together represent a most grateful if inadequate acknowledgement of my indebtedness. I hope that they will induce deeper study. In Tom Dunne's *Comprehensive Bibliography* there are classified lists of some two thousand items up to 1969–70 (including journal articles) on particular poems or topics. The pioneer expositors of Hopkins who were published in the forties (Gardner, the Kenyon Critics, Leavis, Peters, Pick, and contributors to *Immortal Diamond*, e.g.) so shaped my attitudes that although I have tried to assess each poem freshly some of their ideas probably figure in my mind as my own. For all of us the original editors of Hopkins's works (Bridges, Abbott, House, Devlin and Storey) have smoothed the approach: our debt to them is profound. I have made frequent use also of the facts provided by Father Alfred Thomas's valuable *Hopkins the Jesuit*, and the Dilligan and Bender *Hopkins Concordance*.

I would like to thank those to whose encouragement and constant assistance I have owed most while this and other Hopkins volumes have been maturing – though none of them must be held responsible for the opinions here advanced, nor for any slips in fact or doctrine. The Society of Jesus, through successive editors of *The Month*, has given permission for quotations from the published works of Hopkins, and has very kindly released the unpublished variants of the poems and uncollected prose. Three Masters of Campion Hall have in turn offered me the stimulating fellowship of Jesuit scholars during many periods of residence there since 1962. I have been welcomed at St Beuno's, Stonyhurst, St Francis Xavier's in Liverpool, and by the Irish Fathers in Dublin and Clongowes Wood. May I particularly name Fathers Ronald Moffat, Deryck Hanshell, David Hoy, E. J. Yarnold, Benjamin Winterborn, Fergal McGrath, Seán Ó Catháin, and the late Father Basil Fitzgibbon. Father Peter Milward has unselfishly spared time to check the accuracy of my phrasing on doctrinal and other matters: this book would have been more imperfect without his keen eye. Father Anthony Bischoff has been ready at all times to share with me his knowledge, though my interpretation of the facts may sometimes differ from his. Special thanks are due to Mr Ronald Browne for his assistance while he was in charge of the Writers' Library at Farm Street. From the Bodleian Library, particularly through Dr David Rogers, I have received many favours and exceptional helpfulness. My colleagues at Queen's, notably Drs George Whalley and John Stedmond, have given me much aid and advice. Among doctoral students with whom as supervisor I have had a pleasant reciprocal relationship, I must mention Dr Michael Moore for his exploration of further affinities between Hopkins and Newman.

This *Reader's Guide* and my parallel work would not have been possible without the generous assistance of the former owner of much unpublished Hopkins material, the late Edward Lord Bridges, who for some years placed at my disposal Hopkins's autograph poems (MS *A*) along with manuscript collections of letters to and from Hopkins, and who answered queries when I was abroad with a miraculous promptitude – an indication of a keen interest which the present Lord Bridges maintains.

My many return visits to Britain and research expenses have been financed first by the liberality of the Canada Council and more recently by the Social Science and Humanities Research Council, to both of whom I return my sincere thanks. During the final revisions and production of the book I had the privilege of a Killam Senior Research Fellowship.

Finally, my wife Rita and daughter Catherine have given me moral support and practical assistance without which my researches would have foundered: I offer them my deep gratitude. Catherine's exacting and meticulous study of the evolution of Hopkins's handwriting, pursued in her spare time over a period of many years, has greatly assisted me in assigning probable dates to the large number of undated manuscripts.

Norman H. MacKenzie
Queen's University at Kingston, Ontario

Abbreviated Titles of Hopkins's Works

The standard editions, and the titles by which they are quoted in this book are:

Poems *The Poems of Gerard Manley Hopkins*, 4th edn, ed. W. H. Gardner and N. H. MacKenzie, Oxford University Press, 1970

Letters *The Letters of Gerard Manley Hopkins to Robert Bridges*, ed. C. C. Abbott, Oxford University Press, rev. 1955

Correspondence *The Correspondence of Gerard Manley Hopkins and Richard Watson Dixon*, ed. C. C. Abbott, Oxford University Press, rev. 1955

Further Letters *Further Letters of Gerard Manley Hopkins*, ed. C. C. Abbott, Oxford University Press, enlarged 2nd edn, 1956

Journals *The Journals and Papers of Gerard Manley Hopkins*, ed. Humphry House and Graham Storey, Oxford University Press, 1959

Sermons *The Sermons and Devotional Writings of Gerard Manley Hopkins*, ed. Christopher Devlin (S.J.), Oxford University Press, 1959

Other Abbreviations

OED *Oxford English Dictionary*
PMLA *Publications of the Modern Language Association of America*
TLS *Times Literary Supplement*

Some Notes on Hopkins's Life and Interests

1844 Gerard Manley Hopkins was born on 28 July at Stratford (Essex), but as this district was becoming increasingly industrialized and part of London, in 1852 his parents moved to the more fashionable and airy suburb of Hampstead, on the northern fringe of the city. Gerard was both the eldest and the most artistic of a gifted family. His father, Manley, an earnest Anglican, was a successful marine insurance adjuster, author of well-known practical handbooks for owners and masters of ships (yet with unexpectedly learned references to Greek and Latin), who also produced some volumes of verse in which piety, sentiment and humour jostled each other (see *Journals*, pp. 330–2). Gerard was delighted with Ruskin's technique and nature-descriptions and, like his brothers Arthur and Everard who became professional artists, hoped at first to be a painter. Reproductions of his sketches are given in Thornton's *All My Eyes See*, pp. 114 ff, and *Journals*, pp. 453 ff. He also shared an interest in music with his youngest sister Grace, but though he later composed melodies for poems he did not master either piano or violin.

1854–63 He attended Highgate Grammar School, mostly as a boarder. R. W. Dixon, who afterwards became a warm literary friend, was for a short time one of his teachers and encouraged his love for Keats (see their volume of *Correspondence*). After winning the Headmaster's Poetry Prize in 1860 with 'The Escorial' and being made a prefect, Hopkins crowned his school career with the Governors' Gold Medal for Latin Verse, and an Exhibition from Highgate as well as a Balliol College Exhibition.

1863 (April)–67 (June) He read Greek and Latin at Oxford, and wrote poems (Nos 5–24, and 80–133). Some were experimental or imitative: many remained fragmentary, being little more than detailed observations of nature along Pre-Raphaelite lines (see Heuser, *The Shaping Vision*). Others showed deep religious yearnings or misgivings, with hints of his future originality. He came under the influence, first of the Anglican High Church (Oxford Movement), with Pusey and Liddon, and then of the great Catholic John Henry Newman (*Apologia*, 1864). His distinguished teachers included Walter Pater and Benjamin Jowett. Among his friends were William Addis, Robert Bridges, E. H. Coleridge (grandson of the Romantic poet), and Mowbray Baillie: letters to Bridges and Baillie form a significant part of his surviving correspondence (see *Letters to Bridges* and *Further Letters*). Some of his undergraduate essays have been published (see e.g. *Journals*, pp. 74–130). In December 1864 he obtained a First in Moderations, the philological element in which is reflected in his early diary jottings (see especially *Journals*, pp. 4–16, and notes on his intelligent etymological conjectures, pp. 499–527).

1866 He was finally convinced of the Catholic position in July, and was received into the Roman Church by Newman in October.

1867 He completed his B.A.(Hons) degree with a First in Greats (June) and from September till the next April he taught in Newman's Oratory School near Birmingham. Having decided to enter a religious order, he burned some copies of his poems as a symbolic gesture (May 1868), but sent corrected copies of his best work to Bridges for safe keeping: he wrote no further poems except when asked to by his superiors until 1875. His account of a strenuous July spent hiking and climbing among the Swiss Alps makes excellent reading (*Journals*, pp. 168–84).

1868 (September)–70 In the Jesuit Novitiate, Manresa House, Roehampton, south-west London, overlooking the open heaths and beautiful wooded slopes of Richmond Park with its two thousand acres. From these two formative years of strictly disciplined religious life only eleven journal pages have come down to us (pp. 189–200).

1870 (September)–73 At St Mary's Hall, Stonyhurst, near the River Hodder, between the Lancashire fells and the dappled moors of Yorkshire. Here he received lectures (in Latin) on scholastic philosophy, logic and ethics, with some mathematics and mechanics. His views of God and the inscapes of nature became strongly coloured by the teachings of the medieval philosopher Duns Scotus (d. 1308), through an old black-letter volume of his Oxford *Sentences* written in Latin which he found in the philosophers' library at Stonyhurst. The Jesuits preferred the more traditional philosophy of St Thomas Aquinas. Summer excursions to Scotland and the Isle of Man enliven his *Journals* (pp. 213ff, 221ff, 234ff).

1873 (September)–74 During this year he was Professor of Rhetoric at Manresa House, instructing 'Juniors' in the equivalent of VIth Form and Intermediate B.A. studies. A few surviving lecture notes (*Journals*, pp. 267–90) use his theory of inscape to define poetry and verse, and contain brilliant speculations on prosody from which the concept of Sprung Rhythm was soon to emerge.

1874 (September)–77 (October) He studied theology at St Beuno's College, overlooking the lovely valley of the Elwy and the Clwyd, North Wales. His extant journals unfortunately end in mid-sentence on 7 February 1875. That December the wrecking of the *Deutschland*, in which five nuns exiled from Germany were among the many drowned, provoked him into poetry which after seven fallow years was revolutionary in its diction and Sprung Rhythm. Though the Jesuit journal *The Month* refused his ode as too difficult for their readers, Hopkins had another poem, 'The Silver Jubilee', published by his Order and he felt free to resume the composing of verse. His other poems written in Wales are among his most lyrical, 'The Windhover' being the most famous (see Nos 28–40 and 57). They incorporate imitations of Welsh *cynghanedd* (multiple alliteration), which he discovered for himself as he enterprisingly learned Welsh. Bridges continued to preserve the autograph poems sent him, in a fine old album (MS *A*), and later (1883) transcribed them into another album (MS *B*) for circulation among friends. But he and Canon Dixon constituted most of Hopkins's 'public' during much of his lifetime. In September 1877 Hopkins was ordained priest.

1877 (October)–78 This was spent in teaching and miscellaneous parish work at Mount St Mary's College, near Sheffield. Here he wrote 'The Loss of the Eurydice' (No. 41), and met the two brothers described in No. 54. He was transferred to Stonyhurst in April 1878 to coach undergraduates, and there composed 'The May Magnificat' (No. 42) for Our Lady's Gallery, only to be told that it was not good enough to exhibit.

1878 (**July–November**) Temporarily appointed Special Preacher at Farm Street, the Jesuit church in London's West End, he did not come up to expectations.

1878–79 He was in Oxford, assisting the parish priest for nearly a year, though mostly in the poorer fringes of the town and at the barracks. Poems written in Oxford include Nos 43 to 51 ('Binsey Poplars', 'Duns Scotus's Oxford', etc.). See also *Sermons*, pp. 3–25.

1879 (October to 30 December) To his surprise, he found himself in stimulating parish work at Bedford Leigh, near Manchester, a town blackened by foundries, coal pits and steel mills, but with a cheerful and responsive Catholic congregation. See 'At the Wedding March' (No. 52), and his vigorous addresses, *Sermons*, pp. 26–49.

1880–81 (August) This happy spell was immediately followed by exhausting parish work in the Liverpool slums which severely taxed his stamina; but on quite a few Sundays he preached eloquently in the huge church of St Francis Xavier's (*Sermons*, pp. 50–104). However, he composed only a few poems in twenty months (Nos 53–5), though these include 'Felix Randal' and the haunting lyric 'Spring and Fall'.

1881 (August to October) He was given a change of scene if not of work, among Glasgow slums. A hurried excursion to Loch Lomond produced 'Inversnaid' (No. 56).

1881 (October)–82 (August) Relief came with his Tertianship, ten months of religious meditation and devotional study, spent in Manresa House, Roehampton, south-west London. His notes on the *Spiritual Exercises of St. Ignatius* illuminate many of his poems (see *Sermons*, pp. 107–209, 238–52). He took his final vows as Spiritual Co-adjutor in the Society of Jesus in August 1882.

1882–84 (February) At Stonyhurst College, Lancashire, teaching Latin and Greek to their most advanced students (equivalent to undergraduates) for University of London (external) examinations. See *Letters*, pp. 151–2, and the commentary on 'Ribblesdale' (No. 58) for descriptions of the school and its environs at this time. Other Stonyhurst poems are Nos 59 and 60.

1884–89 were spent in Ireland, as Professor of Greek and Latin Literature at University College, Dublin. He taught Latin and Greek to small classes, but shared responsibility as Fellow in Classics in the Royal University of Ireland for examining the scripts of candidates from other colleges, at all levels from hordes of would-be matriculants up to M.A.s. These examinations (which occurred five or six times a year and could produce as many as five hundred papers) proved a nightmare to him, combining with his sense of exile to produce serious depression in health and spirits. Yet the poems of desperation he composed (the 'Dark Sonnets' or 'Sonnets of Desolation' – see article preceding No. 64) have appealed strongly to readers in our own age familiar with modern existential anguish and the energy of despair. Among more buoyant poems written during spells away from Dublin are 'Tom's Garland' and 'Harry Ploughman' (Nos 70, 71). Between gruelling sessions of examining he visited Connemara, sailed under the Cliffs of Moher, forgot the oppressiveness of his work among kind friends at Monasterevan and Howth, and even paid brief holiday visits to England, Scotland and Wales. He met W. B. Yeats, but found him too uncertain of himself at twenty-one to be impressive. 'That Nature is a Heraclitean Fire' (No. 72), written in July 1888, shows Hopkins's capacity to surmount physical debility and melancholia. Yet less than a year later he succumbed to typhoid fever (June 1889) and was buried in Dublin. Bridges acted swiftly to prevent any surviving drafts or autograph poems being thrown away. He arranged for a few to be published, but, concluding that the public was not yet ready to welcome Hopkins's daring innovations, he postponed the issue of the First Edition until 1918. Since the Second Edition of 1930 the poetry of Hopkins has been in such increasing demand that it is still constantly reprinted, while expository articles and entire volumes devoted to him have passed the two thousand mark. The *Reader's Guide to Gerard Manley Hopkins* is, however, the result of my conviction that a great deal which is of basic importance in the study of his poems remains to be said.

Further Reading on Hopkins's Life
A forty-page outline of his career introduces my book on Hopkins (Edinburgh, 1968). There is a full-length biography by Bernard Bergonzi (1977). Father Alfred Thomas, S.J., in *Hopkins the Jesuit* (1969), has thrown much light on his years of training through scholarly research in Jesuit archives.

Part One　　EARLY POEMS

'The Escorial' to 'Rosa Mystica' (Nos 1–27)

The poems in this section of the Fourth Edition, like the experiments in Section III, were written before Hopkins reached his full stature as a poet with 'The Wreck of the Deutschland' (1875–6); and, therefore, in the plan of the Oxford English Texts edition they are intermingled with them in an attempt at chronological sequence. The limitations of that greatly improved arrangement, however, may be illustrated from the fact that 'A Soliloquy of One of the Spies . . .' (No. 5), and fragments of *Floris in Italy* (No. 102) were in process of composition from July 1864 to September 1865, thus between them overlapping more than fifty other poems (Nos 6–18 and 83–125). Specialists who wish to study these poems chronologically are urged to do so in the context provided by his early notebooks or diaries, reproduced in the *Journals* (pp. 3–73), carefully edited by Humphry House and Graham Storey.

But for the less specialized student of Hopkins the separation of the more complete poems from his studio exercises has decided advantages. The fragments and less finished poems in Section III greatly outnumber those gathered here, and as they were never intended for publication in this state, they would dilute the impression of strength which a general reader would gather from those in Section I. Moreover, no fewer than nineteen of the first twenty-seven poems concern the most important factor in Hopkins's life, early and late – his faith. It is surely significant that so large a proportion of poetic attempts which he was sufficiently interested in to complete were religious. Among those left unfinished or unpolished, on the other hand, two thirds of the pages they occupy (111–75) essay the common poet's repertoire of love poems, narratives, embryo plays, thumb-nail nature notes, satiric epigrams and so on – though again some of the ones sustained to greatest length deal with his own highest aspirations or with conflicts involving the spirit. Since both sections are almost entirely pre-Jesuit in origin, the higher vitality of his religious themes argues strongly against the once popular view that Hopkins's natural poetic gifts were throttled and diverted when he entered the Society of Jesus. Engaging though his secular experiments are (and the reader is invited to see the new analysis of them in Part III below) they do not, by and large, possess the same personal conviction and thrust as these in the opening portion of the volume.

The earliest surviving poem, 'The Escorial' (No. 1), is a remarkable effort for a boy of fifteen, and though it inevitably has echoes from earlier poets, it is more attractive and original than a number of prize-winning poems from Oxford or Cambridge during the '60s. 'A Vision of the Mermaids' (No. 2) is less visionary than its title would suggest: it contains accurate pen-sketches of fantastic little sea-creatures introduced to Englishmen by such means as the Marine Vivarium opened in Regent's Park, London, in 1853. Then come two poems characterizing unseasonable weather (Nos 3 and 4). Among other examples of non-religious verse are the two sonnets 'To Oxford' (No. 12), celebrating a genuine affection, and three conventional and imitative ones, 'The Beginning of the End' (No. 14) – how little of Hopkins went into these three may be seen by comparing them with 'Where art thou friend' (No. 13).

And finally in this secular category we have 'The Nightingale' (No. 21). Whereas among his experiments (as my analysis will show) there are numerous ineffectual efforts to use his rich accumulation of descriptive detail, in this narrative monologue Hopkins interests us sufficiently in the tale of a woman lying anxiously awake on a midsummer night, while her love faces danger offshore, to make us attend to the minutely reported sounds she hears while waiting in vain for his returning footsteps. If we remain a little aloof, it is perhaps because the poet failed to make credible the discrepancy between the still weather on land and the storminess of the sea beside it: his elaborate sensory environment does not fit the accompanying plot.

The religious poems (Nos 6 to 9, 11, 16) begin in Anglo-Catholic manner with 'Barnfloor and Winepress' (No. 6), published in *The Union Review*, the journal of an international ecumenical society, the Association for the Promotion of the Unity of Christendom. This had grown from its thirty-four founding members in 1857 to over seven thousand by 1864 (including nearly a thousand Catholics and about three hundred members of the Eastern Orthodox Church). 'See how Spring opens' (No. 17) contains the first of his concealed references to a late discovered truth (cf. No. 19, l. 9): no compromise now seems possible with the claims of Rome to his allegiance – he can no longer rest in 'The Half-way House' of the English church (No. 20). Much the finest of these early poems is 'The Habit of Perfection' (No. 22), examined in some depth below since its use of language is as resonant as in some of the best poems of his maturity. It foreshadows his future development more accurately than the derivative rotundities of the piece that follows, 'Nondum' (No. 23), though his mastery of a public style there appears impressive. Other anticipations of mature subjects emerge in his two delightful poems on the virgin martyr St Dorothea (Nos 10 and 25). We may compare the centrality of the 'tall nun' in his account of the wreck of the *Deutschland* (No. 28), and his long sustained interest in St Winefred and (now St) Margaret Clitheroe (Nos 59, 139, 145, 152, 175).

The section of Early Poems ends with two poems impossible to date with accuracy, 'Ad Mariam' (No. 26) and 'Rosa Mystica' (No. 27). Though written when he was already a Jesuit, probably in the early '70s, they have none of the linguistic profundity of his mature verse discussed in the main section of this *Reader's Guide*.

No. 1 The Escorial Dated Easter 1860, and composed in Spenserian stanzas, it won the Highgate School Poetry Prize. The headmaster gave his boys the challenge of writing on the subject set for the Oxford Newdigate Prize that year. So little was known in England about the Escorial that Hopkins provided notes (printed *Poems*, pp. 245–6), an expedient to which the Oxford prize-winner (John Addington Symonds) was also to resort, though it was most unusual among competitors. The boy's chief sources were Richard Ford's *Handbook for Travellers in Spain* (London, 2 vols, 1845) and William Prescott's *History of the Reign of Philip* *the Second*, Vol. II, just published (London, 1859). Both authors criticized Spanish Catholics from an English Protestant viewpoint. Hopkins mirrored this attitude, and many of his descriptive phrases are also carefully based on details in these two works. The Escorial, built (1563–84) by Philip II among severe mountains thirty miles west of Madrid, was a cloister for the Hieronymites, a palace (till 1861), and a royal mausoleum (st. 1). Its ground-plan was said to represent the gridiron on which St Lawrence was martyred (sts 2, 3).

No. 2 A Vision of the Mermaids Written Christmas 1862, three months before he entered Oxford. This dreamy, fanciful poem crowds together rich detail from his classical studies, from direct observation (e.g. a sunset both described and sketched for the headpiece – reproduced *Poems*, facing p. 8), and from sea-creatures he found in rock-pools or saw under a microscope or in aquariums (then newly popular).

No. 3 Winter with the Gulf Stream Early version was published in *Once a Week*, 14 February 1863 (see *Further Letters*, pp. 16, 437). Westerly winds in December had brought warm air from the Gulf Stream, producing what newspapers called a Christmas summer. See also Jerome Bump, *Victorian Poetry*, Vol. 12, No. 1, Spring 1974, p. 40ff. The tetrameters are arranged in a *terza rima* pattern (*aba, bcb*, etc.). The poem closes (as the previous one had opened) at sunset, with an imaginative interpretation of the western sky 'Where yonder crimson fireball sets'. The 'yellow brim' of Pactolus refers to the gold dust deposited on its shores by that little Lydian stream.

No. 4 Spring and Death Undated, but the handwriting suggests 1863. In tetrameter couplets, some iambic, some trochaic, following Milton's 'Il Penseroso' (see notes to 'Il Mystico', No. 77). It seems a companion piece to No. 3, being exactly the same length, but presenting as a dream a fall-like spring instead of the realities of a mild winter.

No. 5 A Soliloquy of One of the Spies left in the Wilderness The poem was skilfully rearranged by Humphry House from stanzas scattered over nearly sixty pages of the first Oxford diary (July to

August 1864). The title is supplied from *Further Letters*, p. 213. See Numbers (chaps 13 and 14) for the scaremonger reports that Canaan was defended by giants, brought to the Israelites in the desert by ten pusillanimous spies. They wished they were back in Egypt, safe though in slavery.

No. 6 Barnfloor and Winepress A metaphysical religious poem, printed (autumn) 1865 in *The Union Review*, a High Church journal favouring the reunion of the Anglican, Catholic and Eastern Orthodox communions.

No. 7 New Readings An earlier draft dates from July 1864. Closely related to No. 6 in theme and imagery, it plays with literal and spiritual interpretations to show Christ fruitful where His parables seem to predict barrenness.

No. 8 'He hath abolished the old drouth' July 1864. This piece contains reminiscences of the psalms as translated in the *Book of Common Prayer* (l. 4 from Ps. 40: 3; ll. 16, 17 from Ps. 65: 14). See S. W. Dawson, *Essays in Criticism*, 19, 1969, pp. 100–2. The fact that he has adopted the final tone and image, as well as the octosyllabic metre and irregular rhyme-scheme of Christina Rossetti's 'The Convent Threshold' (reprinted Hopkins *Poems*, pp. 346–50) might suggest that these lines were an intended continuation (cf. No. 120), or it was being paralleled to cover a personal situation. At this point he had entered in his notebook only ll. 122–36 of his reply to that poem, 'A Voice from the World' (No. 81).

No. 9 Heaven-Haven: *A nun takes the veil* Earliest draft July 1864. Other versions are entitled 'Rest' and 'Fair Havens – The Nunnery' (printed *Poems*, p. 248). The green pastures and still waters of Psalm 23: 2 are blended beautifully with Tennyson's 'island-valley of Avilion' ('Morte d'Arthur', ll. 259–60; contr. 140–1), and Elysian fields (Homer, *Od*. iv. 562 ff). See E. Mellown, *Victorian Poetry*, Vol. 8, No. 3, Autumn 1970, pp. 263–5. This poem is immediately followed in his notebook (as in the traditional academic exercise, but here both carry conviction) by one in the same verse form breathing the opposite aspiration, to freedom and adventure: 'I must hunt down the prize/Where my heart lists' (No.

88). This urge, reminiscent of Tennyson's 'Ulysses', is also expressed through two images: the desire to scale the mountain tops (the magnified shadow of the eagle recalls the famous Brocken spectre) and the call of the lonely polar wastes. Neither Pole had been reached in 1864.

No. 10 For a Picture of St Dorothea About November 1864. St Dorothea was a Christian virgin of Caesarea, tortured by the Governor (Sabricius or Fabricius) for refusing to worship idols and marry. Condemned to be beheaded (*c*. 303), she exclaimed that in the garden of Paradise grew roses and apples (quinces, l. 9). Tauntingly asked to bring him some by Theophilus the protonotary, she agreed. And though it was winter, presently a fair angel (Hopkins suggests St Dorothea in angelic form) appeared bringing them in a basket. Theophilus was converted by the miracle and was himself martyred. See other treatments in No. 25 and Appendix A (*Poems*, p. 344), a dramatic version.

No. 11 Easter Communion Lent 1865. That year Lent began March 1. A final version of this sonnet, sent to his friend Addis, has not survived. For comments on austerities practised by High Anglicans (e.g. the use of hair shirts and the scourge or 'discipline') see Meriol Trevor, *Newman: The Pillar of the Cloud* (London, 1962) pp. 332–3.

Nos 12 and 119 To Oxford Three 'love' sonnets addressed to Oxford, the first two composed Low Sunday and Monday, 1865 (i.e. 23–4 April). The second one describes an unidentified chapel, the specially ornamental ridge-crest of which had circular holes and flag shaped serrations along its top edge. A similar ridge adorns a building now in the Oxford Union courtyard. The third sonnet (entered about 26 June) was unfinished (No. 119).

No. 13 'Where art thou friend, whom I shall never see' Entered in notebook about 26 April 1865. A sonnet pleading with a friend whom he had not met to accept Christ's love. If intended for Digby Dolben (1848–67 – his name and address occur on the page before the poem), as House suggested (*Journals*, pp. 325–6), the sonnet must predate his meeting with Dolben February 1865.

No. 14 The Beginning of the End 6–8 May 1865. Three conventional sonnets, 'a neglected lover's address to his mistress', derived from sixteenth-century literature rather than experience.

No. 15 The Alchemist in the City Entered about 15 May 1865. Through the mouthpiece of a medieval alchemist striving in vain to create gold in his tower-top laboratory, the poet expresses his sense of the futility of his Oxford undergraduate studies (cf. *Further Letters*, p. 250) or the lack of promise in his art. His lament that he has nothing to show for his labours reflects both the loneliness of the artist, and a personal feeling of being a misfit among the crowds. He ends with a Romantic yearning to escape to the solitude of the wilderness, no matter how bleak.

No. 16 'Myself unholy' Sonnet, about 24 June 1865. The poet contrasts his 'purer' friends with himself: they are bright doves next to his black rook, pure streams against his shallow salt lagoon (or in a variant, white clouds by day compared with 'furnace-eaten regions coaly', either palls of factory smoke or perhaps the profoundly black burnt-out 'Coal-sacks' of the night sky). Yet none is a faultless paragon: only on Christ can he rely.

No. 17 'See how Spring opens with disabling cold' Sonnet, 26 June 1865. The imagery is of winter wheat, sown in autumn (by the Sower of Luke 8 – the Gospel reading for 25 June in the *Book of Common Prayer*), but now retarded by a chill spring (his anti-Catholic upbringing and wasted opportunities?). For a year before his reception into the Roman Church he was virtually a Catholic; verbal parallels in a letter of September 1865 suggest that the field of truth to which his feet should have been led (ll. 9, 14) was the Catholic faith (*Further Letters*, pp. 26, 226–7). The influence of Milton is obvious in the form (octave running into sestet), vocabulary (e.g. *uncouth*, l. 12), and imagery (cf. Milton's *Sonnet* VII).

No. 18 'My prayers must meet a brazen heaven' 7 September 1865. See Deut. 28: 23, 'thy heaven . . . shall be brass, and the earth . . . iron'. His cries to God echo back as from a brazen dome. Cf. *Journals*, p. 212 and n. 1.

No. 19 'Let me be to Thee as the circling bird' Sonnet, about 22 October 1865. The poet turns from varied alluring songs to the one 'authentic cadence' (a disguised allusion to infallible Catholic teaching). At least ten of the terms have technical uses in ecclesiastical music (e.g. *authentic, dominant, range*). The bird of line 1 may be the greenfinch, whose bat-like circular display flight and monotonous call when circling or sitting are identifying characteristics.

No. 20 The Half-way House About 22–6 October 1865. Title comes from Newman's statement in *Apologia* (ed. Svaglic, pp. 185, 422, quoted by Alison Sulloway, p. 18) that Anglicanism was the half-way house on the road to Rome. Instead of the treacherous broken Egyptian *reed* (Isaiah 36: 6, here Anglicanism), the poet chooses the Good Shepherd's *rod* (Ps. 23: 4) or *rood* (the Cross): Victorian philologists treated all three words as related.

No. 21 The Nightingale Dated 18, 19 January 1866, like No. 22, with which its romantic tone makes a surprising contrast. The stanza form gains interest from the shortened fourth line and ingenious rhyme scheme. As in many popular medieval lyrics the speaker is a woman.

No. 22 The Habit of Perfection Dated 18, 19 January 1866. Of all Hopkins's early poems, this is the most enduring and verbally complex – e.g. *Habit* suggests both 'robes' (cf. st. 7) and regularity of endeavour. Though it opens in a pastoral mode, it rejects the delights of all the senses in turn as strenuously as Marlowe's 'Passionate Shepherd' had sought them ('Come live with me'; the model for Hopkins's No. 124). Stanza 1 establishes the paradoxical tone as the poet welcomes into the spirals of an invisible inward ear unheard spiritual music (cf. Eliot's *Burnt Norton*, I). In stanza 2 the warnings against idle gossip found in books on Christian perfection such as *The Imitation of Christ* are expressed in Keatsian synaesthesia as '*Shape* nothing, lips; be *lovely*-dumb'. Behind stanza 3 lies the Platonic exaltation of true vision over the distractions of physical sight: 'The soul when using the body as an instrument of perception, . . . sight or hearing or some other sense . . . is then dragged by the body into the region of the changeable, and wanders and is confused; the world spins round her, and she is like a drunkard' (*Phaedo*, 79c, trans. by Hopkins's tutor, Jowett). The *Lux Increata* of the Neoplatonists contrasts with the created light of Genesis 1: 3. The palate, thought of anciently as the vaulted palace of taste, is demoted in stanza 4 to a mere rabbit hutch. After a fast, the cleansed tongue will greet fresh water and bread as a banquet. Rare and costly perfumes stir up and sustain pride (st. 5), whereas incense may draw the worshipper to the Eucharist at the altar. Stanza 6 originally began 'Feeling voluptuous hands, and feet/That love the yield of plushy grass'. He disparages Nature in this world (the primrose leaf has a velvety underside) in favour of the New Jerusalem in the next world with its street of pure gold (Rev. 21: 21). But on earth the hands of the priest may take the Lord, present in the consecrated elements, from His house, the Tabernacle (in which the Host is reserved) – the height of privilege to which human hands can aspire. The last stanza may be paralleled from Matthew 6: 28–9 and the 'Prayer for Poverty' recited by all Franciscan novices: 'O Lord Jersus, show me the way of Thy very dear poverty . . . , have pity on me and on Lady Poverty, for I am tormented for love of her'.

In its sensuous dismissal of the senses, this reverberating lyric resembles in some ways the Spanish mystics such as St John of the Cross. As John Pick wisely observes of this wonderful early poem, it scarcely matters whether Hopkins was caught in 'that puritanism . . . which is really manichean in its implications' or was 'starting on the purgative path of a true asceticism' (*Priest and Poet*, p. 51).

No. 23 Nondum Lent 1866 (it began 14 February). The title recalls Matthew 16: 9 in the Vulgate, 'Do you *not yet* understand . . .?' Though Hopkins had discounted the impact of science on faith (September 1865, *Further Letters*, p. 227), here he voices the doubts and fears of his contemporaries (from whom he borrows more of his imagery than usual). Discoveries had immensely widened the universe, but its wonders and man's destiny were meaningless and disturbing if the Creator remained hidden as in Isaiah's time (see epigraph). In stanza 2 we may note echoes of Newman (*Apologia*, ed. Svaglic, p. 217), in stanza 4 of Genesis 1: 2, in stanza 5 of Psalm 19 and Keats ('Chapman's Homer'), in stanza 6 of Arnold ('Dover Beach'). From Tennyson's *In Memoriam* come the opening (see LVI: the trusting piety of Man,

'Who rolled the *psalm* to wintry *skies*', may not save him from extinction among *desert* dust), and the close (see LIV: faced with the vastness of the time and space Man is a mere 'infant crying in the night'). Despite touches of Victorian rhetoric (ll. 35–6) and sentiment (l. 38), the poem is among the most impressive of his early pieces.

No. 24 Easter Probably 1866: the fair copy in Campion Hall follows on from No. 23 (dated Lent 1866). Easter fell 1 April. The confident buoyancy contrasts not only with No. 17 on the previous spring, but with other earlier religious poems (e.g. Nos 16, 18, 23). His elation had gone by 2 May (see *Journals*, p. 133).

No. 25 Lines for a Picture of St. Dorothea Undated. See No. 10 for the legend, and also the dramatic version in *Poems* Appendix A (end 1867? to August 1868).

The autograph of No. 25, now at Stonyhurst, may be a fair copy made still later (1869–72?). Both contain anticipations of Sprung Rhythm (e.g. l. 2): Hopkins hoped Bridges would 'master the peculiar beat' (*Letters*, p. 24).

No. 26 Ad Mariam A May poem in praise of the Blessed Virgin Mary. No surviving MS, but Father J. Keating assured Bridges in 1918 that it was by Hopkins; he remembered it as having been hung up with other votive verses near the shrine of Our Lady at Stonyhurst while he was a boy there (in the 1870s and early '80s). When under the initials 'O.S.J.' he contributed a copy to *The Stonyhurst Magazine* (published February 1894) he suggested that it had been written in 1884, but Hopkins was not at Stonyhurst that May. Either 1871 or 1873 seems more likely on stylistic grounds; and the poet did complain about the winters preceding both those Mays at Stonyhurst (cf. st. 2). The poem catches Swinburne's popular melodious rhythms and diction. In stanza 3 'Aidenn' is Eden (Paradise).

No. 27 Rosa Mystica Undated. Handwriting is most compatible with 1874. One of the titles given the Virgin Mary is the Mystical Rose, the Rose without thorns, symbolic of man's innocence before the Fall, or of a state of grace. Here Mary is the rose tree, Christ the blossom.

'The Wreck of the Deutschland' to Dublin Sonnets (Nos 28–76)

No. 28 The Wreck of the Deutschland, December 6–7 1875
To the happy memory of five Franciscan nuns, exiles by the Falck Laws, drowned between midnight and morning of Dec. 7th.

Composed at St Beuno's College, North Wales, during his study of theology, between December 1875 and about the following April or May.

Hopkins submitted the poem in time, as he thought, for inclusion in the July number of the Jesuit journal *The Month*, but on 28 June heard from its editor that it could be considered for August only if he agreed to omit the metrical marks. As the poem contained his first experiments in Sprung Rhythm, Hopkins was sure that readers would misplace the stresses, and believed that 'if the lines are not rightly scanned they are ruined' (*Further Letters*, p. 138). The ode was prefaced by a note to the reader on the rhythm (*Poems*, pp. 255–6) which the editor tried in vain to apply to particular stanzas. Nothing of comparable complexity had ever before been published in that journal, or indeed in any other Victorian periodical. Its rejection was predictable. The syntax and theological musings were both highly involved compared with the Sunday album pieces of sentimental piety which too often passed as religious verse. Among his Jesuit colleagues there was no one else nearly as far ahead of the times in literary technique or sympathies. Today we can recognize 'The Wreck of the Deutschland' as the most substantial proof that Hopkins was a poet of genius, reforging and re-fusing words as he needed them, and moving well beyond Swinburne in the variety of his living cadences.*

To those who, like Robert Bridges, found his long ode a strain to read, Hopkins suggested that it might be best to begin with the narrative portion (sts 11–19), and then the last two stanzas in each part. With the aid of commentaries and notes (such as those in the Oxford editions) students today should have small difficulty in glossing the meaning. If the faith and convictions which dominate the ode are not shared by the reader, he must as with all poetry try to suspend his disbelief – which in this case means accepting the tall nun as a symbol of a Biblical prophetess crying out warnings from her watch-tower.

In each stanza the stresses vary in number as indicated by the pattern of indenting: 2 in line 1, 3 in lines 2 and 4, 4 in lines 3 and 7, 5 in lines 5 and 6, and 6 in line 8. But throughout Part II line 1 has 3 stresses.

HISTORICAL SETTING – THE FALCK LAWS

Tensions within the newly created German Empire (1871) led its first chancellor, Bismarck, into conflict with the Catholic Church. With the aid of Dr Falck, Prussian Minister of Public Worship and Education, he pushed through the Prussian Assembly laws which successively gave the State virtual control of the education, appointment and civil discipline of the clergy (May 1873), dislodged all Catholic bishops from their sees (May 1874), closed all monasteries in Prussia, and expelled from Prussia all members of religious orders except those who cared for the sick (May 1875). To these May Laws were soon added the confiscation of all Catholic Church property and the abolition of all the rights of the Church which had been enshrined in the constitution. The ranks of the priests were also seriously depleted.

The Jesuits, who had been among the earliest Prussian victims (July 1872), were deeply concerned as some half-a-million Catholics were gradually deprived of all spiritual assistance and about three hundred monasteries and convents were closed. Hopkins had himself met some of the displaced priests (*Journals*, pp. 236, 260, 424), and was profoundly affected by one small but

---

* See my 'The Lost Autograph of "The Wreck of the Deutschland" and Its First Readers', in *Hopkins Quarterly*, Vol. III, No. 3, October 1976, pp. 91–115.

dramatic aftermath when in December 1875 five Franciscan nuns, exiled from their Westphalian convent, lost their lives in a shipwreck near the mouth of the Thames. Although they were 'Tertiaries', who spent their working days among the poor and the sick, the sisters had been compelled to emigrate; they were on their way to a Missouri convent hospital because their cloister home in Germany had been suppressed.

THE VOYAGE AND STRANDING OF THE 'DEUTSCHLAND'

The poet has himself in Part the Second recreated the voyage in unapproachable language. Setting out from Bremen to New York on Saturday, 4 December 1875, the *Deutschland*, after anchoring overnight near Bremerhaven at the mouth of the Weser, thrust into the North Sea and headed west, urged by heavy winds and squalls of snow. The officers were not worried. The *Deutschland* was a solid British-built iron ship over 300 feet long with five bulkheads, its single screw driven by powerful 600 horse-power engines. The German company to which the ship belonged had run a regular transatlantic service to New York since 1857 without losing a single life, and on board there were in addition to the Master of the ship, Captain Brickenstein, five officers with Masters' certificates and three river pilots. Over-confident of their 'mastery' of the elements and pleased to have a following gale, they used their foretopsail to increase their speed, although the air was too thick with haze and snow to allow them to check their position by observation. The complicated set of the tidal currents in the North Sea, of which none had a proper *mastery* (contr. st. 32, l. 1), should have made them more cautious, especially when in the total obscurity of snow-blinded night they entered the region of deadly sandbanks off the mouth of the Thames, where hundreds of ships were destroyed every year.

Because of a trade depression the *Deutschland* had sailed without a full cargo and with only a sixth of her peak passenger complement on board. Exact figures were never established, but there were fortunately only about a hundred and thirteen passengers – settlers returning to America, along with some new settlers, including the five nuns. As they lay asleep or ill from the violent tossing, the ship, running before the storm with engines at full speed, drove in the dark towards the unknown. Only when soundings gave results at variance with their dead reckoning did

the Master order the speed reduced. Too late there was a cry of 'Breakers ahead!', but reversing the engines shattered the propellor, leaving the ship to lurch broadside onto a submerged sandbank. The North Sea in the fury of a gale generates some of the highest waves which have ever been measured. Huge breakers cascaded over the ship, lifting her and slamming her down, yard by yard further onto the bank. Rockets were fired as distress signals, but their man-made lightning was swallowed by the snowstorm. The surges swamped and smashed two lifeboats, and snapping three-inch ropes like thread, snatched a third from its davits, and tossed it into the confused currents with three men clinging aboard, on a nightmare voyage which was to last thirty-six hours and to cost two of them their lives. Meanwhile no further attempts to abandon ship were made. When Monday's daylight at last penetrated the pall of clouds, the officers realized that their ship was embedded on the Kentish Knock, a great bank about seven miles long, one of a series of treacherous underwater sand ranges near the mouth of the Thames which run parallel to the east coast. Harwich, the nearest port from which help could be hoped for, lay beyond the horizon, separated from them by banks and shoals difficult to evade even in better light and less tumult.

The ship fought magnificently for her life, enduring the pounding of the seas hour after hour without breaking up. Rescue seemed momentarily at hand. A lightship saw her distress and fired carronades whose flash could occasionally be glimpsed though the roar of the surf drowned their reports. Several ships appeared to be heading to help them, then veered away: not from callousness, as the shipwrecked imagined, but because they were themselves in peril and the stranded vessel was inaccessible among the pounding waves. Ten hours dragged by before distress-rockets, seen after much delay and repeated by intermediate lightships, eventually alerted the coastguards at Harwich. By that time a second night of fury had begun. The would-be rescuers ashore knew only that somewhere among the sea-tormented sandbanks there was a vessel in need, but her whereabouts or actual predicament they had no means of guessing. To have battled their way out into the darkness to investigate would have been suicidal.

As the tide rose and leaks between the strained timbers out-

paced the pumps, the passengers were driven from the lower decks
of the steerage and intermediate saloon to the first class. Then the
first saloon became awash, and in the early hours of Tuesday male
passengers were ordered into the rigging, while the women and
children clambered on to the long table below the skylight. Finally
they too were in danger of being drowned and the stewardess led
them up the companion-way to the deck. But a great wave
catching the stewardess and almost sweeping her overboard, the
nuns (with some other women) returned to the saloon and their
prayers. One woman hanged herself, and a man committed suicide
by cutting a vein. The tallest of the five nuns, thrusting her head
through the skylight, could be heard above the storm calling to
God to come quickly. Some of the survivors found her call as
unnerving as the cry of a woman from the wheel-house, 'My child
is drowned, my little one, Adam!' Many of those in the rigging,
drenched with spray and numbed by the gale, fell to the deck or
into the icy waves (st. 17). By the time Tuesday's dawn broke at
last and the subsiding tide left the deck relatively dry, some sixty of
the passengers and crew, including all five of the nuns, had died,
over a quarter of those who had embarked. Shortly after 10.30 am
a tug, which had set out from Harwich the moment it was light
enough to locate them, at last arrived – about thirty hours after
their stranding – and carried the survivors back to safety.

The bodies of four of the nuns (each with her hands clasped
together in prayer) were subsequently borne ashore; they were
taken to a Franciscan Friary near Hopkins's birthplace, Stratford
in Essex, where Cardinal Manning preached over them a funeral
sermon widely reported (e.g. in *The Weekly Register*, 18
December). He depicted the nuns as unaffected by the confusion
about them, so resigned in the peace, and quiet, and confidence of
God, that they showed not the slightest sign of fear or agitation.
When urged to retreat for safety into the rigging, the nuns left to
others the vacant places which they might have filled. 'We have
reason to know that the calm, composed resignation, the Christian
faith and happiness of those holy Sisters, were an example to all
those who were in the like danger'. The Cardinal expressed his
conviction that their intercession had helped many others to
prepare themselves for a peaceful death, and he ended with a
prayer for the salvation of all those who had been called into God's
presence by the wrecking of their ship.

If Cardinal Manning's eloquent sermon seems to have been based upon unreliable accounts, fault can also be found with virtually every published story of the wreck. Accuracy was reduced by the exhaustion of the sufferers and the difficulty of communicating through a foreign language. Even after the survivors had recovered physically, tense emotions began to distort their recollections, so that some of the narratives given New York papers when they eventually reached their destination in another ship are in conflict with probability in innumerable particulars. Even today we have to exercise great care, sifting evidence from dozens of witnesses and special correspondents in order to reconstruct in fairly dependable detail the events between the stranding and the arrival of rescue. But Hopkins had no such facilities. Though he was writing an ode, not a narrative, he was in search of the facts as a foundation for his poem. Catholic periodicals which reproduced Manning's funeral oration would be easily obtained, but the cuttings from London papers sent by his family at his request disappointed him because they did not cover the actual shipwreck: for this he had to rely upon his memory of reports published in *The Times* immediately after the events (*Further Letters*, p. 135). How well he recalled them may be judged from the passages reprinted in *Immortal Diamond* (pp. 353–74). The extracts sent by his family probably gave the proceedings of the official Board of Trade Inquiry, appointed to ascertain whether the disaster had been the result of negligence or oversight since the vessel when stranded was more than twenty miles further west than her captain thought she was.

The poet's concern was not with the degree of human fallibility uncovered by the Inquiry, which attributed the accident to the 'vessel having got ahead of her reckoning, owing to the disregard by the master of the force and direction of the tide' (*Report*, p. 13). Hopkins explores instead the interplay between the three parties in this tragic drama – the omnipotent but self-limiting God, the powerful but subordinate elements of Nature, and finally the heterogeneous representatives of mankind, varying from the courageous to the terror-stricken. The Sisters figure in the poem in various crucial roles: symbols of God's servants rejected by *dogged* rebellious Man, and yet simultaneously symbols of mankind purged and ennobled by God.

As Hopkins approaches the Creator his exploration is neither relaxed nor conventional. Keating finely notes (*The Wreck of the Deutschland*, p. 17) that the poet is 'first of all concerned, and honestly, tormentedly concerned, with what we may anthropomorphically call the character of God' and His 'contradictory revelations'. The waves and storm emerge in the poem as somewhat wilful creatures of gigantic power, compelled – at any rate when God intervenes – to direct their energies as the divine will requires; yet they also figure as devil-possessed, *endragonèd* (st. 27, l. 8), the embodiment of the great Dragon of the Apocalypse. One moment the element of air in the chilling wind is viewed from man's side as *unkind, horrible* (sts 13 and 15), but almost immediately the cold is described as *God's* (st. 17), and the *wild waters* are recognized as used and therefore, presumably, partly tamed by the Lord of Creation as though the North Sea was a baptismal font (st. 23). God's imposition of Himself on Nature is seen as self-restrained, just as He avoids complete domination of the unwilling will of men. Physical dangers and the so-called imperfections of Providence are designed by a benevolent power to persuade or drive us from material comfort into spiritual safety (*Sermons*, pp. 90–1). If men do not respond to the gentle warmth of His love as plants do in spring, then the Father has recourse to more violent wintry approaches. It is the Lord Who fills the sea with storms and wrecks because men refuse to make their destination 'the heaven-haven of the reward' (sts 9 and 35). Hopkins therefore views God as ultimately responsible for the wreck of the *Deutschland*; yet if the purpose behind this 'disaster' was achieved, those listed as lost in the official statistics might in a truer sense be among the 'saved' (st. 31).

Part the First

The opening ten stanzas (which cause readers most difficulty) are less perplexing if we approach them via stanza 32:

> I admire thee, master of the tides,
>   Of the Yore-flood, of the year's fall;
> The recurb and the recovery of the gulf's sides,
>   The girth of it and the wharf of it and the wall;
> Stanching, quenching ocean of a motionable mind;
> Ground of being, and granite of it: past all
>   Grasp God, throned behind
> Death with a sovereignty that heeds but hides, bodes but abides;

Here a metaphysical parallel is established between the macro-
cosm of the ocean, which the Creator has curbed with granite
walls, and the microcosmic ocean of man's turbulent mind and
spirit, which God alone can control. So too stanza 1 shows God as
bent upon mastering individual men as well as the elements. Just
as divine breath sustains the motions of men so divine wind sways
the sea; the ocean is bound with strands of shore-line as man's
spirit is fastened in flesh. Our prose labours to catch the opulence
of ambiguity in such words as 'sway': God is both the movement of
the waters and their ruler (as Britannia foolishly bragged she was).
His lordship over the *dead* embraces both inanimate Nature and
the souls of the drowned.

Byron had brought his 'Childe Harold's Pilgrimage' to a powerful conclusion with a paean magnifying the overwhelming strength
of the ocean, tossing into wreck flimsy man-made fleets: he had
identified his own spirit with its power, and mocked the terrified
sailors who cried to their gods for deliverance. Hopkins, utterly
different in temperament, sees himself rather as a ship lashed by
lightning, strained by the peaks and troughs of spiritual crises,
swept and hurled as the *Deutschland* was in the North Sea (sts 2
and 13). The God Who can *touch* gently can also lash us into
swifter decision. He acknowledges the anxiety which keeps a man
alert in a gale as a kinder gift than a fatal complacency, such as that
of meadow-grass in a balmy breeze (see st. 11). In the opening
stanzas he refers to his own recurrent experience of spiritual
storms. The particular incident behind stanzas 2 and 3 cannot be
identified with certainty, but the vigil in the chapel is more likely to
have concerned his choice of the priestly vocation or Jesuit order
than his conversion, or entry into the novitiate. In a situation
where he was afraid either to plod doggedly forward or turn back
he had been given the wings of a homing dove to go upward,
towering from the level of grace already achieved to a higher
altitude (cf. *Sermons*, pp. 148ff).

Stanza 4 suggests through a variety of metaphors the insecure
security in which a Christian lives. Tennyson had symbolized what
man would become in a godless world as mere desert dust blown
about by each wind in turn (*In Memoriam*, LVI). Hopkins in
contrast depicts the friable mortality of the believer as sealed
intact within an hour-glass, though his smallest act of mind or body
is scrutinized like the grains trickling through its magnifying

midriff. Though this image may perhaps continue to the end of the fifth line, many of the terms bear a nautical interpretation also. A boat made *fast* 'under the *wall*' (as the first version ran) cannot be swept away, but it is alternately under*mined* by the fall of the tide, tugged by its seaward *drift*, and then lifted as the incoming tide *crowds* and *combs* to the next *fall*. Our mental ocean suffers from ebb and flow. Or we might think of our spiritual resources rather as water in a deep well (ll. 5–8), protected by its shaft from ruffling winds and therefore as smooth as a glass pane when seen from the top; but not unmoving, because its level is in counter*poise* with the water-table of the earth around it. Down the crags of the high hill or *voel* runlets of water twist like silver ropes, then make their way through the veins of the lower rocks to replace what is drawn out of the well. The water corresponds with grace linking us to Christ Who is far above us, like the guide in an Alpine climb to whom we are *roped* for safety.*

The fifth stanza begins a synthesis which occupies the rest of Part the First – an examination of the two contrasting modes in which the mysterious God hidden within creation heightens our awareness of Himself. This 'instress' may come through a romantic star-bright evening which we salute as an embodiment of Love visible but beyond reach, just as we do a brilliant sunset flecked with plum-purple (cf. No. 2, l. 7). But we may be brought into contact with the divine through Nature's forcefulness rather than its liquid beauty, and there will be many days when we are not conscious of anything particularly divine in Nature at all, for as Isaiah exclaimed, 'Verily Thou art a God that hidest Thyself' (45: 15; see epigraph to No. 23).

The sixth and seventh stanzas analyse the real origin of the *stress* flowing from beauty (in stars, e.g.) and of the power-*stroke* delivered by storms. Few even among believers, and certainly no agnostics, realize that this current does not stem from the throne of heaven. Christ, by dying to His heavenly bliss and entering into created matter through His mother's womb, by living a human life from manger-cradle to sacrificial death (His gigantic energies almost totally suppressed), created an immense dam-head of spiritual influence which overflowed as He ascended back to

---

* Todd Bender, *Gerard Manley Hopkins, the Classical Background*, p. 88, contrasts hour-glass and well: 'As the sand which symbolizes physical life runs out, the stream of Christ's gift rushes in, filling the speaker'.

heaven from Galilee. Only dimly sensed in pre-Christian days, this river has ever since been in flood, as unceasing as time itself, able to flush away inhibiting sins and guilt (st. 6, l. 6) or reveal itself to a man in desperate straits (st. 7, l. 8 to st. 8, l. 1). Though John Keating in his thoughtful study of the poem (p. 64) identifies the river as 'the indifference and irreligion that stream through history', I find myself agreeing with Fulweiler (*Letters from the Darkling Plain*, p. 113, n.) that this seems to be ruled out by 'the images of flushing, melting, discharging, swelling, and flooding, that all refer to the mystery of the Incarnation of Christ'.

Stanza 8 suggests that under the lash of disaster we eventually break down, lashing out with the truth about ourselves, whether it is good or bad. Similarly, the sloes (wild plums) in blackthorn hedges may all look equally appetizing, but only the ones that have suffered frost will have had their natural astringency mellowed (an appropriate detail which Hopkins no doubt knew). If, like the hero of Keats's 'Ode on Melancholy' who bursts grapes against his palate, we crush a sloe in our mouth we will become in an instant brimful of either bitter tannin or sweetness. A corresponding awareness of his sweet or sour self impinges upon a man in the crush of physical and mental trials (cf. No. 67, ll. 9–14). Some men turn to Christ as Saviour only as a last resort, but we should welcome their action without asking whether it is fear or longing which has taken them to Him. This musical stanza plays assonantal variations while repeating consonants in a vaguely Welsh way: *best*, *worst*, *last*, *burst*, and *first* intermingle with *lash*, *lush*, *plush*, *flesh*, *flush*, and *flash*. The splitting up of a compound (*tmesis*) in 'Brim, in a flash, full" is followed by the quaint and confusing typography of l. 7, where the apostrophe *s* is separated from its first noun *Calvary* by a parenthesis and from its second noun *Christ* by a comma.

The closing two stanzas of Part the First reconcile God's two masks: a springlike loving Father to the responsive, and a winter-like God of Storms to the rebellious. A man's maliciousness may have to be wrung out of him first; he may have to be half-drowned in black floods before he will creep from his animal cave into the beneficent light. But as soon as the divine mastery has been acknowledged, force is replaced by a soothing and healing touch.

In stanza 10 the poet accepts the need for God to handle stubborn wills like a blacksmith who blasts fierce fire into the cold iron before he can shape it with sledge-hammer blows; but he prays that hearts may be more like closed leaf-buds and blossoms in late winter, needing only the mild warmth of spring to coax them into opening to the sunshine. A sweetness *Beyond saying*, however, can result whether submission has been brought about by lightning strokes or love. Saul, a Dr Falck to the Early Christians, was transformed into Paul the apostle by a sudden blinding light and a voice from the sky (Acts 9: 1–22), while St Augustine was led with patient gentleness until he too capitulated. And the poet, setting out to find what role God played in the wreck, assures us that he has experienced both these treatments himself. Part the First ends on the note with which it had begun – the divine mastery of Man and Nature.

Part the Second

'The roaring of lions, the howling of wolves, the raging of the stormy sea, and the destructive sword, are portions of eternity, too great for the eye of man', wrote William Blake (*The Marriage of Heaven and Hell*). In 'The Wreck of the Deutschland', Part the First opens with the poet in his crisis finding the eternal God, Part the Second with the far more common tale of people, twice removed from awareness of divine action, finding only the instruments used by God's agent, Death. The traditional lists of death-dealers (e.g. in Donne's 'At the round earth's imagined corners') are revitalized by Hopkins through the addition of the most frequent modern cause of a violent end – man's passion for speedy travel. *The Times* for 22 December 1875, which carried details of the cross-examination of the *Deutschland*'s captain by the Board of Trade Inquiry, also gave statistics of British railway accidents for the first nine months of the year – nearly 900 deaths and over 4,000 injuries. In an effort to reduce this distressing total, the Board of Trade analysed the precise reason for each accident: the causes included broken *rails* and wheel *flanges*.

This powerful metaphysical eleventh stanza may, as Keating suggests, owe something to Holbein the Younger's so-called *Dance of Death*, in which a skeletal figure leads an army over a Swiss pass with his drum or blows a trumpet. Though in stanza 11 Hopkins does not, like Donne in his 'Death be not proud', jeer at Death's braggart pretensions to being the ultimate authority, he later shows God throned in the shadows behind His agent (st. 32).

We may remember, too, that in the Apocalypse (14: 15, 16) it is Christ Himself Who holds the sickle. Here the emphasis is rather on human pride, each man's secret confidence that he is in no immediate danger. But death lurks among the waves of grass, age-old symbols of man's mortality (e.g. Isaiah 40: 6), as it does in the ocean waves. The meadow-flower, dust-rooted, sees no warning flash from the scythe (which is bent like a cringer and hugs the ground in misleading humility), but it is wielded by the *sour* reaper death. Next comes the *blear* ploughshare (dull-bladed and undiscriminating in its blear-sightedness), rooting out the stubble.

After this medieval glimpse into the spiritual world, stanza 12 sets out in businesslike fashion to narrate the voyage as reported in the papers. But poet and priest quickly transform the unimaginative facts into the substance of a religious ode. The classification of those on board into passengers and crew was theologically irrelevant: all were *souls*. The reputation of the captain to whose skill they had entrusted themselves or of the company under whose flag they sailed counted for nothing if the individuals had not placed themselves under divine protection. From his many years as an Anglican Hopkins seems to have recalled Psalm 91: 4 in the *Book of Common Prayer*: 'He shall defend thee under his wings, and thou shalt be safe under his feathers'. When 'the blue sky bends over all' it is easy to believe, with Coleridge's Christabel, that 'saints will aid if men will call', less easy to accept that God's silver clouds may sometimes have a black lining, and that the protective vaulted bay above us, which seems to entomb us in a vault, is a mantle woven by a merciful Providence out of a million strands of benefits.*

Stanza 13 continues the voyage, the external circumstances of which have been related in our introduction to this poem. As the ship hurls herself with the powerful thrust of her engines from the physical shelter of Bremer*haven*, who could guess that she is carrying the faithful on board to the 'heaven-*haven* of the reward' (st. 35). All the elements seem hostile or physically transformed from their *kind* or nature; the leading edges of the waves are hard

---

* See No. 60, ll. 34–45, and cf. Chesterton's *The Man Who was Thursday*: '"Listen to me", cried Syme with extraordinary emphasis. "Shall I tell you the secret of the whole world? It is that we have only known the back of the world. We see everything from behind, and it looks brutal. . . . That is not a cloud, but the back of a cloud. Cannot you see that everything is stooping and hiding a face? If we could only get round in front – ".'

and sharp as flint-rock, while the falling snow spirals down like coils of incandescent wire. Yeats in 'The Cold Heaven' later recorded the same paradox under a wintry sky 'That seemed as though ice burned and was but the more ice'. Admiralty charts of the North Sea are strewn with wrecks: those deeps and shoals have torn apart thousands of families, bereaving wives of their husbands and separating for ever children and parents.

The swift and superb mastery of stanza 14 brings us the events of the fatal darkness between Sunday and Monday. Night lures the vessel headlong into a trap, *Dead* both because she is rushing dead straight for the sandbank and because once on that bearing she is as good as dead. The ship's life is choked from her by the grip of the sand, and though she thrashes out in efforts to escape, the sledge-hammer blows of the waves bludgeon away her strength. Without power ever to speed again under wind or steam, or to choose her way with compass or rudder, she lies at the mercy of the breakers.

The leaden metrical feet of stanza 15 drag as did the daylight hours of expectancy for those on board. To *hope* originally meant to await coming events either with fear or optimism, as contemporary dictionaries explained, and here these two emotions interact. The poet's inventive syntax and musical ear enable him to avoid the banal, as he creates out of homely words a resonant dirge: 'And frightful a nightfall folded rueful a day'. By spacing the adjectives away from their nouns he restores some of their eroded significance, aided by the melancholy echoes of *-ful*, *-fall*, *fol-*, *-ful*. The verb *folded* is as unexpected as provocative. More obviously, darkness muffles the light in its black folds, but sheep-imagery runs through Part the Second (sts 16, 22, 31) and we feel overtones from some inhuman Polyphemus folding his sheep, of lambs driven into a pen not for safety but for slaughter. A similar connotation makes *shrouds* so much more vital a word than its technical equivalent 'rigging' (the ropes which support the masts on either side); we sense that some of the victims, frantic to escape their watery enemy, are wrapping themselves in the freezing embrace of a winding-sheet.

Because the tall nun when she presently enters the poem is shown as doing nothing but pray, the poet in stanza 16 seeks to disarm criticism in advance. The courageous sailor, who is the only other figure to be mentioned individually, illustrates the futility of action, even combined with skilful male strength and unselfish heroism, when confronted by a storm of such overwhelming fury. Bridges felt that Hopkins was misusing the nautical term 'rope's end' (where the story in *The Times* of 11 December spoke of him as 'secured by a rope to the rigging'), but Hopkins is supported by other contemporary sources such as the statement made by able seaman Cuddiford, who had been a sailor for over twenty years, when rescued from the sea after the loss of the *Eurydice*: 'A rope's end was thrown to me from the schooner, and I was then picked up' (see *Immortal Diamond*, pp. 368, 385). The poet catches some of the shocking contradictions with his use of *dandled* (the corpse swinging on its rope is like a frail child swung from a parent's arms), and *foam-fleece* (suggestive of the soft warmth they needed that wintry night, but here combined with *cobbled* to accentuate the difference between its appearance and feel: it looks like tufts of lamb's wool but if fallen upon it strikes as hard and cold as the water-rounded cobbles of a road). The forces of Nature seem now to be merely indulging in exuberant play – we might compare Yeats's 'murderous innocence of the sea' – but the swirls of air have the solidity of water-burls from a great fountain, and the waves leap with the deceptive agility of a deer before making their powerful flattening rush.

In stanza 17, like wild animals wrestling for fun with fragile human playmates, the water romps across the deck, rolling lives into eternity. On the survivors locked in a deadly struggle the cold acts as a punishing agency: mostly German Protestants and in a German ship, they must share the guilt incurred by the State in pitting itself against the Church (cf. st. 20, l. 3). Hopkins echoes the Psalmist who cried 'Praise the Lord from the earth, ye dragons, and all ye deeps: Fire, hail, snow, ice, stormy winds, which fulfil his word' (Ps. 148: 7–8). In a later sermon on Divine Providence Hopkins dealt with some of the age-old problems of evil, finding partial explanations in God's preferential treatment of men above animals and things, of believers above those who refuse to obey. God 'takes more interest . . . in a vessel's steering than the pilot, in a lover's sweetheart than the lover'. But although the whole world is 'a million-million fold contrivance of providence planned for our use and patterned for our admiration . . . this providence', he concedes, 'is imperfect, plainly imperfect. . . . the beasts our subjects rebel' (he cites the thousands yearly killed by tigers) and the sea is full of 'storms and wrecks . . . we contend with cold, want, weakness, hunger, disease, death, and often we fight a losing battle, never a triumphant one'. Asking why these imperfections should exist, he replies that good comes from them; 'if we were not forced from time to time to feel our need of God and our dependance on him, we should most of us cease to pray to him and to thank him' (*Sermons*, pp. 89–90). The stanza which begins with *God's cold* ends with God's *lioness*; though symbolized by the much dreaded predatory beast, the tall nun is an agent of salvation, reminding the panic-stricken of Christ.

Out of the flux of shifting gales and breakers and leaderless people there suddenly appears a firm tower, reminiscent of Shakespeare's 'ever-fixed mark,/That looks on tempests and is never shaken' (Sonnet 116). This tower will later function as a lighthouse (st. 29), but first Hopkins exploits the auditory image. The nun resembles a church belfry ('a virginal tongue told' [tolled], st. 17, l. 8), like a passing bell ringing out a clear warning where all other sounds are incoherent blusters, grief-stricken wailings and babble. The remarkable power of this stanza springs partly from the personifications and synecdoche (e.g. 'the heart-break'), but more directly from the elimination of grammatical or explanatory clutter to achieve pace: the parenthetic 'Crushed them', 'and drowned them', the orphaned children 'crying . . . without check'.

Hopkins had (in st. 3) spoken of himself as *tower*ing, but that image was different from this one applied to the nun, being drawn from a frightened bird trying to escape. The poet belittles himself to highlight the nun's bravery. It is his heart, not the lady, who is in a sheltered bower, and in tears. But on both these dedicated Christians the extremity of circumstance impinges with a pain close to pleasure ('an exquisite smart' leading to 'glee'), compelling them into words which, though addressed to Christ, will be overheard by many.

'This madrigal for the nun, which is to become a hymn of praise and finally a prayer', says Professor W. S. Johnson (*Gerard Manley Hopkins: the Poet as Victorian*, 1968, p. 61), 'begins with stanza nineteen. It seems in one sense literally a madrigal, a lyric suitable for music, in its rhythm: "Sister, a sister calling/A master, her master and mine!"' The nun's head was thrust through the skylight of the saloon and therefore she was in danger every time the waves rushed the deck and tried to drag everything there back into the sea. (See my *Hopkins*, 1968, pp. 119–20 for *hawling, rash smart sloggering*.) We may compare Monteith's account of Casement's attempt in 1916 to land on the wild west coast of Ireland, their boat caught on a sandbank in the breakers: 'The smashing of the waves was steadily sapping what strength we had left. Nothing else can deal the stunning blow of a sea wave. It hits you all over at the same time. It feels as though you were slammed from head to foot with a sheet of soft lead twelve inches thick. You have no defence.' (Quoted Roger McHugh, *Dublin 1916*, London, 1966, p. 29). But the nun is undeterred, with a single *fetch* in her (a sustained effort, a direction in tacking). Her cry, though meant solely for Christ Himself, comes through the disorderly shouts of the elements, which were now *brawling* as if drunk with power.

The contrast between devout Germans (such as the five Sisters – see introduction to this poem, p. 30 above) and the German persecutors of the faithful reminds the poet that St Gertrude the Great and Martin Luther were both born in one small German town, Eisleben. In our more ecumenical days some Catholics have proposed the formal canonizing of Luther, founder of the Reformation in Germany. Though readers may resent the description of him as wolf or wild boar ('beast of the waste wood'), the *Catholic Dictionary*, edited by Hopkins's friends William Addis and Thomas Arnold (rev. edn 1893), points out how coarse Luther himself was, even in his Catholic days, in controversy: 'His opponents were asses, pigs, dolts, etc., and were assailed with still viler epithets'. Later 'he made use of vile illustrations to caricature the Pope, the monks, and the teachings of the Church'. His doctrine had precipitated the sixteenth-century split between the Church and the German State, widened by Dr Falck in the nineteenth century. Even before his conversion Hopkins had much preferred the reformer Savonarola to Luther, the 'one martyred in the Church, the other successful and the admired author of world-wide heresy in schism'. [*Further Letters*, pp. 17–18. See also Jerome Bump, 'Art and Religion: Hopkins and Savonarola', *Thought*, Vol. 50, No. 197 (June 1975), 132–47.] The stark difference between Abel the blameless shepherd and his brother Cain who murdered him out of jealousy is delineated in Genesis chapter 4.

The human predicament of the five nuns is contrasted with their spiritual rewards in stanzas 20 to 23. Their country, Deutschland,

was set on a course leading to destruction as surely as their ship the
Deutschland had been (st. 20, l. 3). Given an ultimatum which
forced them to decide whether they loved the Church more than
the State, they had chosen what they were convinced was the way
of Christ and been expelled in consequence (st. 21, ll. 1, 2). In
such famous elegies as Milton's 'Lycidas' personified rivers in
procession join the mourners, but here both the Rhine and the
Thames reject the five Sisters. Literally the mouths of both
estuaries are perilous with sandbanks and complicate the intricate
tidal currents which made North Sea navigation in pre-radar days
so unsafe. Metaphorically the English seamen who eked out a
precarious living near the Thames mouth were widely (though
unjustly) thought to have been slow to rescue the survivors but
swift to loot the abandoned ship. Natural forces appear to have
combined like hunting dogs in a furious attack upon the nuns (the
wild breakers, the concealing snowstorm, river currents and the
Kentish Knock bank), but God is the Great Hunter, the true
Orion of heaven. Hillis Miller quotes many passages from the
classics, the Old Testament and the Church Fathers to show that
Orion was linked with storms and martydom (*Modern Language
Notes*, Vol. 76, No. 6, 1961, pp. 509–14). The ordeal of the
shipwreck enabled God to measure the faith of the five Sisters.
The poet does not directly denominate them martyrs, since their
faith was not the immediate cause of their death, but he associates
them with the blessed martyrs because their 'leader' died pro-
claiming the name of Christ. The undeveloped and original
meaning of the word martyr ('witness') they could claim. Flowers
from time immemorial have been strewn over the dead as symbols
of the transience of beauty: God's lily-coloured curling snowflakes
scattered over the *Deutschland* carried as on inscribed scrolls His
testimony to their unblemished service. The invented word
unchancelling may be interpreted according to various meanings of
'chancel'. As this was the portion of a basilica reserved for judges,
(*OED*, para 1), there may be an allusion to Bismarck as chancellor
of Germany, ultimately responsible for the banishing of the
religious; God defeats the chancellor by converting their
displacement into a welcome home. If we accept the popular use
of 'chancel' for that part of a convent chapel reserved for the nuns,
God is seen as taking them from behind their sheltering screen-
work to measure their heroism in a dangerous public task. Other

explanations may also interact with these in Hopkins's redolent coinage.

Stanza 22 finds special significance in the fact that there were five nuns. Medieval literature was rich in associations with five. The five wounds of Christ made doubting Thomas sure that he had found Him (John 20: 25–9). Five has become a symbol for Christ, used in cinquefoil church windows (l. 7, cf. st. 23, l. 6), and five-porched cathedral entrances or holy wells (*Journals*, pp. 257–8, 261). Modern criticism has only gradually become aware of the numerological basis for many famous poems such as Spenser's. (Here Part the First has five times two stanzas, Part the Second five times five.) Hopkins had devised a special meaning for 'sake' which he explained to Bridges: 'the being a thing has outside itself, as a voice by its echo, a face by its reflection, a body by its shadow . . . *and also* that in the thing by virtue of which especially it has this being abroad . . .' (*Letters*, p. 83, with reference to No. 45, l. 10). In theology the mention of five inevitably brings the Crucifixion to mind: it is Christ's recognized number or *cipher* just as it was once a secret hieroglyph for Him. Scarlet was the martyrs' colour, as the red rose was their flower. Christ alone decides which of His special lambs will be sacrificed, placing His scarlet mark of ownership on them like a farmer reddling his sheep; but man wields the butchering blade. (We may compare Thomas's Christmas sermon in Eliot's *Murder in the Cathedral*: 'Saints are not made by accident. . . . A martyrdom is always the design of God, for His love of men, to warn them and to lead them, to bring them back to His ways.') Because the Sisters were Franciscans, the poet in stanza 23 thinks of the joy with which St Francis of Assisi must surely share in the nuns' triumph. That saint meditated so long on the dying Christ that His wounds were painfully reproduced as *stigmata* in his own flesh, with the heads and points of the nails protruding above the flesh like gnarls on a tree-trunk, and his gashed side bleeding – the whole landscape of Christ's love, a tangible proof (*seal*) that St Francis had been granted the vision of a crucified seraph. His five spiritual daughters ('grouped in a circle of hoods, a five-leaved token', as Heuser finely visualizes them in *The Shaping Vision*, p. 46) are worthy of his favour and pride. Together they pass through the drowning seas, confirmed as Christ's own, into His presence, to be bathed in the golden shower of heavenly blessings, and (being purified) able to absorb new life

from the divine radiance (cf. Rev. 1: 14–16). The imagery in the
final line of the stanza may be influenced by famous hymns
attributed to St Francis, 'The Canticle of the Sun', 'The Canticle of
Love' and 'The Canticle of the Furnace'. When Hopkins speaks of
'fall-gold mercies' bathing the Franciscan Sisters, images of molten
gold, yellow lightning (*Journals*, p. 155) and water falling in
sunlight (cf. st. 34, l. 8) seem to come together.

Just as Homer relieves the strenuous contests around Troy
through epic similes which magically transport us to the peace of
some rural mountainside, so Hopkins in stanza 24 removes us
momentarily from exposure to the merciless easterly storm and the
insecurity of a heaving ship. Compared with the wind-raked levels
of Essex (the eastern English county in which he had been born,
and off whose low coast the *Deutschland* lay stranded) the rich
Welsh valley on which he looked down from the *pastoral forehead*
of St Beuno's College seemed a land of soft delight. We may
detect a feeling almost of guilt at his being so sheltered. Certainly
the tall Sister, hemmed in by impenetrable night, terrifying waves
and freezing snow, was calling, as though to these torturing
elements, 'O Christ, Christ, come quickly'. To her the storm was
Christ and she welcomed Him, though His nearer approach in that
shape meant a sort of crucifixion. Taking a Christ-view of her
surroundings, she renames (*christens*) physical disaster a spiritual
victory. What a splendid Anglo-Saxoning of a Greek concept
Hopkins has created in *black-about*, after the style of such words
as *perimelainomai*, 'to be black all round'. And how fruitfully he
exploits the ambiguities of her calling *to* air, breaker, and the fear-
infected huddle of passengers. On the one hand she seems to the
unbelievers to be throwing away words on the wind and waves; in
another sense those elements are the messengers of God whom
she rightly addresses. Her prayer is directed to Christ, yet its
divinely inspired purpose is as warning and invitation to those
unready for the next world (cf. st. 31).

Stanzas 25 to 28 try to riddle out the motives which made the tall
Sister call for the swift coming of Christ. Hopkins had very little to
work from, since he had seen few accounts of the wreck, and no
reports of private communications on spiritual matters between
the nuns and other passengers during this final crisis have come
down to us. Her cry was in German, and survivors afterwards
differed in their recollection of exactly what she had said and in

their translation of it, interpreting it according to their own reactions. So too does Hopkins. If his arguments seem obscure and inconclusive they have nevertheless produced as an aside (st. 26) one of the most attractive parts of the poem. The special correspondent of *The Times* (London, 11 December, p. 7) reported that the 'German nuns, whose bodies are now in the dead-house . . . clasped hands [i.e. each separately in prayer] and were drowned together, the chief sister, a gaunt woman 6 ft. high, calling out loudly and often "O Christ, come quickly!" till the end came' (reprinted *Immortal Diamond*, pp. 367–8). Hopkins is unlikely to have read the London *Daily News* report of 9 December, which gave the cry as 'O, my God, make it quick! make it quick!' and he had no means of knowing that the tall nun was not the 'chief sister'.

'The majesty!' (st. 25, l. 1), i.e., 'What a majestic cry': these seem to be spontaneous words of admiration which the poet's heart made break from him when he first read the tale of the nun's cry to Christ (st. 18, ll. 3, 4). The 'arch and original Breath' to whom the poet first appeals for inspiration in this difficult portion of his ode is, very appropriately, the ancient Spirit of God brooding over the chaotic deep: 'Earth was still an empty waste, and darkness hung over the deep; but already, over its waters, stirred the breath of God' (Gen. 1: 2, Knox). His second appeal for inspiration is again appropriate: asking whether she had wanted to share with her lover, Christ, a painful death, the poet appeals to the 'body of lovely Death', not the gaunt nun, but the crucified Christ: our imagination of that moving scene has been aided by the greatest artists down the ages. The reference to Christ as her 'lover' is in line with religious language in both the East and the West. 'Although many have been scandalized by the erotic poetry of the *Song of Songs*', says Father Joseph Christie, 'the saints and mystics of the Church have always loved it as a celebration of the love of God' (*The Month*, London, June 1978, p. 216). If the Sister wished to die with Jesus, how utterly different she was from the disciples in their swamped boat who roused their sleeping Master during the sudden storm ('weather') on the Sea of Galilee, not relishing the privilege of drowning with Him (Luke 8: 22–5). Finally Hopkins asks (ll. 7, 8) whether the assault of the elements was too much for her: did she wish the contest over and the prizes awarded? The reference to a crown is most simply interpreted in terms of St Paul's second letter to Timothy (4: 7, 8):

'I have fought a good fight [cf. *combating*] . . . there is laid up for me a crown of justice which the Lord the just judge will render to me in that day; and not only to me, but to them also that love his coming'. Paul goes on to say 'Make haste to come to me quickly', a message for Timothy but close enough to the nun's cry to bring this whole passage to the poet's mind.

Stanza 26 provides another artistic respite from the stormy environment of the Kentish Knock, an exquisite stanza which embodies the surge of relief when the depressing foggy clouds of late winter at last rise heavily above the embracing hills, like some huge winged animal. (The puzzling 'down-dugged' refers to the udder-like droopings of clouds described in meteorological language from 1880 onwards as *mammato-cumulus*, etc. See *OED*. My 1971 *Queen's Quarterly* article, vol. 78, No. 4, p. 501, gives contemporary references to Aryan 'cloud-cows' summarized by James Milroy, *The Language of Gerard Manley Hopkins*, 1977, p. 236.) The month of May, in contrast, its heavy winter clothing peeled off, seems bright and airy as a jay. [Milroy prefers to regard *peeled*, not as Yorkshire and Lancashire for 'stripped', but as Scottish for 'pooled', a reference to showery May: *The Language of Gerard Manley Hopkins*, p. 240.] The monotonous lead colour is replaced with pied beauty:

> Blue-beating and hoary-glow height; or night, still higher,
> With belled fire and the moth-soft Milky Way.

Heraclitus, one of the poet's favourite philosophers, thought of the stars as bowls [bell shapes] filled with fire, and Herbert, once his favourite poet, spoke of prayer as 'Church-bells beyond the stars heard'. The Milky Way is a 'soft mist' of light formed by innumerable tiny specks of light (*Sermons*, p. 238), just as the velvet dust of a moth's wing consists of minute reflective scales. The celestial heavens as usual lead the poet on to their theological counterpart, a place where beautiful but destructive moths do not mutilate treasures we have laid by (Matt. 6: 20). St Paul makes no attempt to spell out the pleasures of heaven, merely quoting from Isaiah 64: 4 that there are 'Things no eye has seen, no ear has heard, no human heart conceived, the welcome God has prepared for those who love him' (1 Cor. 2: 9, Knox; cf. Isaiah). People therefore fill in details according to their own longings. What then did the tall nun have in her mind? (The last clause means 'nor was ever guessed *as a result of* hearing' – i.e. neither visions nor spirit voices have ever revealed what wealth of enjoyment is in store for us.)

On psychological grounds the poet in stanza 27 rejects as implausible two possible interpretations of the cry 'O Christ, come quickly'. 'I gather', he says tentatively (l. 7), that she was not so weary with long-drawn physical stress as to be crying for ease; the 'sodden-with-its-sorrowing heart' (a phrase saturated with emotion) is to be found in those who have endured years of wearing disharmony with circumstances. This *jaded* state of mind was to become all too familiar to Hopkins (see e.g. No. 69, ll. 1–10, *Letters*, p. 178). The metaphor of the jolting cart was probably suggested to him by a book which his father had seen through the press, Sir George Simpson's *Narrative of a Journey round the World during the Years 1841 and 1842* (2 vols, London, 1847), describing an infinitely tedious journey over four thousand miles of rough Siberian roads in springless Russian tumbrils. An acute crisis of danger such as shipwreck (and he further imagines the ship threatened by a violent display of lightning) usually drives people to acts of self-preservation: our adrenalin floods us with energy. As for the nun's wanting to project herself into the sorrows of Christ on the Cross, the wreck was no place for that, with the gale bullying her and the waves attacking like sea-dragons. Meditation demands solitude and quiet. We must look for another explanation.

What his interpretation is has given rise to some dispute. Hopkins in stanza 28 uses broken and incomplete exclamations such as a man actually watching the event might fling out as he shouldered his way to a point of vantage ('make me room there'). In imagination the poet tries to equal the ecstasy of the nun's vision of Christ the King riding to take personal charge of the souls of the survivors, of those dying and dead. He was invisible except to her eyes, and His coming to her fellow-passengers was (the poet assumes) largely through the agency of her cry and the prayers of the other Sisters. Superficially, Hopkins might seem callous and harsh to regard as a divine *triumph* a shipwreck in which a quarter of those on board lost their lives, but we must understand *doom* in the older sense of 'judgment', not 'destruction'. From stanza 31, which should be read along with 28, it is clear that Hopkins believed that many of the 'lost' were perhaps eternally 'saved' through having had to confront the life beyond death during their ordeal on the *Deutschland*.

Dr Elisabeth Schneider (*The Dragon in the Gate*, pp. 26ff) has tried to account for the 'otherwise inexplicably feverish intensity' of these stanzas by suggesting that Hopkins was hinting at a conviction that Christ actually came in some miraculous way to the nun, while she was still alive. The word *fetch* in stanza 19 provides her with the clue: she reads the statement that the nun had 'one fetch in her' as though it meant 'before her' and in Sir Walter Scott's sense of *fetch*: 'wraith or double-ganger'. She then uses as a parallel a remark Hopkins made about an account in the Apocalypse, that it was 'no mere vision but the real fetching, presentment, or "adduction" of . . . Christ' (*Sermons*, p. 200). Realizing that in 'Hopkins's circumstances, and for more than one reason, it would not have been proper for him to proclaim a miraculous event explicitly' she finds here a reason for his otherwise unexplained admission to Bridges that the ode certainly 'needs study and is obscure, for indeed I was not over-desirous that the meaning of all should be quite clear, at least unmistakeable' (*Letters*, p. 50). The suggestion that Hopkins attached a private importance to the nun's experience which went beyond even the claims made in Cardinal Manning's funeral sermon has appealed to many nonreligious readers, and scholars who have felt that the climax of the poem otherwise falls flat have welcomed it (e.g. John Robinson, *In Extremity*, 1978, p. 116). In view of my admiration for Professor Schneider's many other contributions to Hopkins studies, I am sorry not to be able to accept her theory.

The emphasis in stanzas 29 to 31 is not on any physical shape seen by the nun, such as Dr Schneider's theory might appear to entail. The poet seems even to withdraw somewhat from the implication in the preceding stanza (as it is ordinarily interpreted) that she had been privileged with a mystical vision of Christ. Instead he praises the sensitivity of the heart and the divinely oriented mental sight which enabled her to decode the jumble of violent sensations impinging on her. To others the stormy darkness made no more sense than the writing on the wall at Belshazzar's feast (Daniel 5), but the tall nun was spiritually literate: she could *read* the storm. (Someone once remarked that Wordsworth could 'read' a landscape like an inscription on a monument.) In the beginning God made the elements with words such as 'Light!' – and light immediately rushed into existence. Christ the Son was Himself the full embodiment of the Father's 'Word' according to the famous *logos* introduction to St John's Gospel. In his meditation notes Hopkins combines, in a fascinating way which illuminates this section of 'The Wreck of the Deutschland', the beginning of Genesis and of St John: 'God's utterance of himself in himself is God the Word, outside himself is this world' – which in everyday language might be tentatively paraphrased: 'God speaking to Himself is Christ, but His words projected beyond Himself form the universe'. Hopkins continues: 'This world then is word, expression, news of God' (*Sermons*, p. 129). The message, however, may now be doubly difficult to read because the fall has not only blunted men's inner eyesight but injured the harmony of Nature. Scientific explanations concentrate upon the *how* and the *why*, ignoring the *who*. The tall nun has a completely Christo-centric view of the universe, including both time ('present and past') and matter.

'Ah! there was a heart right!' he exclaims, echoing many psalms in which the Vulgate has *recti corde*, rendered 'upright of heart' in English versions (e.g. Ps. 7: 11). Not through a psychic second sight but single sightedness she sees, in an apparent confusion like the return of chaos, the hidden unity in which evil is constrained to contribute towards good; 'if therefore thine eye be single', said Christ, 'thy whole body shall be full of light' (Matt. 6: 22). Peter was declared to be the Rock on which the Church would be founded because he recognized Jesus as the Son of the living God, having seen Him walking across a stormy sea (Matt. 16: 16–18). The nun is hailed as a Simon Peter because she recognizes Christ in the storm itself; moreover, like Peter who was often the spokesman for his brethren, she is the mouthpiece for the Sisters, uttering the name of Christ. And, paradoxically, since the ship was heaving with the surge and shuddering with the gale, she is depicted as unmovably firm on a rock just as the Capitol of Rome (symbolic of the Catholic Church) stood above the solid cliff face of the Tarpeian. Milton had written of Rome's 'Tarpeian rock, her citadel/Impregnable' ('Paradise Regained', iv: 49–50, a description which was relevant enough for Hopkins to echo, though spoken by Satan). The blast has no more effect upon her rock-built faith than on the house 'founded upon a rock' in Christ's Sermon on the Mount (Matt. 7: 24–5). The *but* (st. 29, l. 8) indicates that instead of being weakened by the gale she is strengthened. The metaphor changes, as Hopkins draws on the proverb which tells us that the wind which extinguishes a mere candle will fan a fire. Combining the images, we may think of her as one of those beacon towers which used to be built on rocky headlands, their open bonfires blown into greater brilliance as danger increased at sea.

Following up this metaphor of flame, stanza 30 portrays Christ as light, imagery prepared for by references to God's mild and consuming flames in Part the First (sts 3, 5, 9, 10) and which will be developed in stanza 34. Only by the one woman since Eve's Fall who from her conception was free from all taint of sin could Christ have been born physically – and without pangs. (The Feast of the Immaculate Conception of the Virgin Mary is celebrated on 8 December.) But Christ the (burning) Word can be reborn many times, as He was among these shipwrecked Germans, by a heart on fire with Him, or in verbal terms, a mind which heard the Word, treasured Him and spoke Him again to others. (In st. 30, l. 8, *Word* is a vocative, addressed to Christ, and *that* refers back to *brain*.)

Since stanza 19 the nun, sometimes along with the other Sisters, has been given centre stage. Not that the other survivors have been forgotten: unless the tall Sister's cry had been heard by the 'men‾ in the tops and the tackle', the 'throng that catches and quails' (st. 19, l. 8; st. 24, l. 6), her Master's dealings with those who in body or soul were 'living and dead' (st. 28, l. 7) would have been less effective. The rest of the ode will concern Christ's right to all men's obedience. The transition, movingly managed, is seldom understood. The nun's 'pain' and 'Patience' surely refer not forward to her drowning but back to the image in the closing lines of stanza 30 – spiritual conception, nurturing in the womb (keeping) and birth-throes. After the Last Supper Christ prepared the minds of His disciples for the trials about to envelop them by urging patience and comparing their sufferings to those of a woman in labour, because 'when she has borne her child, she does not remember the distress any longer, so glad is she that a man has been born into the world' (John 16: 21, Knox). Christ has been reborn to the Sister; others have suffered the pangs only for a still-birth. But the poet suddenly stops himself from an unjustified pessimism about the fate of the rest who were drowned. While some were 'unconfessed' (not having acknowledged Christ, and confessed their sins), they had been reminded of the way to salvation through the nun's prayer. Keating has a penetrating comment on the deliberate confusion of syntax (anacoluthon) and image in stanza 31, ll. 5–8 as Hopkins 'halts his judgment on them and ponders on Providence in violently anacoluthic phrasing and incoherently shifting metaphors – devices which suggest his own mood of combined uncertainty and hopefulness' (*The Wreck of the Deutschland*, p. 100). Hopkins shared enough of the wide compassion of 'Christ's lily', St Gertrude (st. 20, l. 5), to turn into a poem a passage from her *Life and Revelations*:

> To him who ever thought with love of me
> Or ever did for my sake some good deed
> I will appear, looking such charity
> And kind compassion, at his life's last need
> That he will out of hand and heartily
> Repent he sinned and all his sins be freed.   (No. 140)

The image of the maiden as a warning bell so delicately poised that the merest touch will set it ringing is usually glossed as a reference to church bells or sheep bells. Yet both these ring out invitations to *come*: they do not 'startle . . . back' (l. 7). Moreover, as bell-ringers will know, a church bell requires a vigorous pull to set it in motion. But the context of the stanza is satisfied by a bell-buoy, which sounds its warning at the slightest swell on the bosom of the ocean. There was one a few miles from the Kentish Knock, though that sandbank was, curiously enough, outlined in Victorian times by buoys known technically as of the 'tall nun' type. (See my *Resources of Language and Imagery in 'The Wreck of the Deutschland'*, Seventh Annual Hopkins Lecture, London, 1976, p. 16.) As the son of a marine insurance adjuster who had written books of advice to master-mariners, Hopkins had considerable familiarity with sea terms, so that the mental leap from 'tall nun' to another sort of marine buoy would have been an easy one. But like Shakespeare in pursuing one metaphor he excites several more into motion. The people warned by the bell suddenly become sheep. The swinging notes of the bell may perhaps be heard in the *cynghanedd* (see Reference Section) of 'sheep back . . . shipwrack'. The ambiguity of *wrack* ('wreck', but also seaweed cultivated by farmers and regularly reaped as fertilizer) bridges the transition to the harvest image, familiar from Christ's use of it in

Matthew 9: 36–7, where people ready to receive the Gospel are also described in these two adjacent metaphors as sheep without a shepherd, and as a harvest ripe for gathering. Hopkins's imagination runs to yet another metaphor as he wonders whether the winds became God's rough but merciful reapers, carrying the sheaves to the barn, or threshing the grain from the chaff.

The 'year's fall' (harvest time) leads naturally back to the Lord of the harvest (Matt. 9: 38), Who is also Master of the tides which had created the sandbanks and baffled the so-called Masters in the ship. In his sermon on Providence Hopkins had described the world as 'patterned for our admiration' (*Sermons*, p. 90): the Latin root of *admire* instils a sense of astonishment as well as respect into its use in stanza 32. God had drowned the earth and most of mankind in the 'all of water' of the great deluge (Gen. 6–8), but Noah's family escaped because they were listeners – heeding God's warning they built the ark (see st. 33, ll. 1–3).

The ebbing and rising tides, the changing seasons, the unstable ocean, men's restless minds (like inland seas subject to wave and storm) all these are examples of the Heraclitean flux. Hopkins as an Oxford undergraduate may have heard Walter Pater talking about Plato's dislike of all this mobility: 'to Plato motion becomes the token of unreality in things, of falsity in our thoughts about them. . . . Everywhere he displays himself as an advocate of the immutable. . . . the insoluble, immovable granite beneath and amid the wasting torrent of mere phenomena' (*Plato and Platonism*, London, 1907, pp. 22, 27). Hopkins turns from the fluidity of water and air to the solidity of the bounding cliffs, which, like the *world's strand* at the beginning of the ode, are images of the divine limits imposed on forces of destruction. Men commonly meet death without seeing God hidden in the shadows behind Death. The poet admires three qualities in the enthroned Lord: first, His *sovereignty*, which is alert though concealed, which decrees but waits for the right time before enforcing its edicts (how compactly the word-play of 'bodes but abides' states this); second, His *mercy*, floating above and surviving the purging punishing floods, like the ark, prototype of the Church as a lifeboat for those who hear the Word and obey; third, His *love*, which pursues the lingerers 'Lower than death and the dark'. This last mysterious statement may, as Father Bischoff has suggested to me, be connected with the prayer attributed to St Ambrose in the Roman

Missal under Preparation for Mass: 'Gently and graciously accept the sacrifice at my hands for the salvation of all mankind, both living and dead' (cf. st. 28, l. 7). Hopkins believed that because God transcends time, He can apply prayers offered in our 'now' to crises in the 'now' of those overtaken by disasters in our 'past' (such as those drowned without warning in the 'Eurydice' – see notes to that poem, No. 41, ll. 113ff, and to 'Henry Purcell', No. 45, ll. 1–4). Charles Williams took over and developed this idea, though perhaps beyond what Hopkins would have approved, in such novels as *Descent into Hell*; it seemed possible to Williams for believers today to be projected into times centuries back and to lighten, by acts of willing sacrifice, burdens of doubt or danger facing our ancestors, for example a martyr afraid of torturing fire.

The second half of stanza 33 refers to Christ's descent into Hell (or Limbo) between His death and resurrection, proclaimed in the creeds and somewhat obscurely described here, as indeed it is in 1 Peter 3: 18–20: 'In his mortal nature he was done to death, but endowed with fresh life in his spirit, and it was in this spirit that he went and preached to the spirits who lay in prison. Long before, they had refused belief, hoping that God would be patient with them, in the days of Noe' (Knox). Here Hopkins depicts Christ's love as a vein of water gliding down to imprisoned spirits who were past praying for themselves, who became penitent at the moment of death. The syntax of lines 5 to 8 is very differently construed by Dr Schneider (*The Dragon in the Gate*, p. 34), but my own reading of it runs: [this prison was] 'the furthest boundary (*uttermost mark*) which Christ – a giant Who was plunged into [a sea of] suffering and rose again, the anointed Son of the compassionate Father – reached (*fetched*) in His triumphant conquering journey' (*storm of his strides*).

The prayer for the return of Christ which constitutes stanza 34 contains some startling imagery. Christ has been reborn through the 'virginal tongue' in the shipwreck (cf. 'The Blessed Virgin', No. 60, ll. 56–65), but (as Father Milward points out) He reappears here as 'The Burning Babe' of Robert Southwell's poem. He is *double-naturèd*, being a blend of the sacred flame and human flesh. In an astonishing metaphor, Hopkins mirrors the violent change involved in the incarnation – from enthroned God to deprived child in a cattle-shed – as His being *flung* out from heaven (one thinks of the indignity suffered by Lucifer and the fallen angels flung from the battlements of Heaven), to become a miracle of flame in Mary. But the poet prays that His return may differ both from the obscure *dark* of His Bethlehem birth and the terrifying brilliance with which He will come again for the Day of Judgment (*dooms-day dazzle*). May kindness and authority unite in His re-entry to claim back a kingdom which is His by right; may He descend like a silvery shower of rain glinting in sunlight rather than an avenging lightning-bolt (2 Thess. 1: 7, 8).

The ode ends with a subject always close to Hopkins's heart – the reconversion of Britain. The idiom in line 1 may hint that through British slowness to mount rescue operations a share of responsibility for these deaths could be laid *at our door*. But the nun had completed her true voyage, passing through English shoals to the heavenly roadstead (Horne Tooke in his *Diversions of Purley*, rev. edn, London, 1840, p. 367, derived both *heaven* and *haven* from the root of 'heave'; Hopkins had already gratefully linked the words in the title of No. 9). Lines 5 and 6 compare the effect Christ would have upon Britain to *easter* (Spring, Mayday, along with resurrection light and happiness), to *dayspring* (i.e. early dawn – cf. 'God's Grandeur', No. 31, l. 12), to a *crimson-cresseted east* (the clouds set aflame by the rising sun and the sun itself, compared to a watch-tower fire or cresset, a word derived by some etymologists from the little cross on those beacons); then finally to the sun rolling in greater and greater splendour to its zenith. The imagery which warms the final crowded and emphatic lines of the poem brings out the willing welcome and heartfelt respect He should be accorded. The storm is over; the blood-tinged lilies of the snowflakes can give way now to the prized *rose*, the chilling thunder-flash to the quiet and comfort of the *hearth's fire*. Infinitely far above the gaunt nun, doubtful heroine to the 'throng that catches and quails', may come the Prince Who can be hero and Lord to all Britain, leaders and throng alike, dominating both the emotions of the heart and the intellectual activities of the mind.

CRITICISM OF THE POEM

Any commentary on an intricate poem is bound to omit many overtones of meaning. There is no substitute for intimacy with the ode itself. From long experience with undergraduates and postgraduates I have found it best to postpone seminars on 'The Wreck of the Deutschland' until students have developed a liking for Hopkins (which the great majority rapidly do) through his shorter and less theological pieces. Although the poet himself did not always regard this ode as his greatest work, preferring 'The Windhover' and, curiously enough, agreeing that 'The Loss of the Eurydice' showed 'more mastery in art' (*Letters*, p. 119), this his longest poem was described in 1884 as his 'favourite' (*Further Letters*, p. 353). It seems to form an excellent climax to the study of his writings. The reader who has grown accustomed to his fresh idiom can take its minor complexities in his stride. Everyone responds quickly to the narrative portion (sts 11–17) – the best port of embarkation for less advanced students – and to those stimulating vistas into space, stanzas 5, 26 and 32. And it may be some consolation to know that nearly everyone has to move with caution through the more mystical areas, such as stanzas 6 to 8 and 33.

Those whose approach is basically devotional – many articles on the 'Wreck' come from religious rather than literary scholars – find no structural weakness in the ode, though they may complain about obscure phrases. But my postgraduates sometimes become uneasy with stanzas 28 to 30. Here the poet is using every rhetorical device to throw emphasis upon the tall nun and to surround her with impressive figures. Thus instead of venturing to say plainly *why* she was crying out to Christ to come quickly, he allows *Fancy* – Keating protests that he should have invoked Imagination – to depict the answer to her prayer. The divine King is half-glimpsed through the poet's own eyes riding across the waves to deliver His *doom* – a scene which recalls the solemn vision in the Apocalypse when the heavens open and Christ, seated on a white horse, rides forth followed by angelic armies in preparation for Doomsday judgment (Rev. 19 and 20). After the poet's eloquent cry to the returning King 'Do, deal, lord it with living and dead', readers tend to expect that Christ will immediately become the focus of attention. Instead the poet takes us back to the nun with what they feel is a great reduction in tension. Hence the appeal of Dr Schneider's theory that in stanzas 28–30 Hopkins is deliberately surrounding a miracle with mystery. Without some such explanation they obviously do not find the tall sister important enough to be held up as a model alongside such central figures of the faith as St Peter and the Blessed Virgin Mary

(cf. Father F. X. Shea, 'The Art of Sinking in "The Wreck of the
Deutschland".', *Hopkins Quarterly*, Vol. I, No. 1, April 1974, pp.
37–42).

Put this way the objection is hard to resist, though in my
commentary I have tried to show that in several metaphorical
senses the nun – though of course in her brief public history she
could not even remotely compete with Peter and Mary – does
emulate them. Some readers would happily omit these two
stanzas, but they are absolutely essential to the poem. Wordsworth had written passionately that the wrong sort of world 'is too
much with us' because we have 'given our hearts away' to tangible
matter; we are out of tune with most aspects of Nature, including
the 'winds that will be howling at all hours'. Deterioration in our
sensitivity means that 'Little we see in Nature that is ours'.
Hopkins in stanza 5 of the 'Wreck', and later in 'God's Grandeur'
(No. 31), indicates how seldom and by how few observers the
creator is recognized as being present in the thunder and lightning.
The simple shepherd, retaining the insights men possessed during
the childhood of the human race, 'owns/The horror and the havoc
and the glory' ('The shepherd's brow', No. 75). If I have understood stanzas 29 and 30 correctly, the nun goes further, revelling in
the storm as the ocean-rousing breath of God, just as the poet in
'Hurrahing in Harvest' sees that the 'hills are his world-wielding
shoulder/Majestic' (No. 38, l. 9). Elijah, immersed in self-pity on
the sacred Mount Horeb, had been unable to find God in the
tornado, the 'great and strong wind before the Lord overthrowing
the mountains, and breaking the rocks in pieces' (3 Kings 19: 11,
Douay, i.e. 1 Kings, A.V.). St Peter, on the other hand, interpreted the 'sound from heaven, as of a mighty wind coming', as the
promised Spirit of the Lord (Acts 2: 2, 17–20). In the tall nun's
sight the *it*, the *Thing*, the *unshapeable shock night*, seem to
become expressions of the Master of the elements, the wuthering
winds are heard as divine words. No lull in the 'burly' is necessary.
If we ask why the nun should *shout* her invocation to Christ to
come quickly, the answer may be simply that the storm *is* God to
her, though not in a pantheistic sense (cf. No. 38, l. 9): she
'christens her wild-worst Best' (st. 24, ll. 5–8).*

* For a much more profoundly philosophical and theological discussion of this crux
– though not, I believe, incompatible with my simplified explanation – see James
Cotter, *Inscape*, 1972, esp. pp. 86–92, 143–66.

A technical study of the Sprung Rhythm of this poem is far too complicated to be attempted here, since particular effects or questions of doubt call for remark in a large number of places. But we should note that (as Dr Schneider has shown in chap. 2 of *The Dragon in the Gate*) Hopkins has for the most part, with the economy of a great artist, freshened the run of his lines by minimal departures from the current practice of writers such as Swinburne. Yet the advance upon ordinary iambic rhythm seems enormous. Among the most successful features of the 'Deutschland' stanza is the long six-footed eighth line. This shares with the Alexandrine at the close of a Spenserian stanza the contemplative prolongation of sound followed (almost always) by a reflective pause. Hopkins appears to have given these stanza endings particular attention, and if they are read separately, one after another, a surprising proportion of his special (and often compressed) turns of imagery, syntax and vocabulary will be found in them.

No. 29 The Silver Jubilee: *To James First Bishop of Shrewsbury on the 25th Year of his Episcopate July 28 1876.* Composed at St Beuno's, Wales, in time for the Bishop's visit in July 1876.

In 1850, Pope Pius IX by Apostolic Brief restored the hierarchy of the Catholic Church in England and Wales to their own bishops, to replace the Vicars Apostolic who had held authority there since the seventeenth century. Bishops were installed in the new dioceses during 1850–1, Dr James Brown becoming Bishop of Shrewsbury (covering North Wales, Shropshire and Cheshire) on 27 July 1851. Hopkins with poetic licence treats the Silver Jubilee of Bishop Brown as the jubilee also of the Restoration of the Hierarchy though strictly speaking that had occurred in 1875 (see *Letters*, p. 65 and *Diocese of Shrewsbury Centenary Record*, 1951, p. 10).

When the Bishop visited St Beuno's in July 1876 after the jubilee celebrations in Shrewsbury, he was presented with a beautiful handmade album, bound in red morocco, containing in manuscript twenty-four congratulatory poems and addresses, composed by members of the college in fourteen different languages, including Arabic and Chinese. As Hopkins was the only one in the college with any knowledge of Welsh whatsoever, he had to struggle with the intricacies of a Welsh poem (No. 172); he also contributed one in Latin (No. 173) and another in English.

His English piece was selected for two honours: it was set to harmony by a 'very musical and very noisy member of the community and was sung as a glee by the choir', and it was also printed above his initials along with the sermon preached on the occasion by the Rev John Morris (*The Silver Jubilee*, London, 1876. See *Further Letters*, pp. 140–1.). Full details of the album and visit are given by Dr Alfred Thomas in his article 'G. M. Hopkins and the Silver Jubilee Album'. [*The Library*, 5th Series, XX: 2 (June 1965), pp. 148–52. See also *Journals*, pp. 191, 259, 403, 440 for John Morris and Bishop James Brown.]

The poem regrets the lack of popular and State recognition of the Catholic bishop's jubilee. The allusion in 'high-hung bells' is to the great cathedrals, no longer Catholic. In pre-Reformation times the mere arrival of a bishop, abbot or emperor at a place under his jurisdiction was heralded by the ringing of cathedral and church bells (Brand, *Popular Antiquities*, 1849, ii. 215–16), but such audible Catholic celebrations aroused resentment in Victorian England. In 1870, for instance, when the large Jesuit Church of St Francis Xavier, Liverpool, began using its newly acquired bells merely to announce the Sunday evening service the minister of a neighbouring Presbyterian church threatened legal action. But Hopkins declares that Nature herself seems to be welcoming the anniversary and offering to senses other than the ear a fine substitute for pealing bells and deafening military bugles. 'Nature's round' (st. 1) serves as a reminder of Newman's famous sermon of 1852 in which he had described the return of the hierarchy as a 'Second Spring'.

The second stanza suggests that when the English Catholic dioceses were restored in 1850–1, spiritual fountains long shut off by the suppression of Catholicism began to cascade openly again like showers of silver in the sunlight (st. 2). The present occasion was unique: whatever celebrations Shrewsbury (bishop or city) might witness in future times, the only true silver jubilee was this one (st. 3). The fourth stanza plays gracefully with the appropriateness of the silver colour of the Bishop's crown of hair while underplaying his ill health from overwork (*Journals*, p. 259). Finally, in lieu of the chiming bells which should have echoed in the Welsh valleys, the poet offers the chime of his verses.

Hopkins was pleased with the poem and encouraged by its reception: 'it seems to me to hit the mark it aims at without any

wrying'. But he classed it, along with 'The May Magnificat' (No.
42), as a 'popular' piece, falling short of his best (*Letters*, pp.
77–8). It is nevertheless markedly superior to the other English
poems entered in the Album, as the community seems to have
recognized. We may contrast in tone and quality the delight in
Wales expressed by his first and last stanzas with the unconvincing
ending of a piece in the Silver Jubilee album written by another
contributor: 'this fair land of Wales, where, cloudlike, loom/Dark
heresies, whose mournful widespread gloom/Have made its
rugged beauty sadder than the tomb'. We recall T. S. Eliot's
condemnation of much religious verse on the grounds that the
poets are 'writing as they want to feel, rather than as they do feel'
(*After Strange Gods*, London, 1934, p. 29).

No. 30 Penmaen Pool *for the Visitors' Book at the Inn*. Written at
Barmouth, Merionethshire, August 1876.

The theological students at St Beuno's College usually spent
their annual fortnight's holiday (or 'villa') in Barmouth, at the
mouth of the Welsh river the Mawddach. One favourite communal
excursion was rowing up the tidal estuary with the flood as far as
Penmaen Pool, a beautiful lagoon which became part of the river
when the waters rose. After breakfast at the George Hotel and
relaxing or climbing, the theologians rowed back to Barmouth
with the falling tide. Boats used to cost six shillings to hire: an
advertisement for the George in the *Gossiping Guide to Wales*
(1883, etc.) offered them for 'River, Lake and Sea Fishing'. It
boasted that the Inn was 'surrounded by River and Mountain
Scenery unsurpassed in Europe', with an endless variety of walks
and excursions.

This poem, which the poet reworked over a period of time so
that many variants exist, was originally written for the Visitors'
Book at the George in August 1876, but when I was staying at
Penmaen Pool in the 1950s the proprietor denied all knowledge of
the book, the poem and the very name of Hopkins himself.

The mountains in this area are for the most part under 3,000 feet
in height, yet Hopkins, in the spirit of the advertisements,
originally wrote 'Here rise the Alps', though he was himself
familiar with the great peaks of Switzerland. Rock climbs certainly
existed, visitors being warned to avoid the precipices, especially in
misty weather. For mountaineers, said the guide-books, there

were many attractions around the estuary. To the north of Penmaen Pool rose the mountain Diphwys (st. 3), to the south the volcanic ridge of Cader Idris (st. 2), also called the Giant's Stool, identified by its three hummocks or knolls (st. 3).

The poet treats Penmaen Pool as a drinking bowl lying between the two old mountains, from which each in turn drinks the health of the other, hobnobbing together (st. 3). Cader, the common Welsh word for a chair, is often used for mountain tops. Idris was reputed to have been a giant, the pebbles shaken out of his shoes being the boulders scattered around the Mawddach valley.

The reflections of the surrounding hills in the tranquil waters figure in stanza 4, where the reversed (trochaic) rhythm of line 3 is contrived to match the inverted ('topsyturvy') images in the Pool. But a slight shimmer on the surface adds brilliance to the reflections of fleecy clouds and the seven bright stars of the Plough, or Charles's Wain (st. 5).

Two stanzas (6 and 8) show cunning rhythmic manipulation to echo the sense. Notice the choking effect of 'throttled' (phonetically five consonants to a single vowel) and 'floodtide', which dam the flow of the lines just as the in-pressing tide holds back the tripping Mawddach. Another slowed line mirrors the snow-clogged landscape at Christmas:

> 'Furred snows, charged tuft above tuft, tower . . .' (st. 8).

The ninth stanza originally had a 'false' rhyme to which his father objected (see *Further Letters*, 141), *renewal*, *Pool*, and was therefore later completely rewritten. It had run:

> While if you're kept perforce at home
> You'll call (and that with fond renewal)
> For ale that mantles like the foam
> That furls an oar in Penmaen Pool.

The technical use of the word 'mantles' for the forming of a 'head' by liquids recalls a seventeenth-century recipe for improving beer: 'the Bran of Wheat, a little thereof boiled in our ordinary Beer, maketh it Mantle, or Flower in the Cup when it is poured out' (John Worlidge's *The Mystery of Husbandry Discovered*, London, 1681, p. 53).

Although this was one of Hopkins's 'popular' poems, such as he sometimes wrote for public occasions and showed to friends, its range of words and technical proficiencies is considerable.

No. 31 God's Grandeur Written at St Beuno's, Wales, 23 February 1877, revised in March and again later that year.

The first quatrain of this sonnet would have to be radically reshaped to bring it into conformity with the interpretations arrived at by many critics. It might then read roughly like this:

> The air is ablaze with the grandeur of God.
> Glory dazzles down like brilliance from noon sun;
> It gushes to a greatness like the run
> Of oil from wells. . . .

Hopkins's *foil* and, more particularly, his *ooze of oil* have seemed such inadequate symbols for the divine glory that the latter has been repeatedly explained in more seemingly impressive terms such as those I have versified above (see Dunne's *Bibliography*, K20–36).

But Hopkins assured Bridges that the starting-point of his poem was the image of gold-foil, which when viewed aslant may look dull but when shaken 'gives off broad glares like sheet lightning and also, and this is true of nothing else, owing to its zigzag dints and creasings and network of small many cornered facets, a sort of fork lightning too' (*Letters*, pp. 168–9). The electrical images ('charged' in l. 1, and 'lightning' which he thought of substituting for 'shining' in l. 2) convey danger as well as power, but their display is rare. The poet constantly emphasizes (as in st. 5 of the 'Wreck') that God's glory is hidden except to the enquiring eye or on special occasions. 'All things . . . are charged with God', he wrote in his meditations, but he added that it was only 'if we know how to touch them' that they will 'give off sparks and take fire, yield drops and flow, ring and tell of him' (*Sermons*, p. 195). Even then there is no gush of evidence, but the cumulative effect of many small proofs of divine wisdom which culminate in an impression of greatness. The electrical charge in an object cannot normally be detected by the eye. What was grey cloud one moment may the next dazzle us as a million kilowatts of energy (built up by the accumulation of innumerable minute charges on raindrops) is spectacularly discharged. In comparing the lightning to shaken gold foil, he may possibly have been influenced, as Pendexter suggests (*Explicator*, September 1964), by the gold-leaf electroscope, in which two filmy pieces of gold-foil hanging limply together are used as indicators of an electric current: the slightest charge will make them leap apart. We may compare the 'feathery delicacy' of the tall nun's reaction to Christ's presence in the 'Deutschland' drama (st. 31).

Contrasted with the violent image of the lightning, the next simile ('like the ooze of oil/Crushed') is mild, paralleling the antithesis in stanza 10 of the 'Wreck' between the blacksmith's bellow-fiercened fire and the genial warmth of spring. 'Oil' in earlier usage rarely referred to petroleum; in religious contexts olive oil was most frequently meant. In Biblical and Classical literature olive oil figures among the prime necessities of life – for food, light, cleansing and the healing of wounds. It had the most solemn associations in Catholic liturgy, since priests, bishops and kings were anointed with it, and it was prescribed for the extreme unction given to the dying. Nor was its general use obsolete in Hopkins's time. As recently as the mid-nineteenth century *oil* (i.e. olive oil) was among the most valuable imports into England from Italy whose oil-presses, while Hopkins was writing these sonnets, produced annually over forty million gallons of it, drop by drop (*American Cyclopaedia*, New York and London, 1875, Vol. ix., pp. 445–7): of olive oil the Victorians could certainly say 'It gathers to a greatness'. An early version of that line continued 'like an oozing oil/Pressed'. Here 'oozing' and 'Pressed' provide double warrant for assuming that the action of a press was intended, through association with the famous lines in Keats's 'Ode to Autumn': 'by a cyder-press, with patient look,/Thou watchest the last oozings hours by hours'. A conviction that God has not disappeared may come only after long patient investigation.

It is no doubt possible to interpret the poem in terms of petroleum (literally 'rock-oil'), but we must then substitute industrial overtones for the sacred symbolism of olive oil, reducing the antithesis between the two quatrains. A contemporary account of oil-fields in the *American Cyclopaedia* of 1875 (xiii., p. 369) emphasizes the 'disagreable pungent odor', surely akin to 'man's smell' reeking from factories (l. 7). 'Crushed' also loses its obvious significance, since both petroleum and shale-oil were products of distillation, not crushing. The violence and volume of petroleum bursting from subterranean depths contradicts the slow deliberation of 'ooze'. Hopkins did, however, mention the use of 'rock-oil for artificial light and heat' when preaching in 1880, though he referred also to the explosions and fires to which oil-wells were prone (*Sermons*, p. 90). If we cannot think ourselves back to the time when *oil* immediately suggested the fruit of the olive, we must at least reject in the present context gushing oil-wells: the ancient method of obtaining petroleum was by digging shallow pits and letting the oil exude into them from the surrounding soil.

Olive oil, like wine, was originally extracted by treading (Micah 6: 15), a practice which Hopkins alludes to in 'A Soliloquy of One of the Spies' (No. 5, ll. 51–3). The unshod feet of those who trod the presses brought an enriching flow, while the shod feet of later generations (not merely those of the Industrial Revolution) only crushed down the natural vegetation. The juxtaposition of 'trod' (l. 5) and 'trade' (l. 6) reminds us of their etymological connection. Richardson's *Dictionary* of 1858 begins its definition of 'trade' with 'A way or course *trodden*, and *retrodden*, passed and repassed'.

The rod which is being ignored (l. 4) is the sceptre or staff of divine authority, perhaps linkable with a 'shaft' of lightning, hardly with a lightning-rod (which adds nothing to the main argument). Hopkins contends that disowning God leads to an abuse of nature, a connection asserted more recently by T. S. Eliot: 'a wrong attitude towards nature implies, somewhere, a wrong attitude towards God' (*The Idea of a Christian Society*, 1939, p. 62). Elsewhere Hopkins expresses more openly his sympathy for the workers driven by the necessities of industrial expansion to 'treadmire toil' (No. 72, 'That Nature is a Heraclitean Fire', l. 8; cf. *Letters*, pp. 27–8). In this poem we feel the mutual impoverishment of men and earth. Farm land and meadow are disappearing under encroaching slag heaps and the blighting smudge of foundry smoke. When two years later he was stationed in Bedford Leigh, 'a darksome place, with pits and mills and foundries', he remembered 'God's Grandeur', as his reminiscent use of 'gather and ooze' in a letter of that time indicates (*Further Letters*, p. 243). Outside the beauty of the valley in which he wrote this poem, Wales itself had numerous areas blighted by mines and smelters.

The sestet shows that God has abandoned neither nature nor man. It begins, surprisingly, with *And* where we would expect

'But'. Nature has resources in reserve, not *spent* or exhausted like
the energies of the toilers. Among the ideas in his mind would
certainly be the amazing surging water of St Winefred's Well, a
few miles from St Beuno's College (*Journals*, p. 261). But even
this holy spring had been converted from a centre of pilgrimage
into a power source for industry, with foundries, smelters, rolling-
mills, lead works and cotton-spinning factories.

The 'last lights off the black West' which have vanished (l. 11)
may refer primarily to the faded sunset colours, but the phrase
almost forces on us the spectacle of an industrialized West dark
under a pall of polluting smoke. The last lines are a vision of dawn,
the physical sequence suggesting the hope of a religious rebirth. The
cloud which hovers over the east seems to enclose the divine Spirit,
like the cloud which rested over the Israelite Tabernacle in the
desert. The Holy Spirit broods fruitfully over a world which is *bent* –
curved, but also warped from the straight path, suffering from
Man's 'selfbent' like Ribblesdale (No. 58, l. 11). And we may fancy
that it is the coming sunrise, as the sun still below the horizon catches
the feathery fringes of the cloud, which shapes the final image of
hope as the poem ends: 'with ah! bright wings.'

Rhythmically, although not Sprung, the sonnet quickly escapes
from possible reminiscences of famous predecessors by departures
from normal types of iambic pentameter. Wordsworth had opened
a resonant sonnet: 'The world is too much with us; late and soon,
. . .' but if Hopkins's two initial iambs suggest that his line will run,
in tame obedience, 'The world is charged, as grandeur flows from
God', he quickly wrests our attention by reversing two successive
feet. In the MSS counterpoint signs indicate that *with* is stressed as
well as *grand*, though most readers probably finish the line with two
anapaests, leaving it a foot short. In line 5, in order that 'have trod,
have trod, have trod' may sound like dogged footfalls, Hopkins
counterpoints (reverses) the two opening measures, *Génerátions*.
He notes in MS *A* that this poem and the next one are to 'be read,
both of them, slowly, strongly marking the rhythms and fetching out
the syllables'. This process lends the sonnet additional weight since
it compels us to give almost full stress to some technically
unaccented syllables in 'Why do men then now not reck his rod?' (l.
4), and virtually converts into spondees such feet as 'bleared,
smeared' (l. 6), 'man's smudge', 'man's smell' (l. 7), 'West went'
(l. 11), 'brink east-' (l. 12), 'World broods', 'bright wings' (l. 14).

No. 32 The Starlight Night Written at St Beuno's the day after 'God's Grandeur', on 24 February 1877.

Like a campfire, the sky viewed from the darkness of a rural slope on a clear frosty night (such as Hopkins enjoyed on this winter evening) lends itself to fanciful pictures. In February from British latitudes one can see such suggestive patterns as sickle or u-shaped citadels in Leo and Corona Borealis, groups of stars like *bright boroughs* in the Pleiades and Orion, the long curved neck of Cygnus the Swan, which could be imagined a swirl of doves rising from the ground, Sirius so diamond-brilliant that it seems to change colour as it twinkles. Above all, the fascinating river of the Milky Way with its countless minute points of light lends itself to reveries, particularly if even such a simple aid as a pair of binoculars is used.

Though the connection seems to have escaped notice, that evening a paper had been read to the St Beuno's Essay Society on 'The Nebular Theory of Creation' (Thomas, *Hopkins the Jesuit*, p. 173 n.) – the hypothesis that the stars had slowly evolved through gravitational and other forces acting upon luminous gases diffused in space. Evidence from the Milky Way was being cited for and against the theory. But in this sonnet in place of cosmological argument we have the free play of reverie – the poet was reacting perhaps from the hard grind of legal and other studies in which he was involved in preparation for a stiff examination (*Further Letters*, pp. 143, 241–2).

At first the stars are treated in fairy-tale fashion as 'fire-folk sitting in the air', an opening which on rereading the poem we may feel in somewhat strained contrast with the equally imaginative but morally imbued final tercet – Christ and the saints feasting in a barn. From the third line onwards he interprets the starscapes above him as though he were looking down from a drifting balloon on a landscape dotted with forests and towns. As with campfire visions, of course, there is no consistency of scale or in the time of day or year represented. Two stars close together – the Milky Way is full of such pairs – may suggest the eyes of an elf like those of a little animal in the darkness reflecting light. Nearby an enclosing belt of stars, not very much larger, may figure as gas lamps ringing a small town. Stars vary from brilliant white, sapphire blue and amethyst through topaz yellow to ruby; books on astronomy almost inevitably match stars with gems. To the naked eye the Milky Way is largely composed of irregular veils of diffused light and of mysterious obscuring matter, against which distinct stars stand out, singly or in pairs or dotted lines, or else in clouds of microscopic specks too faint to be clearly resolved. Some of these misty areas become for the poet *dim woods* and others *grey lawns cold*. Among the woods, sparkling coloured stars suggest diamonds lying ready to be picked up from gem-studded *delves* – 'delf' is a dialect noun for a digging, pit or quarry. In folklore, which Hopkins did not automatically dismiss out of hand, as his *Journals* reveal (e.g. pp. 197–8, 263), elves were associated with mines and underground treasures. On grassy glades (or *lawns* opening within the forest) glint dew-drops of liquid gold (*quickgold*, invented after the pattern of 'quicksilver').

When seen from the right distance and angle, a glossy tree may be a mass of bright points. Ruskin in *Modern Painters* had ventured towards the comparison with stars when he said that 'the crowned and lovely trees of the earth . . . separate into stars', each ray of the leaf forming 'a ray of light in the crown' (*Works*, ed. Cook and Wedderburn, Vol. 5, p. 265). Here Hopkins glimpses a whitebeam (*Sorbus aria*), conspicuous against the dark cosmic foliage around: in a forest it stands out because of the snow-white silky down on its underleaves. Among the star-crowds he notes the equivalent of *airy abeles*, white poplars which in a terrestrial landscape reach sixty to ninety-five feet into the air, glinting silver one moment, olive-black the next as the leaves flare or wave in the breeze (*Journals*, pp. 143, 239). That he is not describing an actual landscape visible in the moonlight (as some critics have imagined) but one conjured up by his imagination is surely shown in the sestet, where we have fruit-tree blossom, which does not offer its *mess* or visual banquet till May (l. 10) side by side with the yellow catkins on the pussy willows (*Salix caprea*), which make their early and somewhat brief appearance in March, and so are used to decorate churches on Palm Sunday. We may compare Keats's 'Ever let the fancy roam', where the poet shows how the imagination may revel in the delights of all four seasons at once.

One line might be selected to demonstrate the complexities underlying the surface: 'Flake-doves sent floating forth at a farmyard scare! – ' (l. 7). Here the imagery is two-deep. Swirls of stars are compared to doves, such as those he had seen on the Isle of Man, where he 'started a shining flight of doves to settle on the roof' in a little hamlet round a mill (*Journals*, p. 235). And in turn the white doves are metaphorically converted into flakes of snow lifted in a winter eddy.

As in 'God's Grandeur', Hopkins associates a respect for nature with right living, and unlike the more ascetic clerics treats the ability to enjoy the temporary beauties of the visible heavens and earth as one of the rewards for basing moral behaviour on the demands of the new Heaven and new earth (l. 9). In the final tercet, the stars are seen as peep-holes in the *piece-bright paling* of the barn where the harvest-home feast is being held, radiant pinpoints of light from the blaze of candles within. And since in a complex metaphor the shocks or sheaves which have been garnered in are His spiritual harvest, this is also a wedding supper celebrating the union of Christ the bridegroom (the *spouse*) and His saints (*all his hallows*). The sonnet reaches an unexpectedly solemn finish with an echo from the parable of the foolish virgins who had let their lamps (their stars as it were) go out and who tried in vain to join the marriage ceremony when 'the door was shut' (Matt. 25: 10). This feast, and its counterpart the Mass, to which everyone has been invited, has to be bidden for with 'Prayer, patience, alms, vows', just as a delight in the splendours of the material universe must be (cf. *Sermons*, p. 79).

No. 33 Spring Written at St Beuno's, May 1877.

The octave of this sonnet is an ecstatic description of spring in terms of fluidity. The weeds are *lush* (succulent, juicy), shooting up in *wheels* – there is some suggestion of a fountain seen from above, with radiating leaves and stems which cascade in spokes (like the wheel of light-drops from wings in 'A Vision of the Mermaids', No. 2, ll. 76–7). British fields in May are also covered with flower-heads like bright pulley-wheels or sprockets, and clumps of tall grasses 'wheel' in the breeze like the surface of a lake. Thrush eggs are tiny pools reflecting the greeny-blue of the heavens; the thrush's song, like a jet of water, rinses the ear; and the sky seems to be flowing with colour, as though it were a rich blue fountain seen from inside its liquid dome.

The happy rapidity of movement is exaggerated (as in a speeded-up film), after the sluggishness of winter. Plants 'shoot up long, lovely, and lush' (so he first wrote); the bird's song beams out with the precipitancy of light rather than sound, striking the tree-trunks and rebounding; the pear-tree puts out leaves and blossoms as he watches it; the azure of the sky is not only *descending* (in contrast with winter skies 'hard as any stone' in 'A Voice from the World', No. 81, l. 8), but *in a rush*; and the lambs race and leap as though in a wild folk dance (cf. *Journals*, p. 206).

In 'Paradise Lost' (following ancient traditions) Milton had envisaged the Garden of Eden as luxuriating in a perpetual spring combined with the fruitfulness of autumn (iv. ll. 148, 264–8: v. ll. 394–5). But after man's Fall, he theorized, God shifted the axis of the earth or else the sun's orbit, to produce the punishing extremes of summer and winter (x. ll. 649–707). Gladstone had compared to the Garden of Eden the Vale of Clwyd in which Hopkins composed this sonnet, and in the sestet Hopkins treats the Welsh spring as an annual reminder of what the earthly Paradise must have been like, an inheritance and survival (*strain*) from it.

Some critics have felt that the 'moralizing' conclusion to this sonnet is not an integral part of it. Seamus Heaney, e.g. in a lecture published by the British Academy in 1974, regretted that 'Spring', while a 'delightful piece of inscaping', is 'nevertheless structurally a broken arch, with an octave of description aspiring towards a conjunction with a sestet of doctrine'. Yet the octave, when more closely scrutinized, shows compatability with if not actual anticipation of the theocentric interpretation which follows it. Even among the luxuriance of the weeds he recognizes order and pattern: the circle ('wheel') is a frequent symbol of the divine, and 'God dwells in . . . plants giving them growth', as he elsewhere wrote (*Sermons*, p. 193). The eggs he selects are in colour a microcosmic reflection of the divine heavens, while the song of the thrush is associated with lightning, the special instrument of the Lord ('Wreck', st. 2). And like all good and perfect gifts (James 1: 17), the richness of spring seems to be flowing down from above, the tree boughs drinking it in as their leaves join the earth to the sky.

In the last four lines of the poem Hopkins invokes a vision of the boy Christ, with His young maiden Mother; and prays that He may possess and preserve the freshness of the spring world in children (their *Mayday*), which the poet compares to an unclouded liquid – such as honey strained from the comb when fresh, which is liable when older to *cloy* (become set, clogging the comb), to lose its pure transparency and (as classical honey did) go *sour*. He uses different metaphors for a similar idea in 'Morning, Midday, and Evening Sacrifice' (No. 49).

In view of the popularity of spring as a poetic subject in all Western literatures, Hopkins is outstandingly successful in striking fresh notes: his selection of weeds for praise rather than flowers, his dazzled simile for the thrush's song, the exuberance which imagines trees in the ecstasy of May growth having their fling along with the new lambs. Rhythmically he has understated his originality by describing it as written in 'Standard rhythm, with sprung leadings' (i.e. with the first unstressed syllables omitted at the openings to octave and sestet, leaving these lines one syllable short). More striking is his approach towards the liberties of Sprung Rhythm with a hurry of light syllables in such lines as 'A strain of the earth's sweet being in the beginning' (l. 10), and by providing contrasts of weight and airiness in the final line of the poem.

No. 34 In the Valley of the Elwy Written at St Beuno's, 23 May 1877.

St Beuno's College, beautifully situated on the Clwydian Range, looks out over the Vale of Clwyd, frequently referred to in Victorian times as 'The Garden of Wales'. Two contributory rivers, the Clwyd and the Elwy, run parallel courses below the college, but Hopkins (as the title of this poem indicates), preferred the upper reaches of the Elwy (more wild and romantic with its lofty wooded banks), to the comparatively placid Clwyd. The precise date, given in a copy Hopkins sent to his sister Grace, shows that the poem was produced at the end of his Whitsun vacation, which ran from Saturday afternoon 19 May till Wednesday 23 May (Thomas, *Hopkins the Jesuit*, p. 179).

But only the sestet refers to the Valley of the Elwy or even to Wales. The household introduced in the octave, which Hopkins remembered with such gratitude, was (as he explained to Bridges in a letter two years later, 8 April 1879), that of the Watsons, friends of his family who lived in Kent, on the airy wooded ridges of Shooter's Hill, surrounded by coppices and farms and grassy commons. Deep finely timbered combes ran down from the hill towards the Thames. Hopkins, who believed that people should live in harmony with their natural surroundings, associated the kindness which met him the moment he walked into their home with the feelings he had when he entered a copse of trees – that he had put on their shelter as though it were a hood or a hat

(*Journals*, 233). His friends seemed a part of the woodlands around them, and made him at home and at ease in their company.

He protests that their welcome was more than he deserved, in case he should appear self-righteous in the moral judgments of the sestet. The contrast between their house and Wales was clearer in the original wording: 'Lovely the woods, waters, meadows, combes, vales,/All the air things wear that make this house, this Wales'. The Welsh are treated (by synecdoche) as a single house-holder, who contrasts with Hopkins's English friends because he is out of unison with the natural beauty he inhabits: *inmate* is used with something of an older sense: 'one not originally or properly belonging to the place where he dwells; a foreigner, a stranger' (*OED*). Yet he also is a *creature dear* to God, and Hopkins prays that God, who weights the scales of justice with mercy, will deal with man's imperfections, since he has the power as Master and the love as heavenly Father. The reference to the shortcomings of the *creature dear* obviously embraces all mankind, not merely the Welsh.

Bridges found the sonnet hard to understand, and Hopkins, after explaining the octave as being factually true, added apologetically that the thought was 'very far fetched'. Among the unexpected twists in its analogies are that the goodness of the family in Kent is stated in terms of their kindness to the poet — yet the first line on its own (if we pause at its end after 'where all were good') and our subsequent deduction from the sestet, lead us to assume that this is only one evidence that they were good people.

Then we would certainly expect from the phrase 'good/To me' that it would be the poet himself to whom the breath of the fresh wood would bring comfort, and who would feel himself clothed with protective warmth. We are tempted to read line 5 as 'That cordial air made the kind people into a hood over me'. But this construing, though possible when the line is taken on its own, makes nonsense of the passage following. Hopkins clearly intended: 'That cordial air made for those kind people a hood all over them, as a mothering wing will [make a hood] for a bevy of eggs, or as mild nights will shield the tender shoots of Spring'.

These complexities may very well have originated in Hopkins's realization that even apparently confident people (such as his friends of Shooter's Hill) are like the 'new morsels of Spring', in need of fostering shelter. The human race, given responsibility for a world of wonderful beauty, of which the first chapter of Genesis tells us many times 'God saw that it was good', has failed to complete the perfection of the universe which was made for them. The paradoxical manuscript description of the metrical form, 'Standard rhythm, sprung and counterpointed', prepares us for special effects. These include the trochaic opening to the octave (suggesting that the line will run like 'I remember homes where all were kindly') and to the sestet (when instead of five iambs the first, third and fourth feet are trochees and the fifth virtually a spondee). Other delightful liberties include four extra syllables in line 6, and in line 10 an introductory hypermetrical full stress which seems to turn the metre into a trochaic hexameter.

No. 35 The Sea and the Skylark Written between 9 and 14 May, 1877, at Rhyl, the 'shallow and frail town' which appears in the sestet, and which might well have shared the title with the sea and the skylark.

Commentators, puzzled by the poet's dissatisfaction, have imagined that he was attacking disfiguring mines or industries, neither of which in fact Rhyl possessed. It was purely a summer resort, to which a tidal flood of English visitors, in annually increasing numbers, poured in from May onwards. During the off-season the Welsh lodging-house keepers were left to themselves in a ghost town.

Hopkins treats Rhyl as a symbol of Victorian 'progress', uniformity and rootlessness. Like the semi-fashionable suburbs being flung up all over Britain, it had no history and little character or inscape. In 1820 it had been no more than a few fishermen's cottages, but the opening of the Chester-Holyhead railway in mid-century brought hordes of visitors from crowded cities to crowd together again on the flat beach and venture knee-deep into the shallow sea. Man had been created to 'have dominion over' the animal and physical creation (Gen. 1: 26), but Hopkins, looking with the eye of an artist at his fellow-countrymen in the mass, felt that so far from having evolved upwards, they represented the dregs of a once noble race.

Most of the visitors to Rhyl used to come from Liverpool, then one of the most unhealthy of British towns. About this time Liverpool's birth-rate was little more than half the average for

England, while its death-rate and marriage-rate were double. Four years later, after watching the May Day procession of horses in Liverpool, he told Bridges in a passage which Swift would have approved that while 'I admired the handsome horses I remarked for the thousandth time with sorrow and loathing the base and besotted figures and features of the Liverpool crowd. When I see the fine and manly Norwegians that flock hither to embark for America walk our streets and look about them it fills me with shame and wretchedness. I am told Sheffield is worse though' (*Letters to Bridges*, pp.127–8).

A similar reaction to Rhyl's indecorous summer visitors (and its featureless winter aspect around 1920) is to be found in the autobiographical novel *Mount Ida* by the sensitive Irish poet, Monk Gibbon: he lived for a while in this neighbourhood.

The poem was first entitled 'Walking by the Sea'. On his right the poet, as he approached the straggling (*shallow*) town from the east, had the sea, which at high tide rushed towards the *ramps* of the protective sea-wall, rearing up like a lion — rampant and roaring. But if he came that way when the tide was out, he found the waves had receded over a quarter-of-a-mile down the shallow slope (*low lull-off*). Hopkins does not really claim that the sound of the sea is eternal. He took his view of the past and the future more from the Bible than such scientific pronouncements as John Tyndall's famous Belfast address on evolution (which Hopkins had criticized in a letter to his mother — *Further Letters*, pp. 127–8). The moon is said to *wear* (l. 4), and the earth's *prime* is in the *past* (l. 12). One day, when Time comes to an end, the present deteriorating heaven and earth, along with the sea, will have to be transformed (Rev. 21: 1). But within Time, and compared with man, the sea and the skylark give out 'noises too old to end', unchanging down the centuries.

Inland on his left were low sand-dunes, a favourite haunt of the skylark. His first version of the skylark's flight and song was too complicated for Bridges to follow, and had to be explained in a lengthy letter (26–7 November 1882 — both are reproduced in the notes to the 4th edn). Though the sense was not exactly 'glaring', it was nevertheless, he claimed, certainly there. Basically the poet thinks of the lark's song as falling to earth along the track up which it has been climbing while singing. The bird does not spiral but ascends almost vertically, in a steep zigzag. As it climbs, Hopkins imagines that its musical score of song (like the skeins of a ribbon creased through having been wrapped tightly round a flat holder), is unlapped from its reel or winch, and falls to the ground, zigzagging downwards. (We might compare the print-out emerging from a computer.) When this winch is completely unwound — the bird may climb to a thousand feet, beyond sight — the lark follows roughly the same track down, still singing. Hopkins imagines crisp folds or curls of song, as they fall into its nest, being there rewound (or in older usage *re-winded*) on yet another wild flat-spindled winch until all of it has been stored ('till none's to spill nor spend'), ready for a future song flight.

The powerful and impetuous quality of the sound from the skylark is emphasized by its being classed with the noise of the sea: both *trench* (furrow) his hearing. It is also *rash-fresh* (l. 6 – cf. 'Wreck', st. 19, 'rash smart sloggering brine'), and is said to 'whirl, and pour/And pelt' (ll. 7, 8). Intermingled with the image of song-skeins is the idea of a stream of music being *spilt* from a height. He pictures the wash of the sea waves and the thin waterfall of singing *poured* from above as sweeping away the *sordid turbid* marsh of the present age. It was out of dust (or *slime* as the Douay renders Gen. 2: 7) that man was originally made. In the last two lines Hopkins sketches the graph of mankind's history, not as rising gradually higher towards the semi-divine stature envisaged by some of his contemporaries, but, after beginning at the peak of its 'cheer and charm' in the Garden of Eden, as deteriorating little by little, eroding away to the featureless materials out of which it had been made.

If this seems a drearily pessimistic picture, it matches quite closely a famous passage in Newman's *Apologia* (chap. V), in which he declared that looking into the living busy world of men he could find 'no reflexion of its Creator'. The history of the roles of men seemed to be full of 'their aimless courses, their random achievements and acquirements, . . . the defeat of good, the success of evil, physical pain, mental anguish, the prevalence and intensity of sin, the pervading idolatries, the corruptions, the dreary hopeless irreligion' — only partially alleviated by high ambitions and gropings after good. This was a vision, Newman concluded, 'to dizzy and appal'.

Like the preceding poem, this sonnet feels its way towards the greater freedom of full Sprung Rhythm: Hopkins described it as

'Standard rhythm, in parts sprung and in others counterpointed'. All sorts of onomatopoeic effects dictate the words and rhythm. The opening conveys the continuous assault of noises by repeating three sounds ('ear . . . ear', 'two, too, to', 'and . . . end' — almost the same in any normal Englishman's delivery). Rhythmic irregularities in the next two lines mirror the impact of waves breaking and rushing up the ramp. Something of the excited stridency and rhythmic variability in a lark's song is brought to us by the sudden change of beat in line 6; and the hypnotically echoing two final lines seem to establish their own authority, bringing the sonnet to a conclusion which satisfies the ear though it may fail to convince our intellect.

No. 36. The Windhover Written at St Beuno's, 30 May 1877.

When Hopkins early one spring morning, in a subdued frame of mind, went out from St Beuno's College and *caught* the flight of the windhover, the sonnet which sprang from his blend of excitement and sober musings about the future was destined to become, out of all the lyrics since the middle of the nineteenth century, the one that has probably attracted the most thought and commentary. Dunne's *Bibliography* records nearly a hundred approaches to it before 1970 alone, contributions we cannot possibly summarize here. Where so much is imaginatively suggested rather than delineated by prosaic statement, each reader feels free to catch his own glimpses of the poet's mood and his maze of ideas, and to disagree with other readings. But as with a diamond viewed from various angles, the impressions created in observers will change as they move, and no 'final' reading of the poem can be claimed by students of literature, linguists, theologians, or naturalists.

Anthony Jack, in one of the most interesting full-scale attempts in English to describe in aerodynamic terms the precise flight characteristics of various birds (*Feathered Wings*, London, Methuen, 1953), begins by quoting 'The Windhover', and goes on to discuss the intricacies of muscular adjustment each different bird has to make in order to combat the gusts and eddies which confront it – to 'rebuff' the wind (l. 7). Each type of bird has its own appropriate shape and size of wing, but whereas most of our aircraft are designed to provide stability at the expense of manoeuvrability, birds have to be far more flexible. They can execute sharp turns like an expert skater, and dive swiftly on to their prey, yet at the last moment rear out wings which not only prevent them from injuring themselves but enable them to twist after their vanishing quarry because of their 'unstable aerodynamic systems'. Only their astounding sensitivity to differences in air pressure and their instantaneous readjustments of complex wing mechanisms enable them to command an apparently effortless flight. Man is still trying to learn all the secrets of their navigational achievements. The marvellous adaptations of individual species to particular environments and needs are analysed in such books as Jean Dorst's *The Life of Birds* (trans. I. C. J. Galbraith, 2 vols, New York, Columbia University Press, 1974), and the beautifully illustrated monograph by Leslie Brown and Dean Amadon, *Eagles, Hawks and Falcons of the World* (2 vols, London, Country Life Books, 1968). Our own hearts ought certainly to be 'stirred' when we study their mastery of the air.

As a bird-watcher, having once 'caught' the kestrel's characteristic flight pattern, I have found it one of the easiest birds to identify on the wing from a distance. The windhover (*falco tinnunculus*) is widely distributed in Europe, Asia and Africa, while in America a close relative, the American kestrel (formerly called the sparrow-hawk), shares its ability to hover. No other birds are as expert in hovering into the wind, their body horizontal, tail and head pointed downwards, while they scrutinize the ground below, looking for the source of some movement which they have glimpsed as they glided along. To remain stationary over one spot they have to fly into the wind at exactly its own speed, with rapidly quivering (*wimpling*, l. 4) wings, missing a. few beats as gusts die, accelerating as they freshen. This requires two separate absorptions (or 'ecstasies', l. 5) – a discriminating searching of the terrain thirty to fifty feet below, and almost computer-speed responses to variations in the wind.

The hover may continue for a full minute. Only one hover in about eight results in a 'stoop' to the ground, so that we must not assume that this diving movement is necessarily incorporated in the poem. When it takes place, it is a short, somewhat slow descent at a slope, with wings held high and tense above the back. Kestrels do not drop inertly like a stone. The application of 'buckle' in the sense of 'collapse' to the controlled stoop of any falcon must, from an ornithologist's viewpoint, be considered as uninformed as it would be if used of an Olympic high-diver. Nor can I easily accept an attacking hunter as a symbol of sacrifice. But these ideas are now deeply entrenched.

If no quarry appears, after the hover the kestrel will be 'off forth on swing' (l. 5), banking against the wind like a skater (l. 6) or side-slipping expertly, and speeding down wind again with planing wings on 'the rolling level underneath him steady air' (l. 3) until with a sudden about turn and upward swoop or 'stride' he is hovering once more. The American kestrel, though he frequently hovers, tends to do less riding of the air, preferring to keep watch from the top of some bare tree or telephone pole. Except when driving off high-flying predators such as eagles and crows, kestrels keep close to the ground. Neither the British nor the American kestrels 'ring' upward in ascending spirals, which would merely take them out of range of their food sought among the grass and vegetation. Windhovers must not be confused with the upward gyring falcons of Yeats's 'The Second Coming'. Though kestrels can be *technically* described as 'soaring', in their case this means that they plane into an ascending current of air (caused e.g. by the slopes above St Beuno's), at such an angle that their height above the ground immediately below them remains more or less the same.

Hopkins's suggestive, but enigmatic statement, 'how he rung upon the rein of a wimpling wing/In his ecstasy' (ll. 4, 5) has been largely responsible for the mistake of attributing to the windhover a climbing spiral. The image is then supposedly drawn from a riding school in which horses attached by a long rein to their trainer in the middle of a circle are taught to run around a ring (though presumably not in much of an *ecstasy*). However, an examination of the first surviving draft of the poem makes clear that the ringing of the rein was during the hover (ll. 3–5):

> and striding
> He hung so and rung the rein of a wimpled wing
> In an ecstacy; then off, forth on swing. . . .

The 'hung' and 'rung' (or 'rang' as we would now say) obviously refer to the hovering, after the abrupt arrest of the riding, and before the kestrel goes off again 'on swing'.

Having tried to catch the inscape of the bird out of which the sonnet arose, let us now examine the poem in more detail. It was begun on 30 May 1877. The fair copy sent to Bridges had several revisions, and was itself replaced some time after 22 June 1879 by an amended copy with further changes. Up to that date Hopkins felt it was 'the best thing I ever wrote' (*Letters*, p. 85). But critics seldom remember that this statement was made in mid-career. He may later have changed his mind since in 1883–4 Hopkins told Patmore that his 'favourite' piece was 'The Wreck of the Deutschland' (*Further Letters*, p. 353). When the poet at that stage came to edit Bridges's copy of the 'Windhover' in MS *B*, he made some further striking alterations, and added 'to Christ our Lord' in the title. To some this is only a dedication, but others have noticed that wherever Hopkins has a similar extension in a title, in the course of the poem he actually addresses the person named. Thus line 14 of 'The Silver Jubilee', No. 29, '*Your* wealth of life is some way spent', makes it quite clear that the subtitle, 'To James First Bishop of Shrewsbury', is not merely a dedication. (Cf. No. 55, 'Spring and Fall', and No. 76, 'To R.B.'.)

The octave presents the windhover as the favourite bird of the daylight, perhaps in contrast with the nightingale, which successions of poets had panegyrized as the 'sweet queen of night' and in similar misleading terms. But this piece is not an 'Ode to a Windhover'; it is a poem to Christ. The windhover in his *mastery* of the element of air (l. 8) seems a representative of Christ, Whose mastery of the tides and the storms and of men themselves Hopkins had celebrated in 'The Wreck of the Deutschland' (e.g. sts 1, 10, 19, 32).

The poem's opening lines crowd in suggestions about the bird's appearance, the circumstances under which Hopkins *caught* him, and the metaphorical role he will play in the sonnet. Dr Geoffrey Hartman remarks on Hopkins's unusual word-consciousness here: 'the poem's very continuity seems to derive from an on-the-wing multiplication of the sound of one word in the next, like a series of accelerating explosions': *morning* to *morning's* to *minion* and the intricate contrasting and echoing assonances and consonant chimes which follow (*The Unmediated Vision*, p. 49). The falcon is not the sovereign, *our Lord* of the title, but the *minion* (darling, favourite) or *dauphin* (a name for the heir to the French throne which dates from the chivalric Middle Ages). The early autographs made more explicit reference to the king-like sun, reading 'king/Of daylight's dauphin'. But when in 1884 Hopkins came to edit the copy made by Bridges in MS *B*, he saw that this phrase was ambiguous: the bird could be mistakenly supposed to be 'king over the dauphin of daylight', the reverse of his intention (which was 'dauphin to the king of daylight'). As 'king' was a rhyme-word, the poet did not wish to tamper with it, so he cleverly added 'dom' to the beginning of the next line.

The idea of an affectionate bond with the royal sun but subordination to him is deducible from the rich word-cluster which follows, *dapple-dawn-drawn*. The dawn leads to sunrise and is outshone by it, as the falcon here leads to Christ, Who is a billion times lovelier (ll. 10, 11).* The bird is drawn into flight by the dawn. He is also drawn or marked to match the early grey sky with its dappled reddish clouds: the kestrel has a blue-grey head, rump and tail, with dappled chestnut upper parts, and buff underparts spotted or barred with deep brown. The shape and dark steel colour of the head and beak when seen full on make him appear to be wearing a medieval helmet with nose- and cheek-pieces. The riding of the 'level underneath him steady air' may be compared to the smooth glide of a powerful boat cutting through oncoming surges.

In this sonnet the kestrel is primarily a knight riding on horseback, corresponding to Christ the *chevalier* of line 11. But just as any good rider learns to move with his mount, leaning and redistributing his weight to ease its every leap or swerve, so here the knight and his horse coalesce in lines 3 and 4 when he is described as 'striding/High there'. He comes to an abrupt halt, like a steed 'wrung' to a stop by the rein — this homonym of 'rung' seems to contribute to the intended meaning. Ringing 'upon the rein of a wimpling wing' (l. 4), as I see it, is an allusion to the ripple effect of the briskly beating wing-tips, like little waves sent down the shaken strap of a rein (cf. the use of 'wimpled' in No. 49, l. 2, and No. 59, 'The Golden Echo', l. 10). He hovers, the wings winnowing rapidly as he scans the ground intently. But while the poet watches the falcon no prey causes him to dive (as I read the poem), and he resumes his planing flight. The simile of a

---

* But Alison Sulloway, quoting Isaiah 14: 12, 'How art thou fallen from heaven, O Lucifer, son of the morning!' suggests that the windhover represents 'the type of Satanic, or diabolic, vision that often intrudes even upon the most pious souls', and that Hopkins in the sestet realizes that he was nearly misled by it. (*Hopkins Quarterly*, Vol. I, No. 1, April 1974, pp. 43–51.)

skater on a tight curve, intermixed with the metaphor of a bent bow, together convey the counterbalancing forces of wind resistance, the bird's own impetus and the pull of gravitation which he manipulates so masterfully (ll. 5–7). The word *Rebuffed* (besides being echoic, imitating the fanning blows of the wings), emphasizes the self-contained distinctiveness of the windhover, separate from the air which he uses to support himself. In a later famous passage among his meditations, Hopkins applied the verb to express the sense of uniqueness which his own individuality impressed upon him: 'when I compare my self, my being-myself, with anything else whatever, all things alike, all in the same degree, *rebuff* me with blank unlikeness' (*Sermons*, p. 123).

In the perfect adaptation of its movements to its way of life the poet recognizes in the windhover a creature acting out superbly the nature he has been given. And Hopkins (always diffident about his own performance) is roused in self-depreciative admiration: 'My heart in hiding/Stirred for a bird' (ll. 7, 8). Whatever his state of depression, of physical or mental exhaustion or temporary lack of enthusiasm (see *Letters*, p. 33; *Further Letters*, pp. 145–6), he was challenged by a mere bird, a *brute*, a *thing,* and the inspiration he caught has been setting readers alight ever since.

In the sestet we reach more debatable ground, and the explication which follows is not intended of course to preclude all other readings. In line 9 animal beauty and courage along with its expression in action, or (in other terms) the wind, the bird's spirit and his distinctive appearance, here gloriously combine (*Buckle!*). And (as any perfect act in a creature reveals the greater glory of the Creator), the flight of the windhover brings a dazzling revelation from the great chevalier, whose splendour is a billion times greater than any from a created being. Christ's fire is *dangerous*, not something which we can admire or ignore as we please, but demanding recognition, obedience and love. Newman once told a congregation which had doubts about the place of fear in the Christian life that the 'Author of Evil' was 'a master who allows himself to be served without trembling', but, he said, any approach to a holy and all-powerful God demanded the combination of love and fear which we call Christian Reverence. 'The Wreck of the Deutschland' shows the fire of God as often gently warming like May sunshine, but when its invitation to love is rejected turning into the terror of lightning, or a fiery forge (sts 9, 10, 34).

No single equivalent for *Buckle* can contain all that the word has
come to mean to the wide diversity of readers who have admired
this poem. Three aspects of the kestrel's achievement are mentioned (l. 9): his physical beauty of plume, his spirit (*valour* or
pride, the latter hinting at a display of mastery and fitness), and *act*
or *air.* St Thomas Aquinas had emphasized the difference between
the 'potential' qualities in a creature and those potentialities
expressed in 'act' (when its imperfection in those respects becomes
a perfection). The three elements of the windhover's inscape join
together (as a belt is buckled into a complete circle). But such an
attainment of unity is often due to the resolution of a conflict, an
inward battle, where separate parts are fused into one; and
therefore those further meanings of *Buckle* which refer to arming
for battle, or engaging in close combat, interact in our interpretation.

Father Alfred Thomas, in a valuable article (*Modern Language
Review,* Vol. 70, No. 3, July 1975, pp. 497–507) has shown that
Buckle was connected with hawking in the Inn sign 'Hawk and
Buckle' (where the buckle is the D-shaped fetterlock in the House
of York's heraldic badge — a device for binding together). Less
helpful but interesting is the technical use of *buckle* in Colonel
Thornton's description of falconry in his *Sporting Tour through the
Northern Parts of England and . . . Scotland* (London, 1804). A
passage which Dr Thomas does not quote explains one sense we
must otherwise guess at: his falcons had flown not less than 'nine
miles, beside an infinite number of buckles, or turns' (p. 143).
Buckle might there be the equivalent of 'loop', though elsewhere it
means 'contest'.

A subsidiary interpretation of 'buckle' may be ventured upon.
The reference to the brilliant fire which results from the buckling
suggests to me that Hopkins may possibly have had at the back of
his mind that the buckling completed an electric circuit AND that
this resulted in the production of a blinding arc of light. No Jesuit
could have used the word *act* (l. 9) without being reminded of
'potentiality', a scholastic term. 'Potential' was the name adopted
in the nineteenth century for the electromotive force or pressure in
a circuit, to which whole chapters were devoted in contemporary
books on electricity (e.g. Henry Noad, *Student's Text-book of
Electricity,* London, 1867). The word 'turn-buckle' applied to a
device for coupling electric wires into a circuit is recorded as an

already accepted term in Funk's *Standard Dictionary* (New York and London) of 1895, but its earliest use remains to be discovered: the coincidence is interesting, but not crucial to my interpretation. By the 1870s electric arcs had been made to produce light equal to a third of the sun's in brilliance, and writers warned experimenters how *dangerous* it was to expose their eyesight to such strong radiation: the whole body could be 'affected as by a powerful sunstroke'. Like the embers in lines 13–14, the carbon elements burned themselves away as they transmitted the light and heat. Even the hardest metal could be melted in its dangerous fire. Yet the electric arc could also produce lovely colours when placed in appropriate gases or with a change of electrodes — rose, blue, violet, orange, or an intense green.

Revolutionary as this supplementary reading of the imagery may appear at first glance, it is clearly in line with others in Hopkins's earlier poems and later writings. God's grandeur (in No. 31, ll. 1, 2) is obviously thought of as an electric charge which will flame out like lightning, and the 'Wreck' repeatedly associates God's power with the 'electrical horror' of the storm (sts 2, 9, 27, 34). In the *Sermons* (p. 195) creatures, the 'works of God's finger' — the windhover being a fine example — are said to be 'charged' with the Holy Ghost, 'and if we know how to touch [or 'catch'] them give off sparks and take fire'. As Geoffrey Grigson puts it, through the nature God has made 'he passes the voltage of the current of his love, his grandeur' (*Gerard Manley Hopkins,* p. 20). That Hopkins should abruptly turn from nature description to a direct address to Christ should surprise no one who has studied the other poems of his Welsh period (cf. No. 33, 'Spring', l. 12; No. 34, 'In the Valley of the Elwy', l. 12).

The final tercet treats the preceding three lines as an outstanding example of some general law of which it proceeds to give two much humbler examples. We might formulate it in some such ways as these: 'When valour leads to action, light breaks out', or 'Fulfilling one's nature reflects the glory of the Creator'. Instead of the knife-edged wings parting the air or the skate-blade cutting a swift curve in ice, the poet presents us with a more work-a-day and attainable model in the laborious plough (ll. 12, 13). Virgil (*Georgics* i. 45–6) and Lucretius (*De Rerum Natura* i. 313) had both remarked how the ploughshare which had rusted in winter was polished as it rubbed against the clods during the spring ploughing. The practical effect is that it slices through the soil with less friction, but a by-product is that the blade mirrors the brilliance of the sun. So the *sheer plod* of the horses and of the ploughman (accompanied, as Lucretius and Ruskin observed, by the wearing away of the ploughshare), brings reflected sunshine into the fields. A *sillion* (or 'selion' as modern dictionaries spell it) is a long, narrow sub-division of an open field, separated from the rest of it only by drainage ditches, and (appropriately in this context) often belonging to a tenant or small farmer.

A rather different interpretation results if we take the 'chevalier' in line 11 to refer to the windhover, not to the Christ of the title; though no major difference might be felt in line 13 whether *ah my dear* is an allusion to his own heart or, as in Hopkins's much favoured poet George Herbert, is addressed to Christ Himself. Since Christ told His disciples that 'No man putting his hand to the plough, and looking back, is fit for the kingdom of God' (Luke 9:62), the ploughman has always been interpreted as a metaphor for a Christian or more particularly a priest.

The second humble exemplar for human life substitutes for the French prince of the octave (whose royal colours, blue and gold, are imitated by the kestrel's plumage) an image of extreme humility — *blue-bleak embers,* which seem dead and cold until they spear themselves open in ultimate sacrifice, giving out to their surroundings their core reserves of golden light and warmth. This metaphor for selfless love seems to point to the crucifixion as the supreme example of 'fall-gold mercies' (cf. 'Wreck', st. 23). It is surely in the self-sacrifice of the collapsing embers rather than in any movement of a hawk that we may most legitimately find the lesson of life-giving abnegation which the poet spells out for himself in this mysteriously powerful sonnet.

No. 37 Pied Beauty Written at St Bueno's, summer 1877.

Although on the surface this miniature or scaled-down 'curtal' sonnet (see Reference Section) seems basically a nature poem, it embodies a theological belief which has been important to many Catholic and Protestant philosophers. The same idea also under-lies 'As kingfishers catch fire' (No. 57, *q.v.*). Cardinal (later Saint) Bellarmino, an Italian contemporary of Francis Bacon, in his Latin treatise on *The mind's ascent to God through the ladder of created things* wrote: 'Though the mere multitude of created things is itself wonderful, and a proof of the multiform perfection of the one God, still more wonderful is the variety which appears in that multiplication, and it leads us more easily to the knowledge of God; for it is not difficult for one seal to make many impressions exactly alike, but to vary shapes almost infinitely, which is what God has done in creation, this is in truth a divine work, and most worthy of admiration. . . . Raise now, my soul, the eye of thy mind towards God, in whom are the Ideas of all things and from whom, as from an inexhaustible fountain, this well-nigh infinite variety springs' (quoted A. O. Lovejoy, *The Great Chain of Being*, Harvard University Press, 1936, p. 91).

The Victorian Age tended to impose a drab uniformity upon England. Dickens in *Hard Times* portrayed industrial Coketown as made up of 'streets all very like one another, . . . inhabited by people equally like one another, who all went in and out at the same hours, with the same sound upon the same pavements, to do the same work' (Bk 1, chap. 5). John Stuart Mill was so provoked by the censorious pressure of Victorian public opinion on matters of convention that he included in his book *On Liberty* a section advocating the development of eccentricity. People in all walks of life, he said, were now asking themselves how it was *customary* for those in their situation to act, whereas each ought rather to enquire 'what would allow the best and highest in me to have fair play, and enable it to grow and thrive?' The result, said Mill, was that 'by dint of not following their own nature they have no nature to follow: their human capacities are withered and starved: they become incapable of any strong wishes or native pleasures'. He blamed Calvinism for some of the tendency to treat self-expression of any sort as a moral misdemeanor. 'Many persons, no doubt, sincerely think that human beings thus cramped and dwarfed are as their Maker designed them to be; just as many have thought that trees are a much finer thing when clipped into pollards . . . than as nature made them.'

He regretted that the differences between the old trades and professions were disappearing (cf. l. 6), and urged his readers to resist the pressures to make them look and think and act all alike. 'Eccentricity has always abounded when and where strength of character has abounded; and the amount of eccentricity in a society has generally been proportional to the amount of genius, mental vigour, and moral courage it contained.' (*On Liberty*, 3rd edn, 1864, chap. 3: 'Of Individuality'.)

However different Mill's philosophical outlook was in many ways from that of Hopkins, in this area of their thinking they had much in common. Witness the very style of this poem, which not only advocates what runs *counter* to the mass, but does so with a rustic unconventionality of image. Who else would be eccentric enough to praise God for skies like a *brinded cow*? The cloud streaks in the sky are never the same two days running, and in a herd of brinded cattle no two cows have an identical pattern. In his *Journals* Hopkins several times refers to a 'brindled' heaven (pp. 210, 216, 218). The type of trout known to Hopkins and to Izaak Walton had delicate pink or red spots: Walton noted in his *Compleat Angler* that the beautiful spots remained only while the fish was still alive and swimming (chap. 7). In a dead machine-made world every chestnut leaf blazing with autumn tints could be mass-produced to match the rest, whereas nature provides limit-less variations.

Later, when Hopkins was writing 'Spelt from Sibyl's Leaves' (No. 61) in Dublin (1884–6), he was willing to exchange the dapple of earth for the black and white of moral judgments. But in 'Pied Beauty' he feels no incompatibility between them. His journals, not merely the Welsh ones, repeatedly illustrate his enjoyment of 'Landscape plotted and pieced'. Surveying the Clwyd valley from a high point he writes: 'it was a fresh and delightful sight. . . . The clouds westwards were a pied piece – sail-coloured brown and milky blue; a dun yellow tent of rays opened upon the skyline far off. Cobalt blue was poured on the hills bounding the valley of the Clwyd and far in the south spread a bluish damp, but all the nearer valley was showered with tapered diamond flakes of fields in purple and brown and green' (p. 261).

The second part of the sonnet (four-and-a-half lines instead of the normal sestet) turns to other philosophical issues: what public opinion condemns as bad or inferior is defiantly recognized as equally divine with the unblemished and radiant. It also artistically reverses the construction of the first part by beginning with the object: for the subject, 'He', we have to wait till line 10: 'He whose beauty is past change fathers-forth all things counter . . .; whatever is fickle . . .; with swift, slow . . . dim'.

That Hopkins saw unity within all these contrasts is quite clear. Like Aristotle, he believed that all change presupposes an unchangeable. On his own creations he imposed an artistic unity within their variety by such subtle methods as the judicious scattering throughout this sonnet of words with a musical resemblance to each other: *dappled, couple, stipple, tackle, fickle, freckled, adazzle.*

It is largely because Hopkins is in style (both verse movement and wording) *original, spare* (in the sense of laconic, not over-explanatory like some of the Victorian poets), and *strange* that his poetry even today remains so fresh. This poem he described as in 'sprung paeonic rhythm'. In a footnote, by means of a great colon between the words he marked 'dappled things' as consisting of two monosyllabic feet (one of many eccentricities in his own scansions of his poems). Only two paeons seem to occur: '[col]ŏur ăs ă brĭnd[ed]' and '[stip]plĕ ŭpŏn trŏut'; most readers probably convert the lines unconsciously into the hexameters which they would have to become in standard rhythm. The economy of means by which Hopkins reached new rhythmic territory may be measured by rereading the first line with 'Oh' in front of it, and interpolating 'the' before *trades* in line 6, reducing them to normality.

No. 38 Hurrahing in Harvest Written at St Bueno's, 1 September 1877.

The summer of 1877 had not been a very profitable one for Hopkins poetically. Of the dozen poems which can be assigned to 1877 (that remarkably productive year in Wales) the great majority had been composed by the end of May. Only one poem, 'Pied Beauty', is definitely ascribed to the summer. If 'The Caged Skylark' was also a summer poem, we must remark on the loss of exuberance which it shows compared to those which had sprung from him earlier in the year.

One reason for his lack of happy summer inspiration may have been the final examination in theology which he sat on 24 July (see Thomas, *Hopkins the Jesuit*, p. 181), and the announcement (which may perhaps have reached him about 9 August, judging from his letters to Bridges immediately before and after that date) that he would not be admitted to the fourth year of theological studies: 'Much against my inclination I shall have to leave Wales', he wrote (*Letters*, p. 43). When he returned to St Bueno's after

three weeks with his parents in London he reported that the
weather was 'sultry and wet'.

This sonnet marks a sudden and welcome change in the seasons,
along with a reawakening of his own animation. Dated 1 September, its opening statement, 'Summer ends now', is part of its
excitement. When he sent the poem to Bridges on 16 July 1878,
Hopkins told him that 'The Hurrahing Sonnet was the outcome of
half an hour of extreme enthusiasm as I walked home alone one
day from fishing in the Elwy'. The rivers in the Vale of Clwyd
abounded in trout and salmon. That he was alone added to his full
enjoyment: already before he entered the community life of the
Jesuits he had noted in an entry in his *Journals* written among the
Alps (p. 182) 'Even with one companion ecstasy is almost
banished: you want to be alone and to feel that, and leisure – all
pressure taken off'.

The sonnet displays much more vigour than most of the others
written that same year. In 'The Windhover' his heart, in hiding,
had merely 'stirred', and the action referred to in the sestet was
'sheer plod'; in 'The Sea and the Skylark' he had been only
listening, in 'The Starlight Night' and 'The Lantern out of Doors'
simply looking. Here the energy in nature infects the poet himself
(ll. 5, 6). The wheat-sheaves, prone on the ground, seem to be
pivoting to their feet and gathering of their own accord into standing
groups (*stooks* or shocks), full of wild shaggy beauty. A field of
stooks to an imaginative eye may seem like a *barbarous* dance of
grass-skirted tribesmen, though the word was often closely
associated with the 'bearded' appearance of grain. The sky reveals
two levels of cloud: lower down, a succession of silk-sacks (more
glossy and neat than the cumulus formations commonly called
'wool-packs') gliding in orderly fashion along their aerial pavements; and high above them the cirrocumulus, in contrasting
disorder, continually appearing out of nothing and moulding
themselves into fantastic speckled shapes, only to melt again into
invisibility (ll. 3, 4). That the sunset-colours had not yet begun we
may gather from an earlier version which ran: 'never swan-wing-
whiter ever or wavier/Meal-drifts moulded and melted across
skies'.

The buoyancy of the scene gives springiness to the poet's steps
and to his feelings. Everywhere he looks he picks up evidence of
Christ's presence until he seems to be in dialogue with Him (ll.

5–8). Though he had recently written to thank his father for his kindness to him while he was in Hampstead (*Further Letters*, p. 146), the difference between his own religious convictions and those of his family muted their sharing of his life and poetry. Letters written to his close friend Bridges the previous month bravely conceal his profound disappointment that the great poem into which he had poured so much of his pent-up aspirations and admirations, 'The Wreck of the Deutschland', had drawn in reply a witty parody, and a (fortunately short-lived) resolution not to read it again 'for any money' (*Letters*, pp. 42–7). In communion with Christ through the glory of the harvest scene, he draws from above a sense of rapturous encouragement which his detached human friends had been too self-immersed to offer.

The Vale of Clwyd lies in a basin surrounded by hills, with the mighty Snowdon itself visible to the west. In the rich mistiness of autumn the hills themselves seem to be hung with blue, cut off from the fields below them, heaved up into the air as though by the sustaining shoulder of a divine Colossus. They have the virile strength of a stallion, paradoxically combined with the sweetness of a violet – a godlike combination of contraries such as he had recently celebrated in 'Pied Beauty' (No. 37).

The final lines (11–14) muse on the fluctuating sensitivity to such animating sights, even in himself (as he confirms elsewhere in his *Journals*, e.g. p. 254, and *Letters*, p. 66). When the recipient is ripe for the experience, the surging pleasure which results seems to transcend the limitations of human joy – but only very briefly: the sensation of hurling away the earth, that is pushing it down out of his way (an absurd illusion for any of us to entertain) moderates to the more sober *half hurls*. His mounting spirit is still *scanted* in his physical cage (No. 39, 'The Caged Skylark', l. 1).

The rhythm of this poem shares with 'The Windhover' two innovations with which he was revitalizing the sonnet form: Sprung Rhythm used throughout, and 'outrides' – hypermetrical unstressed syllables, sometimes in clusters, which he considered it necessary to mark, by means of loops below them, as additional even to those which the laws of Sprung Rhythm allowed him to crowd into a line. In his metrical note above MS *A* of the poem he claims that outriding feet are 'not to be confused with dactyls or paeons, though sometimes the line might be scanned either way'. In line 1, by replacing the original 'It is harvest' with 'Summer ends now', he seems to have produced an inevitable hexameter, but in MS *A* Hopkins ignores *Summer* (a slight I cannot justify), allocates his five stresses to *ends barb beau stooks rise*, and somewhat unnecessarily marks as outrides the first *now* and the last two syllables of *barbarous*. His reasons are hard to follow: 'The strong syllable in [before?] an outriding foot has always a great stress and after the outrider [there] follows a short pause'. I certainly don't pause after *barbarous* nor feel that the relationship of *in* to the rhythm of the line is any different from that of the two syllables before it. But he insists that the 'paeon is easier and more flowing'. Other reservations trouble me when I find line 5 marked in MS *B*:

I wálk, I líft up, Í lift úp heart, éyes,

where *heart* seems far more deserving of stress than *I* or *up*; but we must content ourselves with allocating *heart* a secondary stress, and feeling almost a muscular exertion in *up* even if that takes away something of the spontaneous buoyancy of the poet's responsiveness.

Such quarrels with prosodic theory, however, must not damp our awareness of the excitement of this occasion, when nature for a short half-hour became the smile and voice and physical presence of Christ.

No. 39 The Caged Skylark Written at St Beuno's some time in 1877 before 25 July.

When Henry Mayhew, the Victorian economist, interviewed street-vendors in preparation for his book *London Labour and the London Poor* (1851), he found that catching and selling wild song-birds occurred on an extensive scale. He estimated that among larks alone some 60,000 were captured each year, but that a third quickly died. He remarked on 'the restless throwing up of the head of the caged sky-lark, as if he were longing for a soar in the air', but from the evidence of the bird-catchers he maintained that this was not due to their impatience at restraint, because in fact 'the lark adapts himself to the poor confines of his prison – poor indeed for a bird who soars higher and longer than any of his class – more rapidly than other wild birds'. This view Hopkins also takes, believing that the caged bird is 'beyond the remembering his free fells', the wild moorlands from which he was taken. Mayhew throws light too on line 8: 'Like all migratory birds, when the season for migration approaches', (September in the case of some skylarks), a caged skylark or nightingale may show 'symptoms of great uneasiness, dashing himself against the wires of his cage or his aviary, and sometimes dying in a few days'. (Since the British Protection of Birds Act of 1933 the catching of any wild bird for purposes of sale has been illegal.)

All his life Hopkins felt that the inadequacies of his body (for he was unimpressive physically, and continually running out of energy) imposed unwelcome limitations on his spirit. Shortly after his graduation, when he was coaching boys at Newman's Oratory School in Birmingham, he began to complain of tiredness (*Further Letters*, p. 231), and this refrain runs through every phase of his life until the final frustrations of his days in Dublin. His inward being, like a bird in a cage, found 'a resistance in the body' which it could not overcome; 'there is a degree of effort, pain, weariness to which it yields' (*Sermons*, p. 124).

In the octave of this sonnet he compares the spirit to a captive lark and the body to its cage. The analogy implies that the spirit by itself would be charged with courageous energy (*dare-gale*, like a free skylark or windhover), but when barred in by the body its existence is physically limited (*scanted*), dull, demeaning, and like that of the blinded champion in Milton's *Samson Agonistes*, mere *drudgery*, the mind compelled to earn money to support the enclosing body. *Bone-house* had been used to describe the human body since Anglo-Saxon times (see *Beowulf*, 2508, 3147, e.g.), but its other meanings ('coffin', 'charnel-house') emphasize the fatal effect upon the spirit which follows, making it *droop deadly* in its cell (l. 7).

In depicting a lot common to all men, Hopkins nevertheless seems to have had himself specially in mind. Born with a poetic voice, he could on occasion produce hauntingly beautiful songs (*sweetest spells*), but more often he lacked time and motive, as he told Bridges in a letter of 15 February 1879 e.g., and in his last sonnet, dedicated to his friend. Though Jesuits may jestingly refer to their monastic *cells*, the prison overtones of that word here predominate. The octave offers other traces of the extra stress which a religious man with a *mounting spirit* inevitably experiences as he struggles to lead a life of perfection in a fallen body. In writing line 4, Hopkins was consciously echoing the complaint voiced by the blind Milton: 'Doth God exact day-labour, light deny'd?' Every day the distracting body brings recurrent temptations to the spiritual man, and further demands for care and support.

Because the sestet deals with a profound Christian mystery – the post-resurrection relationship between a believer's soul and his *bones risen* (l. 14) – Hopkins has to imply rather than state. The image of the liberated human soul as a bird is to be found in very old traditions, in the Jewish Kabbala, ancient Egypt, Greek mystery religions, Japanese myth, and in the neo-Platonic writings of Plotinus and his followers. English poets as various as Marvell and Yeats employ it. Readers may therefore, if they prefer, think of the ideal unity of the spirit and body after the resurrection as here embodied in the skylark singing and flying in full natural freedom.

A closer look at lines 9–11 shows that the analogy is more complicated. Just as the octave represents the mortal body as an imprisoning cage, so this tercet appears to see the unimpeding resurrection body as the bird's 'own nest, wild nest, no prison'. The nest has no confining bars, providing instead an enveloping security and place of rest. To some the implied relationship between body and spirit may seem too loose, but the wild skylark does not roam over distant fields: in singing it usually ascends from and descends to the close neighbourhood of its home. From his rather laborious explanations to Bridges of 'The Sea and the Skylark' (reproduced in the notes to *Poems*, 4th edn, pp. 265–6), we know that Hopkins felt that each skylark was attached to his base on the ground by an invisible cord of melody, paid out from the singer as he soared and rewound on the grass as he dropped down again (*Letters*, p. 164). In some such indefinable way man's soul in its best (i.e. resurrection) state will be *flesh-bound*, but in no way encumbered by its partner.

The last two lines of this sonnet suggest that the resurrected body will no more weigh down the spirit than the foot of a rainbow does feathery balls of thistle- or dandelion-down, which are themselves so light that they can float through the air.

The rhythm, which Hopkins described as 'Falling paeonic . . ., sprung and outriding', gives the sonnet a most unusual movement. The first line could be reduced to a commonplace iambic pentameter by the omission of the two indefinite articles, *a*, but Hopkins wanted both *dull* and *cage* stressed, each a monosyllabic foot. The inclusion of eleven, or twelve and even more syllables in many of the lines makes for an unconventional freshness. When read aloud, the rhythms of the sonnet superbly reflect the energies, frustrations and ultimate freedom to which it refers.

No. 40 The Lantern out of Doors Written at St Beuno's in 1877, perhaps as early as March or April.

Like its companion piece, 'The Candle Indoors' (No. 46), this poem begins with a speculation about the owner of the light, and what he is doing. To emphasize the connection between the two poems, when he edited MS *B* in 1884 Hopkins expanded the title from simply 'The Lantern' to 'The Lantern out of Doors'.

The opening quatrain describes how the eyes, looking into the darkness, are fascinated by a moving light, and automatically follow the lantern as it goes *wading* into a bog of black (a countryside devoid of lights). Like a sentry on watch, the poet cries (but only to himself) 'Who goes there?' The recollection that 'friends pass' may have brought to his mind the sentry's challenge.

In the second quatrain the lantern which brings interest to the stagnant emptiness is compared to men he has met who were outstanding in *mould* – the soul, the 'moulding force' behind physical features – or mind or some other gift which irradiated the company around him. The effect of both literal and figurative rays on his sensitivity is shown by his description of how the 'Rich beams' 'rain against' the fog (like pellets of water on a window). We may compare his physical sensations from the candle beams in 'The Candle Indoors', which *truckle* at the eye. The effort involved in reading aloud the consonants clustered in *much-thick* imitates the resistance of the fog to the lantern rays. Max Müller had pointed out how little differentiation there was between *very* and *much*, the latter meaning the same as the former but being confined to use with participles [e.g. 'much-polluted air']. Yet, he exclaimed, 'the smallest rule of English', such as this usage, 'cannot be changed or moulded by the taste, the fancy, or genius' of any individual or academy (*The Science of Language*, London, 1861, p. 38–9). Hopkins, however, was always willing to challenge a convention to achieve a needed effect.

Although Hopkins loved the Welsh countryside, his allusion to his human environment in terms of a marshy fog might possibly be taken to indicate a feeling of mental stagnation at St Beuno's which he was presently to complain of at Mount St Mary's, where life was 'as dank as ditch-water' (*Letters*, p. 47). With his gifts for enquiring beyond the edges of revelation, he found 'dogmatic theology, moral ditto, canon law', and so forth, very dry (*Correspondence*, p. 95; *Further Letters*, pp. 124, 143). There was no one to share his interest, e.g. in Bridges's poetry, and the college's grunting harmonium brought his music to a stand (*Further Letters*, pp. 147, 127). Once the brilliant passers-by had been bought up (like slaves) by death or despatched to a distance, the mental atmosphere darkened into night.

In the background is a loneliness which could have been developed in this sonnet into the sense of isolation found in 'The Alchemist in the City' (No. 15), whose protagonist stands by while the world passes, or even Tennyson's lady of Shalott, watching through silent nights the torches as they recede down the winding road to Camelot. But, with one of those twists in direction we have noted under No. 34, 'In the Valley of the Elwy', the sestet tries to change the object of our sympathies from the poet (shorn of radiant companionship) to those he has lost sight of (consumed by death or distance – bought only to be squandered). It is they who are deprived – robbed of the poet's priestly comfort 'at the end', namely death. Hopkins was on the verge of ordination, which would enable him to bring relief and assurance to the sick and dying such as Felix Randal (see No. 53). But after separation from his friends, not seeing them he would perhaps not remember them in his prayers (l. 11).

Christ, however, has no such limitation of vision and of sustained interest. Whether to *avow* (support them by showing His approval) or *amend* (lead them to better ways), He follows them on their journey, ransoming them from their captor (Sin and Death), and proving Himself a friend who never leaves them in the lurch.

In the sestet the convolutions of thought and syntax suddenly straighten into a homely proverb, 'out of sight is out of mind'. We cannot help reflecting that a poet who used to complain that his friends or family forgot to write to him or reply promptly to his letters must have been at least subconsciously afraid that he himself might fade from the minds of those who no longer had him in sight. And many readers may feel that the final tercet appears more heartfelt and in closer accord with the octave if its ultimate origin is thought of as being his own need for a true and lasting friendship after those he had most admired and liked had faded into the distance.

Much less adventurous rhythmically than the three poems printed before it in the Fourth Edition, this sonnet may possibly have been composed in the early spring. Its position at the end of the sonnets of 1877 can be justified by the fact that we do not know during what part of the year it was written. With my discovery (incorporated in a correction of 1970) that the first line in the authoritative version ends, like the original autograph, with a full stop after 'night', the awkwardness in rhythm and diction which I had felt in the opening has disappeared (as something we had created ourselves). The first quatrain has since then appealed to me as perhaps the best part of the sonnet.

No. 41 The Loss of the Eurydice Written at Mount St Mary's College, Chesterfield, near Sheffield, April 1878.

The *Eurydice* was a wooden-hulled frigate, about thirty-five years old, which had in February 1877 been converted into a training ship for second-class ordinary seamen attached to the naval reserves. Instead of her twenty-six original guns, she carried only four new ones for gunnery practice, but the large gun-ports on her main-deck had been kept for ventilation. A few years before the disaster, naval architects in a survey of the British fleet had reported that out of twenty types examined, the *Eurydice* carried the largest square footage of canvas (13.1) for every ton of displacement [some 12,000 square feet] – twice as much as the *Caledonian* and more than four times that of the *Hercules* (*The Times*, London, 29.3.78, p. 9). Nevertheless she was found capable of withstanding heavy gales, though her old gunports had to be closed if she was rolling because they were only four or five feet above the water-line.

On 24 March 1878, she was returning under command of Captain Marcus Hare from a training cruise in the West Indies which had lasted since November. On board were over three hundred officers and seamen, a number of them mere lads. She had reached the Isle of Wight ahead of expectations, eighteen days from Bermuda, and could be seen from the cliffs above Ventnor pressing home to Spithead in the bright sunshine under full sail.

An admiral who observed her through his telescope from the shore later reported that her forecastle and afterdeck were filled with men — no doubt exulting in the sight of their homeland again. She was keeping close inshore to reduce the effect of the outward rushing tide which almost halved her speed: she wished to complete the remaining ten miles of her voyage before evening. But the proud ship was too near the high cliffs and the great dome of St Boniface Down (787 feet) to see an immense storm cloud advancing overland upon them. Other vessels further out to sea having observed this were shortening sail, but Captain Hare, despite the falling barometer, was apparently confident that his large and nimble crew could furl the sails at the last moment. The squall which struck them, however, was to make meteorological history by its violence and the suddenness of the wind's shift in direction. The men had no sooner been sent aloft to take in the upper sails than they were recalled for fear they would be carried away. The squall, funnelled by a chine or cleft in the cliffs, and laden with snow, struck them on the beam with such force that the ship capsized, dipping her sails into the water. The sea deluged in through the open ports of the gundeck, and cascaded down the hatchways leading to the lower decks, trapping everyone below. Within ten minutes of the first blast the ship sank, righting herself as she did so, and creating a gully into which she dragged those who had jumped into the sea for safety (l. 61). Only two men survived the freezing waters to tell the story of her disaster. When the snowstorm cleared half an hour later, nothing but the tops of her masts could be seen from the shore, as she lay in water 11½ fathoms deep. *The Times* carried details of the inquest on the bodies of those picked up, of the salvage operations which required five months to complete, and the court martial on her foundering (28 August–3rd September). Some early reports are reprinted in *Immortal Diamond*, pp. 375–92. There is also a rather rare little book by Captain E. H. Verney, R.N., *The Last Four Days of the "Eurydice"*, Portsmouth, 1878, written immediately after the disaster in aid of the *Eurydice* Fund for the relatives of the victims. Its frontispiece shows the ship in full pride of sail. Bergonzi (*Hopkins*, p. 93) mentions the fact that among onlookers from the cliffs was Winston Churchill, then a small child, who never forgot the sight of the grand ship and the subsequent wreckage after the storm.

Hopkins had felt no poetic inspiration since he had left the rural beauty of Wales in October 1877 for Mount St Mary's College, Chesterfield, 'smoke-ridden' from the neighbouring industrial city of Sheffield. He found his duties as bursar or sub-minister inconsecutive and burdensome, particularly when in addition to helping the parish priest he had to take over classes taught by a master who was ill.

But just as the story of the *Deutschland* had roused him from long poetic silence, so here too the thought of so many fine lads precipitated into eternity *unwarned* (ll. 3–4) worked on him, and by April 2 he was able to send Bridges the rought draft of what are now lines 73–84. The pitiable waste of skilled dexterity touched him. He reflects ruefully on one of the men whose body was recovered:

> Oh! his nimble finger, his gnarled grip!
> Léagues, léagues of séamanship
> Slumber in his forsaken
> Bones and will not, will not waken.

He marked some of the stresses for Bridges because the use of Sprung Rhythm created considerable variations in pattern between lines of equal prosodic length. The metre was tetrameter, except for the third line which had only three stresses, but that short line could hold as few as five syllables ('Every inch a tar', l. 75) or as many as eight or nine (ll. 3, 23). Just as he had defended earlier metrical experiments by citing rather distant precedents in Shakespeare or Milton, so now he ingenuously described the rhythm of his new poem as 'a measure something like Tennyson's *Violet*'. Tennyson's title (as Abbott points out) is actually 'The Daisy' (though Hopkins might have been remembering the reference to violets in a neighbouring poem, 'To the Rev. F. D. Maurice', written in the same metre). Occasional lines may approximately match:

> 'He was but one like thousands more'   ('Eurydice', l. 85)
> 'How best to help the slender store'   (Maurice, l. 37)
> 'Three hundred souls, O alas! on board'   ('Eurydice', l. 2)
> 'Crocus, anemone, violet'   ('Maurice, l. 44)

Tennyson's invented metre is comparatively inflexible. Hopkins, however, can produce dramatically appropriate effects through his Sprung Rhythm as in the last line of the fifteenth stanza:

Sydney Fletcher, Bristol-bred,
(Low lie his mates now on watery bed)
　Takes to the seas and snows
As sheer down the ship goes.

Here omission of an unaccented syllable in the middle of *shéer
dówn* and again in *shíp góes* prevents the metre from devolving
into sing-song.

But few readers will persuade themselves that they are always
following the poet's intentions. When Bridges queried line 41,
'Then a lurch forward, frigate and men', Hopkins replied (*Letters*,
p. 52), 'I don't see the difficulty about the "lurch forward"? Is it in
the scanning? which is imitative as usual – an anapaest, followed
by a trochee, a dactyl, and a syllable', i.e. a monosyllabic foot.
Only when we read the line with the designed scansion do we feel
that sudden jerk, such as the ship made as she began her fatal
dive: 'Then a lúrch ∧ fórward, frígate and mén'. We might note that
Bridges liked the poem as much as he had disliked 'The Wreck of
the Deutschland', paying it compliments which embarrassed the
poet because they included tributes to his spiritual concern for the
souls of the men (p. 52). Bridges's detailed criticisms led to
modifications and explanations which Hopkins scholars have
found most enlightening. Bridges even considered composing an
ode on the subject himself (p. 54).

The ode on the drawn-out miseries on the *Deutschland* had been
prefaced by an introductory 'Part the First' of eighty lines, and
even the second Part opened with a symbolic preliminary stanza.
But since the ill-fated *Eurydice* had no sooner been sighted from
the shore, her sails resplendent in the spring sunshine, than she
had vanished Hopkins tried to reproduce the stark event by the
abruptness of his opening: 'The Eurydice it concerned thee, O
Lord'. This he later altered to 'The Eurydice – Christ, they are thy
concern – /Three hundred souls in her, stem to stern'. Bridges
seems to have found this 'too sudden' and Hopkins proposed a
reversion to the earlier form (p. 54). When Bridges challenged line
6 with its two-layered metaphor, asking how hearts of oak could be
furled, Hopkins replied, 'You are to suppose a stroke or blast in a
forest of "hearts of oak" (. . . sound oak-timber) which at one
blow both lays them low and buries them in broken earth' (*Letters*,
p. 52). The stately grove of masts and rigging had been instan-
taneously felled by the squall (cf. *Journals*, p. 192). A famous

eighteenth-century patriot song had run 'Heart of oak are our ships,/Heart of oak are our men', and Hopkins thought of the drowned sailors as being furled 'in sand and sea water'. The next lines contain two beautiful coinages – *flockbells*, rung by the sheep in the *forefalls* of the lofty suspended ('aerial') downs overlooking the fateful channel. In the Isle of Wight and Hampshire, where the Hopkins family had enjoyed many a holiday, 'falls' were steep cliffsides: the prefix 'fore' (suggestive of 'foreland') indicates that these overhung the sea.

The third stanza contrasts with the *Eurydice's* the cargoes of the Elizabethan galleons with their hoards of Spanish gold, along with the great ships of more recent times bringing bales of silk and wool. No material treasure could compare with the *Eurydice's* freight of skilful sailors. Their value must have been borne in on Englishmen all the more by two coincident items in *The Times* of 29 March: a leader on the lost lives and the announcement that because of the imminent risk of war with Russia and Turkey reserves were being called to the colours, and all troopships were being readied to embark an expeditionary army corps. The ordinary seamen who had been trained in the *Eurydice* might have been mobilized with those reserves.

Lines 17–28 deal with the paradox that the *Eurydice*, having successfully withstood the notorious hostility of the Atlantic, was overwhelmed by a *blow* from her mother-country: the use of a nautical word for a gale combines with his conviction that England was not a responsible parent to these young lives, having failed to give them the religious training they deserved. Everything had conspired to lull the officers into deluded confidence — the serene spring sky (the startling personification in *liar* avoids the commonplace dead metaphor in 'treacherous weather'), their closeness to the longed-for destination. The black north wind rides the storm clouds as Boreas in Greek legend rode his swift horses to wreck the Persian fleet. The enmity of the elements (*deadly-electric, wolfsnow*) recalls the 'endragonèd seas' around the *Deutschland* ('Wreck', st. 27).

There was much argument in the newspapers, at the inquest, and finally at the court of inquiry into the disaster, as to whether the *Eurydice* had been carrying too much sail in view of the falling barometer, but expert witnesses agreed that since the captain was too close to the cliffs to observe the approaching storm front, and

had every right to be confident of the speed with which his
well-disciplined crew could take in the sails, he was justified in
pressing on under full sail till the last possible moment. Such
tactics were often essential in a man-o'-war striving to overtake a
fleeing enemy or endeavouring to escape from superior forces. But
popular opinion remained unconvinced. In a magnificent stanza
Hopkins catches the impressions of onlookers from the lofty cliff-
walks above Ventnor:

> Too proud, too proud, what a press she bore!
> Royal, and all her royals wore.
>   Sharp with her, shorten sail!
> Too late; lost; gone with the gale.

Royal sails were 'never used but in fine weather', according to
Admiral Smyth's *Sailor's Word-book* of 1867. The squall struck
the vessel on her beam with such appalling suddenness that the
topgallant men sent aloft to take in the upper sails had no time to
carry out their orders before the ship heeled over, soaking her vast
sails in the seas. Through the eight large open gun-ports on the lee
side of the middle deck tons of water deluged in, drowning the
men who at seven bells (3.30 pm) were messing there. Of these
Sydney Fletcher, being near a hatch, was one of only three or four
to escape even as far as the upper deck. Those on the lower deck
stood no chance whatever. And when the vessel sank below the
surface, the vortex she created 'wound . . . with her' nearly all
those struggling in the water (l. 44).

The three stanzas (ll. 45–56) on the captain, Marcus Hare, are
less successful. They embody something of the tragic picture which
emerged at the court martial: none of his rapid and lucid
commands had served to save his ship, and as Benjamin
Cuddiford, who had been on watch, stood near him on the side of
the hull with the keel plainly visible, he heard the captain say 'It is
of no avail'. A revision of lines 48 and 50 could have easily avoided
the undignified associations of 'wallow' and 'rude of feature'; but
Hopkins had made as many concessions to Bridges's criticisms as
he was prepared to (having sacrificed his coined 'grimstones' in
l. 28 and 'mortholes' in l. 39 or 40). When Bridges pointed out that
lines 53 to 56 seemed to imply that Captain Hare had previously
been a 'duty-swerver' (which at first glance seems the implication of
this comment on the captain's nobility in going down with his

ship), Hopkins replied: 'You mistake the sense of this as I feared it would be mistaken. I believed Hare to be a brave and conscientious man: what I say is that "even" those who seem unconscientious will act the right part at a great push' (*Letters*, p. 53). But the editor of *The Month*, in deciding not to publish the poem when it was submitted to him, may possibly have been influenced, among other things, by the risk of an action for libel. The disaster had been referred to a court of inquiry under Admiral Fanshawe, commander-in-chief at Portsmouth, and Captain Hare, who had had an outstanding record, did not have his name posthumously cleared of all blame until 2 September.

In contrast with this section comes a fine account of how 'Sydney Fletcher, Bristol-bred' managed to survive. He was only nineteen. Hopkins told his mother that he had become 'very fond of the boys I have had to do with as pupils, penitents, or in other ways' (*Further Letters*, p. 150), and chose to mention this young lad here rather than a second survivor Benjamin Cuddiford, who had served twenty-one years at sea, and on this voyage was one of the crew, not a trainee. But perhaps the most moving passage in the poem follows (ll. 73–84) – the description of the manly body rescued too late from the ice-cold seas, all its practised skills frozen by death.

Comparisons between the two shipwreck poems are inevitable, especially as Hopkins himself aimed at avoiding the features which had made 'The Wreck of the Deutschland' so difficult to master. Up to line 84, 'The Loss of the Eurydice' is entirely narrative, providing an easier beginning. But the 'Deutschland' swells to a triumphant visionary ending, whereas the later poem in coming to a gloomy close reflects Hopkins's own disappointments. He finds an analogy to England herself in the foundering ship, dragging down with her her precious crew – the valiant *daredeaths* and the sweet *wildworth* of English men and women – all *rolled in ruin* as she capsizes (ll. 94–6). He pictures the devout pilgrims of Catholic times wending their starlit way through Norfolk to Our Lady's Shrine at Walsingham (in his day a deserted ruin), guided by the Milky Way overhead as the Magi had been led to the infant Christ at Bethlehem by the star. (The shrine was destroyed in 1538, and not restored until 1938, but pilgrimages resumed in 1922.) The 'one' writer he starts to mention in line 103 was Duns Scotus (*Letters*, p. 77; see No. 44, 'Duns Scotus's Oxford').

The last four stanzas have some complications of syntax which
Hopkins was called on to explain (e.g. in *Letters*, pp. 53, 77–9).
Having shown deep sympathy with the tears of the widowed and
bereaved (ll. 105–8), he urges them to kneel in prayer to Christ,
the Lord of storms as well as the supreme example of manhood,
beseeching the Hero who saves the faithful to save the souls of their
beloved heroes (l. 112). The 'awful overtaking' of their death by
drowning was in the past as human thought measures time, but
God's actions transcend the passage of days, and in answer to their
requests He can already (though in our future) 'Have . . ./Heard'
the prayer of the bereaved, and have granted grace to the
drowning men at the moment they needed it, although humanly
speaking that opportunity vanished with the 'past'. Hopkins later
attempted to fill out this idea in his sonnet to 'Henry Purcell' (No.
45). Finally, though rejecting the idea that those in hell itself could
be redeemed, he declared that 'Fresh . . ./Prayer' could draw
eternal pity for souls who might appear to human judgment to be
lost, 'sunk in seeming'.

All Hopkins's poetry demands reading aloud. How much this
poem calls for a rhetorical declamation Hopkins himself realized
when, having sent it to someone for comment, he at last had it
returned to him a year after its composition. Rereading it silently,
as people normally treat both prose and verse, he tells Bridges 'it
struck me aghast with a kind of raw nakedness and unmitigated
violence I was unprepared for: but take breath and read it with the
ears, as I always wish to be read, and my verse becomes all right'
(*Letters*, 79).

Modern readers tend to find the double and triple rhymes
distasteful, such as *crew*, *in/ruin* (ll. 95–6), and *burn all/eternal*
(119–20). But in the second half of the century efforts were being
made by a number of poets to win acceptance for new techniques,
and to introduce into English such devices as feminine rhymes.

Hopkins had found, when he attempted to stir English readers
through 'The Wreck of the Deutschland', that he was too remote
from current practice to win a hearing. With his second shipwreck
poem he exerted himself to achieve a more popular style, making
it simpler, shorter, and with more narrative than the 'Wreck' had
offered. In modern judgment the ode on the *Deutschland* has so
eclipsed the story of the *Eurydice* that we learn with surprise that
his inner circle of critics greatly preferred the second poem.

Bridges embarrassed Hopkins with praise of it, declaring that of the two (and Hopkins agreed with him), 'the *Eurydice* shews more mastery in art' (*Letters*, p. 119). Dixon wanted to have it published in a Carlisle newspaper. Edmund Gosse, himself a poet and an influential critic, is mentioned in February 1879 as having liked pieces shown him by Bridges, so that he too probably approved the poem. He was prepared to pay Hopkins some compliments in one of his reviews (*Letters*, 65–6). But because the official Jesuit journal, *The Month*, had rejected the second wreck also, Hopkins shrank from a publication which his change in style could have brought him.

We must not, however, forget the misgivings which Hopkins expressed at the time and later – his awareness of his tendency towards oddity. Few readers, unless their attention is drawn to it, would notice that in lines 23–4, 67–8 and 91–2 Hopkins has once again used the run-over rhymes he had borrowed from nineteenth-century Welsh innovators (e.g. *coast or/M*[ark] rhymes with *snowstorm*). Discussing this practice in a letter to his brother Everard in November 1886 (not published until 1972 when Father A. Bischoff, S.J., contributed it to the *TLS* of 8 December), Hopkins admitted that the 'run-over rhymes were experimental, perhaps a mistake; I do not know that I should repeat them. But rhyme, you understand, is like an indelible process: you cannot paint over it.' Like many poets, Hopkins established his rhyme words at an early stage and tended to retain them through all the changes in his drafts. As we have already noted, when Bridges felt the opening stanza of the 'Eurydice' was too abrupt in the version he saw ('The Eurydice – Christ, they are thy concern – /Three hundred souls in her, stem to stern'), Hopkins changed it to rhyme on 'Lord' and 'board'. But this then meant a further revision, since his third stanza had run: 'For what had she aboard, or was she stored/With bounden bales or a bullion hoard? – ' Little though we may like the rhymes he substituted, 'fully on'/'bullion', they were popular innovations when he was writing, and no poet can be wholly independent of his own age.

For us today it is likely that as we read 'The Loss of the Eurydice' we may feel ourselves lifted by passages of exceptional and delicate beauty one moment, and confronted the next with a rhyme which arouses too many memories of Byron's irreverent triple jingles to be taken seriously. Yet (to judge from my own experience and those of others) the poem as a whole is likely to make an increasing appeal the more familiar with it we become.

No. 42 The May Magnificat Written at Stonyhurst, May 1878, for the statue of the Virgin Mary, but, as Hopkins notes on an autograph copy, 'it did not pass'.

When Hopkins sent his only text of 'The Loss of the Eurydice' to Bridges for criticism he was no longer at Mount St Mary's, but back at Stonyhurst College on the edges of Lancashire and Yorkshire, to coach Catholic students writing University of London degree examinations. He arrived at the end of April 1878, and was immediately encouraged to compose a poem in honour of the Virgin to be hung according to the college custom before the statue of the Madonna during the month of May. He was already developing a reputation for eccentricity as a poet.

The authorities who disapproved Hopkins's contribution would have been entirely unconvinced by any suggestion that it was based upon Horatian Alcaics. 'The Loss of the Eurydice' was in theory ultimately derived from that source, if we believe Tennyson's claim for the inspiration behind the metre of 'The Daisy'. In 'The May Magnificat' critics have detected the influence of Marvell's 'Horation Ode upon Cromwell's Return from Ireland'. Though nine months later Hopkins mentioned to Dixon that he knew Marvell only in extracts (*Correspondence*, p. 23), he may certainly have encountered this poem and been interested in its alternation of tetrameter couplets with trimeter couplets. But its subject would have been repugnant (glorifying the man who had massacred Catholics in Ireland), its metre is in rising instead of his own falling measures, it is not divided into stanzas, and it uses comparatively little metrical substitution.

The Fathers who vetted the literary submissions would probably have mistaken his Sprung Rhythm for lame metre, and wanted to supply his missing slack syllables, just as the editors had emended Shakespeare. His second stanza could easily have been 'regularized':

> . . . Candlemas [and] Lady Day;
> But the Lady Month [of] May,
> Fasten that upon her?
> Feast it in her honour?

Moreover his language could have been 'improved' at various points: lines 11 and 12 e.g. with 'opportunest' ('the most fitting') could have been reduced to plain English 'poesy':

> Is't most opportune,
> Finding flowers so soon?

The very first number of *The Stonyhurst Magazine* (May 1881, pp. 14–16) printed some of the May verses which had been accepted as (anonymous or initialled) offerings to Our Lady – in Greek, Latin and English. One by 'J.G.' in 1880 (presumably Rev John Gerard, S.J., later editor of *The Month*) is dignified but unmemorable. Another had been written by Newman, and was reproduced mainly because it was accompanied by a Stonyhurst translation into Latin – to my mind a great deal more interesting than its original. When Newman wrote his poem, 'The Month of Mary' in 1850, the custom of dedicating that month to Our Lady had only recently reached England from Europe, having been introduced into England about 1840 by Father Aloysius Gentili. The standards of acceptable religious verse may be conveyed by quoting Newman's second stanza (*Verses on Various Occasions*, 1868, p. 276) in its Stonyhurst version:

> Green is the grass, but wait awhile,
>   'Twill grow, and then 'twill wither;
> The flow'rets, brightly as they smile,
>   Shall perish altogether.
> The merry sun, you sure would say,
>   It ne'er could set in gloom;
> But earth's best joys have all an end,
>   And sin a heavy doom.

Newman's second May poem, 'The Queen of Seasons', raises the question dealt with also by Hopkins, the reason for assigning May to Mary. He concludes that to her belong all the months,

> And we give to thee May, not because it is best,
> But because it comes first, and is pledge of the rest (p. 280).

As Hopkins was later to remark with some justification to Dixon, 'The Lake School expires in Keble and Faber and Cardinal Newman' (*Correspondence*, p. 99).

In his 'May Magnificat' Hopkins points out (ll. 3, 4) that the feasts officially in honour of the Virgin are placed logically in the calendar. Lady Day, which commemorates the Annunciation, when Mary conceived Jesus by the Holy Ghost, is fixed for March 25, nine months before Christ's birth; and Candlemas (February 2), falls forty days after the birth, when a boy's mother was by Mosaic law required to present herself at the temple for purification. But the dedication of May to Mary ('Lady Month' is formed on the analogy of 'Lady Day'), though indulgenced by Popes Pius VII and Pius IX, had no such ancient and rational justification.

Appealing to the 'mighty mother', the earth or Nature, in stanza 4, Hopkins is guided by the etymology of 'Spring', which implies the springing up of everything, its growth. His invented *green-world* embraces 'greenwood', 'greensward' and all 'greenery'. But Mary's colour is blue, and she is identified in the Apocalypse with the woman 'clothed with the sun, and the moon under her feet, and on her head a crown of twelve stars' (Rev. 12:1). These symbols may have influenced his selection of detail as he pictures the song-thrush or throstle, *star-eyed*, brooding upon her blue eggs. The thrush's breast is olive-brown with dark triangular spots, which (once Hopkins has drawn our attention to it, l. 19), we recognize as rather like the seeds mottling a yellow ripening strawberry (a favourite treat to a thrush in season).

The 'bugle blue' of the eggs (l. 21) has occasioned some dispute. The common English bugle flower, *Ajuga reptans*, is perhaps too bluey-purple to have matched in the poet's mind the pale greenish blue of thrush eggs. But in Hampshire, where the Hopkins family often holidayed, Viper's bugloss (*Echium vulgare*) was known as 'bugles', and it is rather closer in colour to the eggs when fully open. Small bugloss is another candidate. However, we cannot altogether rule out a reference to beads, since the term 'bugles' was rather loosely applied, and we do come across allusions to small beads of 'bugle blue'. A possible but faint resonance might be to the beads of a rosary, 'Mary's Garden'. In 'A Vision of the Mermaids' (No. 2, l. 95), 'bubbles bugle-eyed' suggests the gleam of beads and their shape.

The second part, Nature's answer, runs from stanza 4 to stanza 8: the swelling of the wildflower seeds and bulbs in the sod of the meadows, and blossoms opening out of their sheaths (l. 24), while Mary looks on in approval at 'all things sizing', i.e. growing in size (like the 'sizing moon' of 'Lines for a Picture', No. 25, l. 20). She is 'the universal mother', as Hopkins notes in a Rosary Sunday address (*Sermons*, p. 29). This 'magnifying of each its kind' represents the first phrase of her Magnificat: 'My soul doth magnify the Lord'. The remaining four stanzas take up its second phrase: 'And my spirit hath rejoiced . . .' (Luke 1: 46–7).

May was traditionally sung as the 'merry month'. The examples offered by the poet have as their liquid underthought a great flood of bliss, a sea of colour and joy, sweeping the countryside. The apple-blossom is like pink foam – an image which he had developed at greater length in 'A Vision of the Mermaids' (No. 2, ll. 84–97). The cherry is 'silver-surfèd', like a glistening white scud on the sea; while the wooded slopes and thin undergrowth are awash with lakes of *greybells* azuring into the familiar blue-bells. All these details are brought into harmony by the *magic* notes of the cuckoo – Spenser's 'herald of the Spring', whose call assures the listener in the English countryside that spring has at last arrived.

The final stanza sees the growth and gaiety of spring as reminding Mary of her ecstasy between the Incarnation of God within her, and the birth of Christ, which according to ancient tradition was without the pangs of labour (*Sermons*, p. 170). I very much doubt whether those whose task it was to select May poems at Stonyhurst had been offered such original flashes of poetic beauty since Hopkins's 'Ad Mariam' (No. 26), or were again before his poem on 'The Blessed Virgin compared to the Air we Breathe' (No. 60).

No. 43 Binsey Poplars: *felled 1879* Written at Oxford, 13 March 1879.

A long letter to Dixon, begun in February 1879, discussing Sprung Rhythm and promising to send the Canon his two ship-wreck poems, opens with memories of the Oxford environs they had both known as students, and nostalgic regret that its beauties were being gradually extinguished. A terse postscript written on Thursday 13 March adds, 'I have been up to Godstow this after-noon. I am sorry to say that the aspens that lined the river are everyone felled' (*Correspondence,* p. 26). They would then have been rich in catkins, full of the promise of spring. Though he had just told Dixon that in his parish work he was 'called one way and another', and could find little time to write, the Muse took command and that very evening, probably as he retraced the bared path in a mutilated landscape, he began the composition of this poem.

A summer stroll beside the upper river from Medley Weir northwards to Godstow, with the flat expanse of Oxford's Port Meadow on the right and Binsey Village on the left, would prove hot and rather featureless without the curving line of trees which now once more surmount the river embankment as they had done in Hopkins's undergraduate years. His journals relate various student excursions by boat or on foot towards Godstow or Binsey, mostly accompanied by a remark about the warmth of the day. In 1866 we hear of four such trips, three when the weather was warm or hot in May – by which time the aspens would be in leaf – and in June of an evening walk when the slowly setting sun would have crouched behind the full-leaved branches (pp. 135, 137, 139). Aspens, like other poplars, send up tall straight polelike trunks. This row of them was transformed by Hopkins's poetic imagination into the bars of a cage behind which in winter the westering sun appeared like a fierce animal *quelled* by captivity (l. 1). In summer the leaves of the aspen shimmer like water in the slightest breeze; among them the burning ball of the sun might seem to be *quenched* by their quivering liquid sparkle (l. 2). The antiquity of some such image may perhaps be judged by a common interpretation of the Chinese ideograph for 'east', which as Ezra Pound explains it in his *ABC of Reading* (chap. 1), shows the low sun tangled in the branches of a tree.

The disruptive Sprung Rhythm of the third line haunts us like the ring of the labourers' blows, if we read it with the intended rhythm:

> My aspens dear, whose airy cages quelled,
> Quelled or quenched in leaves the leaping sun,
> Áll félled, félled, are áll félled; . . .

The onomatopoeic effect is so keen that it seems strange that in one of his revisions he omitted any attempt at it. In 'The Loss of the Eurydice' he had compared the downthrow of young sailors and their ship to the felling of oaks. In this poem he sustains such a comparison, for which moving precedents could be found in the epic similes of the *Iliad* and the *Aeneid*, where the fall of some hero in battle is paralleled by the toppling of a tall tree in the forest. The aspens, the steep slope of their branches like long spears, constitute a chevron column (*folded rank*) of young men caught in a defile by a ruthless enemy and struck down in turn as they follow bravely on – 'Not spared, not one . . .'.

The 'strong dark shadows of trees through grass' had arrested the poet's attention in the meadows around Binsey (*Journals*, p. 137), but their description here is particularly rich; *sandalled* not only forms a bridge from the military image in *following folded rank*, since Roman soldiers wore sandals with thongs, but accurately depicts the cross-hatched lines thrown by a network of branches in sunshine. The substitution of *dandled* for 'dangled', as elsewhere (e.g. 'The Wreck', st. 16), replaces an ugly clash of consonants with an imitation of a Welsh chime (*dandled a sandalled*). It also reproduces the up and down dancing movement of the strapwork shadow on the surface of the wind-rippled meadow and river, the pattern disappearing and re-emerging under the ruffling breeze. The lushly-vegetated banks seem to wind like a snake as their tall weeds sway and their trailing fringes of water-plants spread out and retreat in the current – earlier drafts included 'weed-weeping', 'weed-wound' and 'broidered bank'. Putting together lines 8, 10 and 17, we glimpse an implied contrast with the straight embankments of a man-made canal: the river's edge in this reach still owns something of nature's freedom to curve like a wild creeper.

The second and longer stanza, not symmetrical with the first, protests against the maiming of Nature as irreversible damage. Hopkins in his Welsh sonnets (such as 'God's Grandeur', No. 31) associates respect for the natural world with deference to the Creator. We are therefore entitled to assume in his lines 'O if we but knew what we do/When we delve or hew – ' a deliberate allusion to Christ's words on the cross concerning those who were destroying His physical life, 'they know not what they do' (Luke 23:34). Ancient legends claimed that the aspen trembles with horror because the Cross of Calvary was made from its wood. The great ball of the world, in spite of its size, is as vulnerable as the sensitive microcosm of the eyeball. Hopkins is here not merely echoing Milton or following a favourite metaphysical analogy in John Donne: he feels an injury to himself in the hacking down of what he claims to have been '*My* aspens'. Such outrages against divine inscapes will produce a spiritual blindness, even when executed in an effort to improve upon Nature. We are depriving coming generations of their heritage – their share in the self-expressive shapes of the *growing green*, landscapes of unique rural beauty, unselved by zealous *strokes of havoc* from misguided modernizers. The poem ends with dying cadences, the repetitions being characteristic of his treatment of poems when he set them to music (see *Journals*, pp. 457–97). But the reduplication of *especial* points directly to Duns Scotus, who had emphasized the stress exerted upon the mind of observers by the 'special' form peculiar to an object, *species specialissima* (in this case the horizontals of the Binsey landscape completed by the verticals of the graceful aspens).

This lyric deserves a place far above the one which Cowper earned himself by 'The Poplar Field', once a much-anthologized recitation piece, as any old edition of Granger's *Index to Poetry* indicates. Bridges was unduly sensitive to possible criticism in 1893, when, having persuaded Miles to include a number of Hopkins's poems in his *Poets and Poetry of the Century*, Vol. 8, and being invited to send a further one, he felt that Cowper's piece was too familiar for this poem to be acceptable. Yet Cowper's metre is comparatively insensitive. Moreover Cowper has lost what Hopkins preserves, a sense of the sacredness of the poplar, dedicated to Apollo, such as is found in the famous lament of Antipater of Sidon in the Greek Anthology (London, Bohn, 1852, p. 480). Hopkins translates this Greek sentiment into profound Scotist terms. Homer's idyllic landscape in *Odyssey* Book ix included a fringe of poplars: Ruskin was sure they were aspens (*Modern Painters*, in *Works*, ed. Cook and Wedderburn, Vol. 5, p. 236).

Many Victorian writers shared Hopkins's love for trees, and it is interesting that an almost exactly contemporary letter to *Jackson's Oxford Journal* (15 February 1879) expressed great approval over the planting of an avenue and the creation of a footpath beside the Southam Road, Banbury.

No. 44 Duns Scotus's Oxford Dated 'Oxford, March 1879' in one manuscript, but 1878 in another.

As an Anglican undergraduate Hopkins had written sonnets to Oxford in which he listed some of the 'charms' which soothed his 'inmost thought,/The towers musical, quiet-wallèd grove',

'Meadows . . . inexplicably dear'. Nothing, he declared, could sour ('unendear') her sweetness for him ('To Oxford', Nos 12, 119). But returning as a Catholic priest after an absence of eleven years he found that changes in himself, in the university and in the city had tempered his pleasure. This sonnet looks back with maturer judgment beyond his own happier days in residence to the remote dawn of the fourteenth century when Duns Scotus, the great Catholic teacher and philosopher, was at Oxford.

The octave depicts the city at its best as the perfect meeting ground of town and country. When the mayor of Oxford used to make his annual circuit of the bounds claimed by the city (a custom which dates back to the fourteenth century), starting from Magdalen Bridge he proceeded by boat down the Cherwell, across Christ Church Meadow to Folly Bridge, and thence by a route which, mainly following rivers and streams round the 'island' of Binsey to Godstow, embraced neighbouring fields and pastures (H. E. Salter, *Medieval Oxford*, Oxford, 1936, pp. 66ff). The city was 'river-rounded' (l. 2) on the east, the south and the west. On all four sides it included meadows belonging to the city or colleges, where flocks and herds grazed or where corn and hay were harvested. These fields remained intact for many centuries – in fact Christ Church Meadow and Port Meadow preserve even today that 'neighbour-nature' (l. 6) which makes such a perfect base for the beautiful grey stone of the colleges and chapels, though an ugly brick skirt spoils the western fringe.

From any vantage point Oxford offers a silhouette of towers and trees — man and nature in superb conjunction. The second line encapsulates in five hyphenated phrases the tussle of emotions with which the poet views her. 'Cuckoo-echoing' seems wholly pleasurable: his journals note the welcome sound of these heralds of the spring calling and answering each other, heard as he returned by river or on foot from excursions to Godstow or Cumnor (pp. 135, 137). The next phrase, however, hints at irritation: 'bell-swarmèd'. The bells had sounded more musical to him in the days when he was himself an Anglican. But the religious life of the colleges was now so perfunctory that even the Anglican-oriented *Oxford and Cambridge Undergraduate's Journal* of 6 February 1879 entitled its leading article 'Are College Chapels Worship?' Relying upon the mechanical rule that members had to attend four chapels a week and two on Sundays, the authorities, (it declared), 'pay a man to ring a bell; to stand behind a door and to tick down upon a greasy slate' the names of the bored worshippers. 'Meanwhile a chaplain rattles through the prayers that cannot be entirely divested of their beauty'. The evening services might in some colleges be attended by perhaps two or three, but in others the chaplain, knowing that no one would respond to the tower bell, left a servant to ring it for ten minutes as a matter of form before locking the empty chapel again.

The phrases alternate attraction and repulsion: from the meadows on all sides sounds the 'charm' (song) of the skylarks, but the cawing of the rooks puts listeners upon the rack. The description mellows again with 'river-rounded', and no one familiar with the poet's delight in pied beauty could miss his interest in the 'dapple-eared lily' on the streamy fringes of the city.

The second quatrain alludes to the nineteenth-century *skirt* of terrace houses in red or yellow brick which had been allowed to separate the quiet grey of the ancient buildings from Nature's green. Lecturing at Oxford in 1872, Ruskin maintained that to improve the city it would be necessary to undo 'the greater part of what has been done to it within the last twenty years; . . . what was once the most beautiful approach to an academical city of any in Europe . . . is a wilderness of obscure and base buildings'. Cheap lodging-houses now heaped their brick-bats on one side, and the manufacturing chimneys of Cowley with their ashes and smoke fouled it on another (*The Eagle's Nest*, in *Works*, ed. Cook and Wedderburn, Vol. 22, pp. 192, 204–5).

But there was at least one angle from which Oxford remained unspoiled. Standing near the tree-canopied river Cherwell, and looking across Christ Church Meadow towards Merton, where Duns Scotus is believed to have taught around the year 1300, Hopkins could see some of the few *walls* (l. 10) which were certainly there in the time of Scotus, including parts of Christ Church Cathedral, of Merton Chapel, begun just before Scotus's arrival, and the towers or spires of such ancient churches as St Mary the Virgin in the High. As the sestet opens, the poet seems to be making a conscious effort ('this air I gather and I release') to fill lungs and spirit with the heavenly atmosphere on which Scotus *lived* during that long-past age: his mind was as subtle as air. Hopkins senses in the medieval philosopher a delight in the wild plants as God made them, each with its own 'thisness'. Through his surviving works, his spirit haunts the poet, like a soothing breeze in the branches, swaying him into peace (l. 11).

The final tercet of the sonnet attempts to summarize the claims of Duns Scotus to our respect. One title conferred on him by contemporaries was 'the Subtle Doctor', an epithet picked up in *rarest-veinèd*. The *realty* which Scotus unravelled refers to the philosophical doctrine of 'Realism', a belief traceable from Parmenides and Plato to St Thomas Aquinas and Scotus, who was the last of its great exponents before William of Ockham introduced the Nominalism which persisted into the Oxford of Hopkins's own time. Though Plato had believed in a 'real' world of Ideas (universals such as an ideal tree of which earth's varieties were indifferent copies), Duns Scotus taught that the essence of individuals, which included particular universals, had in addition something specific to themselves which was also 'real'. His doctrines were very complicated. It is interesting to note that the *Catholic Dictionary of Theology* (London, 1962), uses Hopkins to explain Scotus, not the reverse: 'The ideas of Scotus about the individual existents of this world have been much illuminated by their being taken up by the poet G. M. Hopkins' – and they quote from 'As kingfishers catch fire' (No. 57) and this poem. We might without serious distortion perhaps substitute for 'realty' such a phrase as 'theory of real individuality'. Scotus unravelled the great cable of being into the finest strands or veins. Though Aquinas, his Italian predecessor, was also a Realist, he compromised, choosing a less explicit form than Scotus discovered and (to Hopkins's mind) with less insight. In his understanding of the subtleties of the infinite variety among essences, Scotus seemed to outvie even the great thinkers of Greece – Plato and Aristotle (l. 13).

The last line, 'Who fired France for Mary without spot', may strike many readers as a sudden intrusion, unprepared for – unless we are to suppose some dubious contrast intended with the 'dappled-eared lily' (l. 3), since the pure white lily has been an age-old symbol for the Virgin. Yet the spotlessness of Mary is inextricably bound up with the name of Scotus. The *Catholic Dictionary of Theology* affirms that the controversy as to who was the first champion of the Immaculate Conception of Mary has now been settled in favour of Duns Scotus: he it was who argued most persuasively the soundness of the doctrine that Mary had been conceived free from 'original sin', the deprivation of sanctifying grace as a result of Adam's Fall. The doctrine was not officially defined as an article of faith until 1854. In ending his sonnet about Oxford with a reference to this contribution to Catholic doctrine from one of her sons, Hopkins reintroduces the fundamental dissonance in his Catholic portraits of Britain: it was France and not English Oxford that caught the fire of Scotus's enthusiasm.

The technical achievements of the sonnet deserve recognition. The opening line ('Towery city' is so much lighter than Milton's 'Towered cities') preserves the airy gracefulness of the Gothic architecture which predominated in Oxford (cf. 'The Escorial', No. 1, st. 6). The towers at the start and the end of the line enfold the trees between them as they do in the city itself. In March these would still be 'branchy', the leaves not yet out. Onomatopoeic effects of a complexity possible only in Sprung Rhythm cluster in line two, which has seventeen syllables. Since any number of slack syllables can in theory hurry between the stresses, we do not absolutely need to invoke or identify 'outrides' to scan it. Its vowel-chimes and busy movement contrast admirably with the stark monosyllables in line 5 ('Thou hast a base . . .'). The poem is, in fact, full of contrasts in sound and sense: an octave about Oxford leads on to a sestet about Scotus. And what sonnet before those of Hopkins could incorporate both the nimble hurry of the opening and the emphatic conclusion with its two Sprung leaps: 'Who fíred ∧ Fránce for Máry withóut ∧ spót'?

No. 45 Henry Purcell A sonnet in alexandrines, probably one of the two which Hopkins had 'soaking' – i.e. baking in a slow oven – in February 1879 (*Letters*, p. 73) but did not complete till April.

Of all composers Henry Purcell was the one who impressed Hopkins most deeply. Just as Milton's verse 'seems something necessary and eternal', he told Dixon (*Correspondence*, p. 13), so too did Purcell's music. He borrowed his compositions from Bridges, read the book on Purcell by W. H. Cummings and called on its author near Hastings to look at Purcell relics and discuss his genius. Purcell, one of the greatest English composers, was born about 1659 in London, and after sixteen years as organist in Westminster Abbey, was buried there in 1695. In addition to much church music for choirs and solo voices, he wrote royal odes and birthday pieces, a number of operas, incidental music and songs for plays, as well as instrumental compositions. He is mentioned in 'To what serves Mortal Beauty?' (No. 62), and may be the composer whom Hopkins had primarily in mind in two of his uncompleted pieces, the mistitled '(On a Piece of Music)' and 'What being in rank-old nature' (Nos 148 and 141). Purcell's reputation had been reinforced by the establishment of the Purcell Society in February 1876, to publish his music and (in the Society's earliest years) to give performances of his work.

Looking back on it four years later, Hopkins regarded this sonnet as 'one of my very best pieces'. Although earlier drafts have not survived, from a study of other complicated poems I believe that he reworked it into successively more and more elliptical shape. He was dismayed to find he was 'so unintelligible' and was making himself *mis*understood (*Letters*, pp. 171, 174). Bridges, interested in the poem in spite of its grammatical obscurity, kept on asking for further elucidation. The prose paraphrases which Hopkins sent him, to be found in the notes to the Oxford Fourth Edition of the *Poems* (pp. 273–4), form the basis for this commentary.

The poem may have had a remote origin in a visit to Westminster Abbey, where Purcell lies buried beneath the organ with an inscription on a nearby pillar, 'Here lyes Henry Purcell Esqr. Who left this Life And is gone to that Blessed Place Where only his Harmony can be exceeded'. The reference in line 4 to Purcell being laid low 'here' places us imaginatively before the tomb.

The main source of obscurity is the syntax – the relationship of the clauses to each other and even of the words within the clauses. The first quatrain (the punctuation of which is particularly unhelpful) might be rearranged in this way, a few of the terms being simultaneously modernized: 'May so arch-especial a spirit as heaves in Henry Purcell, so dear to me, have fallen fair, O fair, fair have fallen, by the reversing of the outward sentence which here lays him low, enlisted among heretics, [even though] there stretches a whole age since he passed away, since he departed'.

As with the young seamen overwhelmed in the *Eurydice* within moments by the swift rush of squall and sea, Hopkins assumes that time is a human illusion, that to the divine Lord the 'past' can still be acted upon in the 'future' (No. 41, ll. 109–20). His prayer, which he hopes may be given a retrospective answer, is for a favourable spiritual destiny to have been awarded to Purcell,

because of the rarity of his genius, in spite of the fact that his life
was given to the service of the heretical Anglican Church.

The second quatrain seeks to explain what is 'arch-especial'
about Purcell. 'What finds me (i.e. makes an impact upon me) is
not mood or meaning or anything which he, just like other
musicians, might nourish (*nursle*) in listeners – proud fire or sacred
fear, or love or pity. [Hopkins implies that Purcell expresses or
calls out all those emotions.] No, what impresses me is his unique
hand-forged feature, the constant revelation (*rehearsal*) of his own
individuality, his distinct self, which so thrusts on the ear
(impinges upon it) so fills it.'

The sestet maintains that this self-expression is involuntary,
incidental. Hopkins uses in turn the analogy of two different birds
(the effort to identify a single bird with all the characteristics in
lines 9–14 is stultifying). First there is an angelic bird which carries
him aloft and lays him down, in a new place perhaps – all the while
unaware that the poet in the midst of his aerial transports of musical
delight (carried safely in the talons) is busily studying the quaint
moonmarks ('crescent shaped markings on the quill-feathers') and
the under-wing plumage of the bird, his individually distinctive
characteristics (ll. 10, 11). On 'sakes' see the note to 'The Wreck
of the Deutschland', stanza 22.

Another parallel is added for clarification (ll. 11–14): Henry
Purcell is compared to a great seabird, which seems to share the
power of the storm and the 'thunder-purple' colour of the clouds
reflected in the wet beach. The great 'stormfowl' strides at first
along the sand until he is ready to fly off again. As his wings open,
ruffled by the wind ('wuthering'), the poet sees a 'colossal smile'
scattered from his snowy feathers. The bird, 'but meaning motion'
(i.e. simply intending to take off), is not trying to impress
onlookers by the size of his wing-span or the features of his
plumage, but by showing his beauty and valour in action like the
windhover he stirs in them a sense of wonder and a delight at this
sudden change in mood. The 'colossal smile' may be the cupid-
bow effect of the gracefully curved wings seen front on as a bird
flies. A marginal sketch of a heron in his *Journals* (p. 225)
approximates very roughly to this impression.

In an age when the 'fascination of what's difficult' lures readers
back to a poem time and again until they have mastered it, we are
not so liable to protest against the obscurity of this sonnet. We

may nevertheless be thankful for Bridges's queries and Hopkins's clarifications. There were times, of course, when Hopkins did not wish his meaning to be too easily gathered, as in parts of 'The Wreck of the Deutschland'.

J. A. Westrup, who opens his learned book on Purcell in the Great Composers Series, revised edition, Collier Books, New York, 1962 (Master Musicians, Dent, London, 1975), with the second quatrain of Hopkins's sonnet, rounds off his three-hundred page study by declaring that Hopkins has shown greater insight into Purcell's work than the musicologists who have laboured upon it. 'Gerard Manley Hopkins's sonnet on Purcell seems to me to sum up better than any critical account I know the fundamental reasons for admiration . . . "The forgèd feature"! Could anything better express the stubborn individuality of a great artist?'

No. 46 The Candle Indoors Written at Oxford in 1879, some time before 22 June when he sent it to Bridges, remarking that it had developed into a companion piece to the 'Lantern'. He later altered that title to 'The Lantern out of Doors' (No. 40), as an indication that it was one of a pair. He had been discussing the earlier poem in some detail with Bridges in February 1879 (*Letters*, p. 66).

Hopkins was fascinated by the phenomenon of light, as his many references to starlight, moonlight and the rays of the sun, both in his *Journals* and his *Poems*, make evident. Towards the end of his life he began writing a 'sort of popular account of Light and the Ether', because he felt that the scientific books on the subject were very unsatisfactory (*Correspondence*, p. 139). No trace of this survives.

Between this sonnet and the 'Lantern' there are interesting contrasts. At St Beuno's he had been indoors, looking out through the darkness of the Welsh countryside upon the receding light of a bright lantern beating onto surrounding mist. Here he is himself out-of-doors and in motion, approaching a candle set on the window-ledge of a city house, and he is conscious of the impact of the wavelets of light upon his eyes, as well as a sort of hypnotic pull upon him. In all other directions the city seems given over to 'night's blear-all black'. The persistence of the poet's speculations as to why the candle has been placed in the window indicates that the circumstances are unusual. The sixth line was repeatedly revised from its first surviving form: 'Not answered, I plod past and, yes, for lack/Of knowing, wish more, wish much, this Jane or Jack/There . . .'. It must surely be very late at night. 'I plod past' is the same humble gait of the ploughman-priest going about his duty as brings brightness to the share in 'The Windhover'. It suggests that Father Hopkins is walking wearily back (from an emergency call to the sick or dying perhaps), all too conscious of the *fading fire* of his own physical and spiritual energies. He told Canon Dixon in May that he found his parochial work 'very tiring'; but like St Paul, he was always ready to 'spend and be spent' for his parishioners – even if the outcome was that his spiritual salt, leached out, became 'spendsavour' (l. 14).

'Some candle clear burns': here the prime meaning of *clear* is 'brightly', as in the parallel passage in Shakespeare's *Henry VIII* (III: ii. 96–7) where Cardinal Wolsey, referring to Anne Boleyn's life and character, exclaims 'This candle burns not clear, 'tis I must snuff it'. Hopkins might have called it her *vital candle* (l. 10). But from the Oxford window happy wavelets of light ripple out, gently pressing back the surrounding darkness with their *yellowy moisture*. We might compare Milton's references to 'liquid light' and the 'Fountain of light', several times quoted by Hopkins. The candle has its own *being*, like the ocean waves in No. 141 ('What being in rank-old nature').

Line 4 presents fewer difficulties if we accept the metaphysical idea, familiarized by Donne, of the light rays running to and fro as they issue from the candle and are reflected back from the eye. The distinguished scientist Tyndall, whom Hopkins had met in the Alps (*Journals*, p. 182), had described a 'beam of light' as a '*train* of innumerable waves' (*Fortnightly Review*, 1869, p. 228): Hopkins brings that metaphor to life by imagining the beams as running on rails backwards and forwards between their source and his eye. The use of the same word (*beam*) for both a shaft of light and a shaft of wood (cf. l. 12) has ancient parallels. 'Trams' was a term applied to timber beams used as railtracks. To *truckle* was to run or roll. But other interpretations enrich the line. There was, for example, the game of truckles, which consisted in rolling a reel back and forth between players. And another 'tram' was a technical weaving term for 'silk thread consisting of two or more silk strands loosely twisted together; used for the weft or cross threads of the best silk goods' (*OED*). The image in line 4 would then be of delicate beams of light like silk threads woven by a shuttle speeding to and fro. The eye of the onlooker is held as by the tug of a light line to the bright flame. One thinks of John Donne's 'Ecstasy', where the two lovers were linked by hand and eye: 'Our eye-beams twisted, and did thread/Our eyes, upon one double string'. If all these images seem far-fetched, we must remember how widespread such metaphors are in literature, and that in an exactly contemporary letter to Bridges (26 May 1879) Hopkins praised Coventry Patmore's poetry for its 'exquisiteness, farfetchedness, of imagery worthy of the best things of the Caroline age'. And in a previous letter (3 March) he had commended Dixon's work for its 'Very fine metaphysical touches'.

The first quatrain has pondered over the physical nature of the light waves which push away darkness and mesmerise the onlooker. The second quatrain worries about the nature of the person who has set them to work. We move from philosophy to religious symbolism. In the Sermon on the Mount (from which the whole of the sestet will be seen to derive), Christ had used the rays of a candle set on a candlestick as an image for 'good works', the sight of which would cause men to 'glorify your Father who is in heaven' (Matt. 5: 15–6). The poet eagerly hopes that this solitary candle may symbolize the good character of its owner. But as the priest plods on past, his questioning unsatisfied, his buoyant wishes turn to misgivings and gloomy suspicions. How else can we account for the severity of his self-scrutiny in the sestet?

'Come you indoors, come home', he cries to his inquisitorial mind. The Sermon on the Mount had warned that those who judge others will be judged with equal vigour themselves. And Christ, comparing the eye to a window giving light to the body, pointed out that if the eye were obscured by evil, the body would be full of darkness (Matt. 6: 22). The poet reminds himself that his own inner fire needs fresh fuel and his secret spiritual flame needs trimming (ll. 9–10). Unable to dictate standards of conduct in the house he has passed, he should make his own life a model home. (Compare the ending to 'The times are nightfall', No. 150.)

In the last three lines he wonders whether his feeling of being in the right is due to blindness – as with the New Testament 'hypocrite' ('stage-actor' as the Greek means, a *liar* who lives a lie). In a famous hyperbole, Christ told of men who claimed such precise vision that they offered to remove 'motes' (tiny fragments of chaff) from their neighbours' eyes, though in fact their own eyes were obstructed by a *beam* (rafter). The poet implies a contrast between his own fingers, *deft* at plucking out faults in his neighbours, and the probably hard-working fingers lit by the candle. And in final mistrust, he wonders whether his purified will, which should like salt preserve him among the world's corruptions, has not lost its potency and ought, as we would say, 'in all conscience' to be thrown out like the savourless salt in the Sermon on the Mount (Matt. 5: 13).

When Hopkins sent 'The Candle Indoors' to Bridges along with 'The Handsome Heart', he confessed 'I am afraid they are not very good all through'. But neither then nor when editing his poems in 1884 did he make any but slight emendations to 'The Candle Indoors', though the other poem was subjected to a long series of revisions. We must always remember, nevertheless, that what may seem an objectionably obscure line to one reader may be a delight to another. Charles Williams, recalling in 1945 the enthusiasm which the few Hopkins pieces published before 1918 inspired in him, singled out as the 'line which, with a sigh of pleasure, I remember from that time most clearly' a surprising one, hard to explain, 'Or to-fro tender trambeams truckle at the eye' – though he smiled at it even while he admired. (*Time and Tide*, Vol. 26, No. 5, 3 February 1945, pp. 102–3.)

No. 47 The Handsome Heart: *at a Gracious Answer* Written at Oxford, between Easter 1879 (13 April) and 22 June, when it was sent to Bridges.

Just before Holy Week, Hopkins's superior Father Parkinson, while giving a retreat in the country close to Oxford, had a carriage accident in which he broke his collar-bone. All the church and parish work descended upon Father Hopkins, but he came through this busiest liturgical season buoyantly with the willing help of some members of the congregation. Two boys, for example, greatly assisted him in the sacristy; though they were from poor families (one was the son of an Italian ice-cream seller) when Hopkins urged them to accept some payment for their services they refused. Eventually, however, the older of the two agreed to let Hopkins buy him a book. The sonnet is about the younger lad's reply (*Letters*, p. 86).

Like several other poems written at Oxford, this one admires the rightness of conduct which occurs when a being expresses itself in the instinctive way it was intended to; 'wild and self-instressed' action (l. 7), untutored, could not be improved by ten years of teaching. If the boy had been trained at school and university he could not more surely have chosen the right course. In this case the lad's answer to his spiritual Father is in line with the sort of request which Christ taught His disciples to make to their heavenly Father: 'Thy will be done'. After all, He 'knows well what your needs are before you ask Him' (Matt. 6: 8–10).

The image in the first quatrain is of a magnetic needle on a mount which allows it to swing and dip freely: no matter how it is twisted or pressed down, it swings back to its original direction and balance. The poet could scarcely have guessed how this metaphor harmonized with the imagery in the second quatrain: birds are now known to have a built-in sensitivity to magnetic forces, their skill in homing and migration depending partly upon their capacity to guide themselves instinctively as though by compass. When Hopkins was writing, *carriers* (l. 5, i.e. carrier-pigeons or doves), were thought to steer entirely by sight. The encyclopaedias of his day recommend that they should be kept in darkness for six to eight hours prior to being released: hence the *Doff darkness* of line 6. Once they are let out into the light, their instinct takes command. The Christian parallel is obvious: once we have 'stripped off the works of darkness' (Romans 13: 12) like soiled clothes, nature will be free to direct us. In line 8, *Falls light* means that the heart like the pigeon reverts *lightly* to its own marvellous special function, namely finding its way home (as in st. 3 of 'The Wreck of the Deutschland'). No doubt there is some play on the two homophones in *light*.

The poet's problem is not which gift to buy him with money but what gift he does not already possess to buy him with prayer. He is already *mannerly* in heart, an adjective which means doing the right thing, morally and/or socially. An early draft is clearer: 'A mannerly heart! handsomer than handsome face'. (See notes to No. 62, 'To what serves Mortal Beauty?') Whether his face was handsome or not, his heart certainly was, and (though the syntax leaves room for guessing) he seems to have had a fine bearing, a grace of movement, a soaring poetic spirit. To these natural graces had been added divine grace: together they were responsible for

the 'Gracious Answer' of the title. What more could the priest ask
on his behalf? The answer rushes out suddenly – the gift of
perseverance, to keep on to the end in the same track along which
he is pacing, but with the added strength to break into a *run*,
exerting himself more strenuously than before. In October
Hopkins was able to tell Bridges the first results of his prayerful
interest: 'The little hero of the Handsome Heart has gone to
school at Boulogne to be bred for a priest and he is bent on being a
Jesuit' (*Letters*, p. 92).

Sending the poem to Bridges, Hopkins expressed his misgivings
about its unevenness in quality and the need for polish. After some
eight weeks, writing to his friend again, he said 'I send you a
corr[ected]' which he changed to 'an improved copy' and then (not
apparently being sure that he had improved it) 'a recast of the
Handsome Heart' (*Letters*, pp. 84–6). He expressed some surprise
that Bridges liked the sonnet so much. 'I thought it not very good'.
Its chief problem is not the one hesitation expressed by Bridges –
the de-emphasizing of the rhyme 'buy' because the sentence
hurries forward to the enclitic 'You' in the next line. His 'recast'
had in fact repeated 'the offence' by running the end of the first
quatrain into the second: 'push what plea one might and ply/Him'.
The real weakness, as Hopkins himself realized, was syntactical.
The second quatrain consists of an exclamation ('What the heart
is!') to which an explanatory clause is loosely attached (ll. 5, 7–8).
But line 6 is another exclamation injected into the middle of this
clause parenthetically ('Throw off the cloak of darkness and your
spiritual homing instinct will work!'). In the sestet three more
exclamations carry the meaning, but the first ('Mannerly-
hearted!') is not clearly related to the rest of the line ('handsome
face') nor to 'Beauty's bearing' and the 'muse'. Why the dash after
'face' and three dots after 'grace'? During his revisions Hopkins
converted these lines into a rather prosaic statement: 'Mannerly
the heart is more than handsome face,/Beauty's bearing, or Muse
of mounting vein;/And surely it is in this case, bathed in high
hallowing grace?'

The metre is common rhythm 'counterpointed', so described
because of the reversed stresses in 'carriers' (l. 5), 'Mannerly' (l.
9), 'Beauty's bearing' (l. 10) and 'sterner' (l. 14). Some of the lines
are very irregular if treated as pentameters – for example, 3 and 4.
His efforts to improve the poem by using alexandrines instead of

pentameters was hardly a success. There are altogether six
different versions of the poem if we include the draft. The one
printed in the Fourth Edition is close to the original sent to
Bridges, and I agree with Hopkins's first editor that the recasting
lost as much in freshness as it gained in clarity.

No. 48 The Bugler's First Communion Written at Oxford, 1879,
about 27 July. In sending it to Bridges Hopkins added a note at the
bottom of the poem that the bugler had been 'ordered to Mooltan
in the Punjaub; was to sail Sept. 30'.

A successful teacher or priest tries to make each person for
whom he is responsible feel of unique interest and value. In the
impersonal life of the army, the bugler of this poem was only a
cipher among the hundreds of lads and men living in Cowley
Barracks, which in turn was only one among several hundred
barracks scattered across Britain. But to Hopkins the priest he was
an individual, just as for Hopkins the artist it was necessary to
select out of all those he had instructed one striking example if he
was to create a poem. As we see the lad kneeling for his first
communion we are unaware that anyone else is present. But the
occasion was definitely a Sunday, for we know he started the poem
that 'very very day' (though in dating it he could not quite
remember whether it was 27 July or 3 August); and the scene was
the church, for line 9 in an early draft reads 'And knelt at chancel
in regimental red'. We may presume that a whole congregation
also heard Mass, and perhaps others among them were receiving
their first communion: from stanza 6 it is clear that the priest had
been instructing a number of youths. But, like Christ, the priest
has to be intensely personal (as well as impersonal, detached).
Preaching a few Sundays earlier in the drab old chapel at St
Clement's, Hopkins had stretched the imagination of his hearers
by assuring them that while Christ was going about His work in
Palestine, He 'was thinking of us every moment of his life, of each
of us separately' (*Sermons*, p. 15).

Visiting an army barracks, however spiritually rewarding, would
be an ordeal for a shy man – and Hopkins even years later in
Dublin was mistaken for a rather small highly-strung youth of
fifteen or twenty. He found this part of his pastoral work the most
strenuous (st. 8), and yet the most satisfying (st. 6). If much of his
other parish duty was mortifying, like walking barefoot on stony

ground, the responsiveness of the young Catholic recruits made
him 'tread tufts of consolation' for days afterwards (st. 7). Later he
spoke of the majority of soldiers and sailors as being not only
morally 'frail' but 'foul' (No. 63, '(The Soldier)', l. 3). Here we are
told that though these young Catholics are *limber liquid* under the
priest's instruction in the catechism and their Christian duty, they
show vehement energy in following their moral well-being when
left on their own. The adjective *limber* means pliant, resuming
natural shape once pressure is released. Its military homophone
inevitably resonates in this setting: the limber of a field-gun
enables its crew to move it rapidly into action. For a decent lad to
survive unscathed in the crude life of the barracks, he needed to be
(st. 4) *dauntless* (*Christ's darling* jeered at as 'mama's darling').
Hopkins as a boy had himself overcome ridicule in a school
dormitory by his quiet determination in reading a portion of the
New Testament every night in obedience to a promise given his
mother (*Further Letters*, pp. 394–5). He knew that a Christian
soldier had to remain *vaunt- and tauntless*, not provoked into
retaliation by the boasting and jeering around him. 'Breathing
bloom of a chastity in mansex fine', as Jim Hunter remarks, 'is a
most perilous phrase, though we ought to take it seriously and
thoughtfully' (*Gerard Manley Hopkins*, p. 88).

But the sacraments of the Church, communion and confirmation, provide miraculous gifts and protection. The Mass is
accompanied by 'sendings' from heaven (st. 4) – a courageous
heart, true tongue, chaste nobility of physique – far more valuable
than the sendings in long-awaited parcels and letters sent from
home. The holy chrism (the 'sealing sacred ointment' of st. 9,
solemnly applied by the Bishop during confirmation) is a charm
more potent against evil than the superstitious lucky objects
carried by many soldiers (even today) to ward off the physical
'evil' of death. From a priestly point of view death before collapse
into mortal sin is to be preferred to dishonoured survival. A
'sudden death *need* not be a bad death', Hopkins used to tell
retreatants; 'it has its advantages, for if we then are in the grace of
God we have no time to fall away' (*Sermons*, p. 247). This explains
his seemingly shocking remark to Bridges about this poem, that he
was 'half inclined to hope the Hero of it may be killed in
Afghanistan' (*Letters*, p. 92). With such high hopes for a new Sir
Galahad, whose purity led him to the Grail, the poet can scarcely

contemplate the moral disaster he dreads against hope (sts 10, 11). Knowing only too well from hearing confessions the tremendous temptations of a soldier's life, he has hurled himself in fierce prayer against the forces of darkness. His pleas have been vehement enough to shake (*brandle*) heaven if they go un-answered, like the up-surge (*ride*) and jarring of breakers against an adamantine cliff (st. 12). But favourable heaven may have heard his prayers already.

Many readers may feel that the 'Bugler's First Communion' provides more evidence for Hopkins's success as a priest than as a poet. While it was still in progress, he told Bridges that the poem he was busy with was a 'finer thing' than 'The Handsome Heart' (No. 47) and 'Brothers' (No. 54) (*Letters*, 86) – though that would still not place the poem high in his canon. The allusion to its metre being 'something like the Eurydice' makes the identification uncertain, though they look similar on the page. Perhaps he was trying too hard. Much contemporary religious verse, such as Keble's, Faber's and Newman's, was to his critical judgment watered-down Romanticism, and, we might add, often conveyed in a childish singsong metre. Hopkins errs in the opposite quarter, endeavouring to make everything startlingly new. His vocabulary runs the whole gamut, from the homely (Christ's *treat* fetched from a *cupboard* instead of 'tabernacle' — a reminder that the communion is a feast providing spiritual nourishment), to the mysteriously poetic (such as the transubstantiated body of Christ in the consecrated wafer: 'Low-latched in leaf-light housel his too huge godhead' – st. 3). He deliberately reverses our expectations: in defiance of normal usage he calls lads who are true to their own noble inscape of gracious personality 'headstrong' (st. 6); instead of putting a 'ban on' someone (a curse or anathema), the sealing chrism 'bans off' evil (st. 9). So too the 'divine doom' in stanza 11 is, surprisingly, a favouring providence.

At times the syntax is too complicated for use in an uninflected language. In stanza 4, 'ah divine' is marooned from its original noun, as we realize from the first fragmentary draft: 'Your sweetest sendings, ah divine/Heavens befall him! a heart . . .'. In stanza 10, 'own Galahad' is qualified by two possessives, both 'our day's' and 'God's' – reminiscent of the last line of 'The Wreck of the Deutschland'. And the poem ends with colloquialisms beyond the reach of most modern readers (and surely Victorian ones):

'Forward-like ['Presumptuously' – referring to his prayers which refused to take No for an answer] but however ['nevertheless'] and like ['it is likely that'] favourable heaven heard these' [i.e. 'pleas'].

In contrast to this rather critical analysis, Dr Gardner (*Study* ii, pp. 296–303) feels that it is this 'eager, inchoate expression which saves the poem from sentimentality'. He adds: 'In no poem by Hopkins does the conversational and dramatically spontaneous style combine more successfully with the grand style of resonant yet imaginative declamation.' His analysis of the poem is accordingly much more sympathetic than mine. On the other hand Father F. X. Shea judges the poem 'overrich with holy-card imagery, and . . . corrupted with sugar' (*Hopkins Quarterly*, Vol. 1. No. 1, April 1974, p. 39).

Some images are drawn from trees (leaf, blossom, fruit): the airy 'leaf-light' (st. 3), 'bloom' (st. 4) which is breathed like the 'goldish flue' on Harry Ploughman's arms (No. 71, ll. 1–2), and the less appealing metaphor for moral ripeness in 'pushed peach' (st. 6) – no doubt meant to *un*prepare us for the independent vigour displayed in the next line. In stanza 8, 'freshyouth fretted in a bloomfall . . .' was clearer before he had worked it up: 'boyboughs fretted in a flowerfall all portending/Fruit', where *fretted* refers to the ruffled blossoms as their petals are shed.

Associated also with trees is the image of the 'hell-rook ranks [which] sally to molest him' (st. 5). In England these great black birds converge in long ragged trains upon their roosting place, or descend in voracious hordes on newly sown fields like the 'fowls of the air' in the Parable of the Sower. No inanimate scarecrow will frighten them off for long; a man has to appear to make them *squander* – a word in common country use in the poet's time for the scattering of birds or people, and formerly a military term (very appropriate in this context) for the dispersing of enemy forces or ships. His guardian angel is asked to be to him what the Greeks called a *parastatēs*, a 'comrade on the flank'. 'Dress his days to a *dexterous* and starlight order' plays on the familiar command to a marching column to 'dress by the *right*': the guardian angel is implored to keep him in line on a route approved by the heavens. And finally there is the image which originates in 'liquid youth' (st. 6), and picks up 'bloom*fall*' (st. 8), though it is asserted only in stanzas 10 and 11: water 'by a divine doom chánnelled', i.e. drifting down a natural river-bed on its way to the sea. The water is certain to find its way *home* in the end, but it may *rankle* (a word which represents the dialect 'rangle', to wind about, ramble) in back-eddies or *wheels* at every bend of the river, delaying its ultimate safe arrival. Anyone who had lived at Stonyhurst would know the favourite salmon holes in the River Hodder there, such as Sail Wheel, and Sandbed Wheel.

The metre is 'Sprung Rhythm overrove', one line overspilling into the next line so that a falling rhythm in one line (basically trochaic) may be followed by rising rhythm (basically iambic) in the next, as in the first two lines of stanza 6. These two features permit great elasticity – more in fact than the poet took since he insists on an awkward stress upon 'in' with the ninth line. The last line of each stanza has an outride or flurry of extra-metrical syllables, recorded in notes to our Fourth Edition. Its closest metrical resemblance to 'The Loss of the Eurydice' lies in the shortened third line with three stresses: to the ear the movement of each poem is utterly distinct.

No. 49 Morning, Midday, and Evening Sacrifice Written at Oxford, August 1879.

The differences between Youth, Manhood and Age have been epitomized and embodied in the proverbs of all nations. Aristotle in his *Rhetoric* (Bk 2. 12–14) emphasized the changeability and lack of control in the young who were in the 'morning of life', the chill absence of desires and ambitions in the old, their lack of courage, while those in the prime of life he presented as uniting the virtues of youth and age without the handicaps of either. But in this poem Hopkins is thinking more positively about what each age group can offer in terms of the Pauline injunction to 'present your bodies a living sacrifice, holy, pleasing unto God' (Rom. 12: 1). In stanza 1 youth is characterized by beauty, in the middle stanza manhood by power, and in the final stanza age by mastery and ripeness. Youth offers the bloom (as with the bugler of No. 48, l. 30), age the mature fruit like the architect in No. 148, '(On a Piece of Music)', and in between them, the prime of life the fulfilment of Nature's inscape in the co-ordination of all powers (tellingly illustrated by 'Harry Ploughman', No. 71).

In describing 'beauty that must die' (a Keatsian phrase very much in his mind here) Hopkins in the opening stanza makes every

feature seem as evanescent as a morning mist or the dying fall of
an exquisite melody. The cheek is *die-away*: he avoids the cliché of
'fading' as skilfully as the 'war of white and red', or of the lilies and
roses to which Shakespeare and his fellow poets had accustomed
readers. Architecturally to 'die away' is used when one part of a
structure merges smoothly into another – as here the two colours
in the cheek. The *wimpled* lip not only catches the cupid's-bow
effect of the Elizabethan headdress, but implies the transitoriness
of ripples in water (as in No. 59, 'The Golden Echo', l. 10). The
golden hair is a mere *wisp* like a thin cloud at sunrise; the eye is
airy-grey; and all this beauty is like the short-lived blossom in an
orchard doomed to a 'bloomfall' or *fuming* into the air like the
morning sacrifice of sweet incense on the golden altar, enjoined in
the laws of Moses (Exod. 30: 1–7). The Psalms warn us that beauty
will be consumed away during life as by moths and after death by
the grave (39: 11 and 49: 14, A.V.); but Hopkins later elaborated
in 'The Golden Echo' what he merely hints at here, that if beauty
is freely surrendered while still 'worth consuming' (its ownership,
as it were, transferred back to the donor), it will be transformed
into the spiritual equivalent.

The syntax of the second stanza was misunderstood by Bridges
and therefore incorrectly published by Beeching in his *Lyra Sacra*
(1895) as: 'told by Nature tower'. All surviving autographs read
'told by Nature: Tower'. The colon followed by a capital letter
surely indicate that Nature's instruction to 'thought and thew' is
that they should tower – increase in strength and height. Compare
the message from the heart in 'Spelt from Sibyl's Leaves' (No. 61,
l. 8). In a sermon preached the month this poem was composed
Hopkins spoke of the dangers of godless good health, but added,
'which leads me to say, brethren, by the way, the man or woman,
the boy or girl, that in their bloom and heyday, in their strength
and health give themselves to God and with the fresh body and
joyously beating blood give him glory, how near he will be to them
in age and sickness and wall their weakness round in the hour of
death!' (*Sermons*, p. 19).

Although the last stanza depicts Death with his finger already on
the latch, the portrait is again positive, showing age at its best. The
imagery is reminiscent of '(On a Piece of Music)' (No. 148 –
'scope', 'overvaulted', 'masterhood', 'ruder-rounded rind'). 'In
silk-ash kept from cooling' is no deathbed picture of 'blue-bleak

embers' ('The Windhover', No. 36, l. 13): Hopkins explained to Bridges that he was comparing grey hairs to the 'flakes of silky ash which may be seen round wood embers burnt in a clear fire and covering a "core of heat", as Tennyson calls it. . . . "Your offer, with despatch, of" . . . is "Come, your offer of all this (the matured mind), and without delay either!" ' (*Letters,* p. 98).

The little lyric is superbly musical, basically in trimeters but handled with some of the freedoms of Sprung Rhythm, particularly in stanza 1. The rhyme scheme gives it a flavour of its own, the first four lines alternating in sound, and the next three in each stanza, with matching double rhymes, chiming their way to the climax of the last line.

No. 50 Andromeda Written at Oxford, 12 August 1879.

Within a few days of writing this poem Hopkins, who often took a long time to reach satisfying finality, sent it off to Bridges with an invitation to subject it to 'minute criticism. I endeavoured in it at a more Miltonic plainness and severity than I have anywhere else. I cannot say it has turned out severe, still less plain, but it seems almost free from quaintness and in aiming at one excellence I may have hit another' (*Letters*, p. 87).

In the classical legend as told by Apollodorus and Ovid (*Metamorphoses* iv, 663ff), a country vaguely called Aethiopia had been visited with floods and the ravages of a sea-monster because of the wrath of the god Poseidon. It was prophesied that the evils would cease if the king sacrificed his beautiful daughter Andromeda to the monster, by chaining her to the sea-cliffs. Ovid speaks of the hard rough pointed rocks (*duras cautes*) to which she was bound, and Josephus, in his *Wars of the Jews* (Bk 3, chap. 9), describes the scene according to popular tradition – the semi-circular harbour at Joppa (near the modern Tel Aviv), which had two curving cliffs bending towards each other, with great rocks jutting out at their base. Hopkins catches the crescent shape of the bay with his 'both horns of shore'. The hero Perseus, flying back with his winged sandals from slaying the Gorgon Medusa, fell in love with Andromeda's beauty as he hovered invisible above the rock, and when the dragon came with its fearful roar across the waves, he slew it with his adamantine sickle (the *barebill* of l. 14). Hopkins implies that he also turned the monster to stone by exhibiting the Gorgon's head. Andromeda, released from her terrible ordeal, became his bride.

Although Hopkins does not tie the allegory down, the most obvious interpretation would see Andromeda as representing the Church, which Christ set on a rock (Matt. 16: 18). Her arms stretched wide in sacrifice show her as being crucified with Christ, sharing his sufferings and injuries. Very movingly, the author of Lamentations portrayed Jerusalem, that city set on a rock, as a beautiful princess rejected and exposed to scorn, crying out in her desolation, 'Is it nothing to you, all ye that pass by? behold, and see if there be any sorrow like unto my sorrow' (Lam. 1: 12, *A.V.*). Since Jerusalem is regarded as a symbol of the Church, we are not surprised to find an echo of that passage here: Andromeda has 'not her either beauty's equal or/Her injury's'. Perseus plays the role of Christ, Whose mystical marriage to the Church in heaven follows His deliverance of the Church on earth.

But just as Browning conflates the Perseus-Andromeda legend with that of St George and the Dragon, so Hopkins in referring to 'Time's Andromeda' seems to be associating her with the mysterious woman in the Apocalypse (chaps 12–17) against whom and whose seed the dragon waged war, forcing her to flee to the desert for 'a time and times, and half a time' (chap. 12: 14). In one of his meditation notes he records 'I cannot help suspecting that the attack on the woman which the dragon makes was, though I cannot yet clearly grasp how, the actual attack which he made, is making, and will go on making on the human race' (*Sermons,* p. 200). Hopkins sees her as in some degree a picture of the Virgin Mary, without contradicting her other traditional identification with the Church on earth. The Apostles and early Fathers continually urged their persecuted congregations to hold out with patience because their sorrows were limited to Time: 'For I reckon that the sufferings of this time are not to be compared with the glory to come' (Rom. 8: 18).

The greatest problem lies in interpreting the extreme crisis of the 'wilder beast from West' in the second quatrain: what is Hopkins most likely to have had in mind? Dr Gardner suggests that it was 'rationalism, Darwinism, the new paganism of Whitman, and all similar forces' (*Study* i. p. 186). Let me commend the solution proposed by Dr Michael Moore, whose doctoral dissertation on the lifelong influence of Newman upon

Hopkins I had the pleasure of supervising. Moore quotes from the much publicized speech which Newman made in Rome three months before this poem was written, on the occasion of his elevation to the College of Cardinals.

> For thirty, forty, fifty years I have resisted, to the best of my powers, the spirit of Liberalism in religion. Never did the Holy Church need champions against it more sorely than now. . . . There never was a device of the enemy so cleverly framed and with such promise of success.

That Newman was the prime inspiration behind the sonnet seems to be clinched by another passage quoted by Dr Moore:

> Our light shall never go down; Christ set it upon a hill, and hell shall not prevail against it. *The Church* will witness on to the last for the Truth, *chained indeed to this world*, its evil partner, but ever foretelling its ruin, though not believed, and in the end promised a far different recompense. For in the end the Lord Omnipotent shall reign, when the marriage of the Lamb shall come at length, and His wife shall make herself ready.
> (*Parochial and Plain Sermons*, 1844, i, pp. 189–90, my italics).

Hopkins had reason to be pleased with this sonnet, but he was, of course, perfectly right in recognizing that its style was not 'plain'. His phrases inevitably resonate: e.g. 'looks off by both horns of shore' (1. 3) shapes the entrapping bay and simultaneously invokes a semi-conscious image of a victim impaled. Hopkins knew that dragons were often represented as horned, especially when thought of as typifying the Devil (*Sermons*, p. 199). Equally resonant are the last three lines, especially 'her patience, morselled into pangs,/Mounts'. The unexpectedness of the rescue, when the invisible hero hovering aloft suddenly appears and alights, is contained in the absolute, almost parenthetic, phrase, 'no one dreams'. The oblique stroke after 'barebill', while roughly equivalent to a comma, restrains readers from construing 'thongs and fangs' as part of Perseus's equipment, along with his 'barebill', instead of recognizing them as the object of 'disarming'.

Metrically the sonnet is so conservative that when in 1881 Dixon asked Hopkins for some sonnets for an anthology of them being published by Hall Caine, Hopkins thought that 'Andromeda' might be suitable. The extent to which his poetry was considered out of line with the norms of his age is indicated by the fact that

Hall Caine, after consulting 'a critic of utmost eminence' (D. G. Rossetti), not only rejected the sonnet, but threatened to devote a special paragraph in the preface to 'refute' the principles on which it was constructed (*Letters*, pp. 127–8).

No. 51 Peace Written at Oxford, 2 October 1879, on the eve of his departure for Bedford Leigh – a Curtal Sonnet the abruptness of which reflects a fatigued and distracted mind.

Hopkins as an undergraduate was strongly attracted to George Herbert, the Anglican divine and poet, and traces of that influence can be found throughout his writings. Herbert was fresh in his mind (*Letters*, p. 88) when he composed this poem, which, though called 'Peace', might with more reason be given a title from Herbert, 'Affliction': in fact its central image bears some resemblance to one found in Herbert's first poem under that name:

> I read, and sigh, and wish I were a tree;
>   For sure then I should grow
> To fruit or shade: at least some bird would trust
> Her household to me, and I should be just.

Hopkins, imagining himself a tree, finds no such satisfaction. He produces no fruit, and the birds distrust him. Round and round, afraid to return to her nest, circles a wild wood-dove. Though the turtle-dove is a symbol of peace, the wary wood-pigeon or -dove is startled from its hiding place by the least hint of disturbance. During no stage in his life did Hopkins lose the tension which keyed him to strenuous exertion, though at the cost of serenity and health. As an earnest Anglican, in a poem he first called 'Rest', he had fancied that a nun taking the veil was entering a haven of peace (No. 9, 'Heaven-Haven: A nun takes the veil'). After he entered a strict religious order himself he discovered that he was still within reach of storms. It is true that when he decided to become a Jesuit, he could report that he had 'enjoyed the first complete peace of mind I have ever had' (*Further Letters*, p. 51). But he found the life of a religious, like any other, 'liable to many mortifications' (*Correspondence*, p. 28). During his years of training he fortunately discovered Duns Scotus, whom only a few months before this poem he had described as the one 'who of all men most sways my spirits to peace' (No. 44, 'Duns Scotus's Oxford', l. 11).

The disturbed syntax here mirrors his disturbed 'wonderings' (to quote a draft of l. 6). What is in store for him in the appointment to which he is about to move, and will he be considered more successful there than he had been so far? It is easy enough to reduce the words to a more normal Victorian poetic style, simultaneously shortening the alexandrines to pentameters: 'O Peace, wild wood-dove, when wilt thou make end/Of roaming round me, and (thy shy wings shut),/Nest 'neath my boughs?' But this is neither Hopkins nor, for that matter, poetry. In line 5 he plays, characteristically, with homonyms opposite in sense – *peace*, which results from unity in mind or spirit, and *piece*, a disunited fragment. Against '*pure* peace' is pitted '*poor* peace'. The four-fold repetition of *peace* in that line makes one wonder whether he ever heard the pigeons at St Mary's Hall, Stonyhurst, being wooed by some Scottish brother with the call 'Pease, pease, pease, pigeons; here's some crumbs to you' (*English Dialect Dictionary*, under Pees', and *Journals*, pp. 231–2). It is more likely that he is remembering Jeremiah's allusions to the peacemongers who cry 'Peace, peace: and there was no peace' (6: 14, etc.).

In an earlier version of lines 5–6 he had asked 'what true peace allows/Of breaks, awakes, wars, wonderings, fears for the end of it?' Later, in Dublin, he was to write of those 'awakes' – sleepless anxious hours spent after waking in the dark – of 'war within' concealed by an outward placidity, of living by a spirit of fear, of losing his peace even during periods when he had no soul-fraying examination work through letting his mind dwell on the approaching end of his brief respite.

The sonnet attempts some reconciliation, but it became less reassuring as he revised it. In line 7 the reference in the early version to the Lord (landlord of an estate) 'taking Peace' turned into the violence of 'reaving Peace' – to reave being to 'rob, plunder, carry off', as he explained to Bridges (*Letters*, p. 196). Instead of the dove-winged Peace, his Lord has left him a mere fledgling, Patience, which in the first version 'will be Peace hereafter'. In the revision however, it is simply preening its feathers in the hope of turning into a dove of peace: the verb *plumes* can mean to prepare the wings for flight, but it also carries some unpromising overtones of false pretensions. The final sentence differentiates between peace and rest: true spiritual peace must produce tangible works to prove its presence. We are reminded of

Herbert's poem cleverly entitled 'The Pulley', since this is a mechanical device for transforming the downward drag of gravity into an upward lift. In that poem Herbert imagines God, in the process of making Man, almost emptying a glass of blessings over him. When only rest remained, He stopped, being afraid that if man were given rest, he might 'rest in Nature, not the God of Nature'. Playing on 'rest' as Hopkins here plays on 'peace', Herbert imagines the divine benefactor saying:

> Yet let him keep the rest,
> But keep them with repining restlessness:
> Let him be rich and weary, that at least,
> If goodness lead him not, yet weariness
> May toss him to my breast.

His lack of peace drove Hopkins continually back to his Maker.

No. 52 At the Wedding March Written at Bedford Leigh, 21 October 1879, in Sprung Rhythm tetrameters, the last two lines expanding to pentameters. In line 11, *his* claims the additional stress.

On 21 October 1879, an important wedding took place in St Joseph's, Bedford Leigh, Lancashire. The marriage of Mr John Fairclough to Miss Maggie Unsworth, both of Leigh, was solemnized by the 'Rev. Father Fanning, assisted by Fathers Hopkins, Kavanagh, and Wright' (*Notes and Queries*, March 1971, article by Tom Dunne). If we may interpret Hopkins literally, this little lyric was made actually at the wedding (*Correspondence*, p. 132). He probably began it in his head and committed drafts to paper that night. The final autograph is dated November.

Hopkins had arrived in the parish less than three weeks before, and could scarcely have known the couple well enough to have composed the poem for them as a wedding present. Moreover, it would be unlike him to offer it: he was at that very time trying to prevent Canon Dixon from publishing 'The Loss of the Eurydice' in a Carlisle newspaper – 'notoriety' as a poet among his colleagues was the last thing he desired (see *Correspondence*, pp. 29–31). But apart from that, the poem was not likely to please the pair, being strange in rhythm and syntax, and (as Hopkins felt years later when considering whether it would be suitable for

Dixon's *Bible Birthday Book*) it was 'too personal and, I believe,
too plainspoken' (*Correspondence*, p. 132).

The opening line is arresting and (on reflection) a little dis-
quieting, yet it was the result of careful revision. The poet moved
from 'God hang his worship on your head', through 'God with
worship hang your head' (vaguely suggestive of civic honours), to
'God with honour hang your head', below which the idiomatic 'to
hang the head in shame' insists upon being heard. Does it in some
way incorporate the priest's concern about the frequency of
dishonoured marriages, evident in the last stanza from the tear-
fulness of his prayers for the prosperity of their marriage? But the
imagery may derive from the rich-crowned head of a willow tree
hanging down, and so interact with *grace*, *bed*, and *lissome scions*.
The basic meaning of *scion* is an offshoot or graft. *Lissome* means
supple, and is applied in the *Sermons* (p. 36) to the perfection of
body in Christ the man.

The middle stanza is the most attractive. The pitting of 'divined'
(probed by human insight) against the 'deeper . . ./Divine charity'
(love like a hidden intertwining of God-given roots) emphasizes
the sacramental character of true marriage. This is the allusion in
the last stanza: the 'wonder wedlock' is no earthly honeymoon, but
the mystical union of Christ with His Church, referred to in a
sermon the next month in St Joseph's: Christ 'is the true-love and
the bridegroom of men's souls' (*Sermons*, p. 35). It is through this
rather than mortal marriage that He 'Deals triumph and immortal
years'. The March which (violent metaphor) *treads* the ears of the
poet is a foretaste of the apocalyptic one in Revelation (chaps
19–21), when the Bridegroom on a white horse leads the great
armies of heaven, and the visionary is overwhelmed by a voice 'as
the voice of many waters, and as the voice of great thunders,
saying . . . the marriage of the Lamb is come, and his wife hath
prepared herself' (19: 6, 7).

No. 53 Felix Randal A sonnet of alexandrines, with outrides, dated
at Liverpool, 28 April 1880.

On 21 April 1880, a young Liverpool farrier who, at the age of
thirty-one should have been in the prime of his strength, died in
that part of the city slums where Hopkins's parish duties lay. For
two years he had been treated for pulmonary tuberculosis, during

the last months having been seriously ill and wasting visibly away. (See Rev. Alfred Thomas, *TLS*, 19 March 1971, for historical details and exposition.) Liverpool had been expanding with an unhealthy, greedy speed – it boasted that since 1740 its population and revenues had been escalating. But in the second half of the nineteenth century, and about the time the poet was stationed in Liverpool, its death rate was twice the average for the whole of England. Besides Felix Spencer (the farrier's real name), four other parishioners who had died that week were commended to the prayers of the faithful on Sunday, 25 April, in St Francis Xavier's. The entry in the church notice book is in Hopkins's own hand, and it was he who preached the morning sermon. In this superb sonnet, though he has naturally disguised the surname, the poet has kept the Christian name, Felix, for a subdued feeling that the farrier was 'happy' does pervade the poem. As for the surname, whatever other reasons may have influenced Hopkins's choice of a pseudonym, we may note the additional tonal unity (a quality he valued in verse) given by *Randal, rambled, ransom, random*. James Milroy uses the poem as an illustration of the importance in Hopkins of consonant rhyme and syllable rhyme for reinforcing meaning (*The Language of Gerard Manley Hopkins*, 1977, pp. 139–42).

The sonnet begins deliberately in a low, minor key, reflecting the strain of a protracted illness where death arrives as a relief to both sufferer and friends: 'Felix Randal the farrier, O is he gone then? my duty all ended . . .'. This more colloquial earlier phrasing (*gone*) is less stark, pointing forward to a *return* in strength at the resurrection. The reference to *duty* is warmed for us as we read Hopkins's striking first Liverpool sermon: '*Duty is love . . . . There is nothing higher than duty* in creatures or in God' (*Sermons*, p. 53). The opening quatrain rehearses the last desperate stages at the finish. We see only the outer shell, the *mould* formed by the soul (*Further Letters*, pp. 306–7) — an image specially matched to metal-working – the obtrusive physical frame (built broad and tall, as he had needed to be to handle great drayhorses). His virile attractiveness is ideally caught in *hardy-handsome*. Neither the poet's earlier portrait of the *Eurydice*'s captain as 'rude of feature' (No. 41, l. 50), nor his later attribution of 'Churlsgrace' to Harry Ploughman (No. 71, l. 16), inscape so satisfactorily the combination of strength and a fine physique which he admired.

In his delirium his reason wanders ineffectively in a rambling mansion too large for him, unable to eject the disorderly usurpers who have one by one thrust their way in, and who are wrecking the house as they brawl with each other for control. *Fatal four disorders* (contrasting perhaps with the three Fatal Sisters of classical mythology) refers to the medical complications or cross-infections, each deadly in itself, which had made their home there, like the roaming evil spirits who invaded the demoniac of the Gospel story. To a writer as well versed in Shakespeare as was Hopkins, however, *fleshed* would carry some Elizabethan overtones of 'fierce, eager for slaughter, bent upon destruction'.

The confusing time-sequence of the second quatrain corresponds with the natural blurring of recollections as he looks back over visits during a long-drawn and fluctuating illness. We can, if we like, rearrange the phases in logical rather than emotional order: 'at first' the young Samson rebelled, cursing. Then came the tendering to him of the communion for the sick, 'our sweet reprieve and ransom', his acceptance of Christ's sacrificial payment leading to a more heavenly heart. Though line 5 begins with *broke* and concludes with *mended*, both refer to the same advance, to opposite sides of a single process, a physical loss which is a spiritual gain – the crucial point in his illness when heaven broke through into the farrier's life. We may recall from 'The Wreck of the Deutschland' the poet's prayer for God, 'Father and fondler of heart thou hast rung', to show cruel mercy to the 'rebel, dogged in den': 'With an anvil-ding [the smith's sledge-hammer blow]/And with fire in him forge thy will' (sts 9, 10). Last chronologically but not in the priest's memory of events, is the viaticum and the anointing, with their infusion of grace. However many the wrong turnings along which he had blundered in the past, like the Prodigal he had come home. We may remark that the poet, always ready to help revive a dead metaphor, here and in his Lancashire sermons uses the comfortable North Country phrases 'all road', 'any road', 'this road', where conventional English would say 'all *ways*', 'any *way*', 'this *way*' (*Sermons*, pp. 47, 73).

The first tercet originally opened more personally: 'This often seeing the sick endears them, me too it endears'. The revision of 1884 ('endears them to us, us too') is not only more neatly turned: it distances the statement, while emphasizing the reciprocal reach of the affection and the poet's membership of a priestly community. To have 'taught comfort' means more than to have brought it: a sufferer will inevitably go on casting for comfort which he has no hope of getting by groping in his own comfortless mind (in the phrases of 'My own heart', No. 69), until he is taught the secret of recognizing the voice of the Comforter for himself. Hopkins had used homely illustrations of how the Holy Spirit cheers people on and comforts them in a sermon preached the Sunday after Felix Spencer died, and just before he began the poem (*Sermons*, p. 70). Even towards the end when the sturdy blacksmith was reduced to speechless weeping, priest and penitent were still in contact: Felix's tears 'touched' the priest's heart, and the priest's touch in benediction penetrated the feverish haze, quenching the sick man's tears. 'How far from then forethought of' such a relationship – as well as his own physical helplessness – would have been to the smith in the days of his rough and thoughtless strength! Hopkins's capacity for friendship and his selfless devotion to his parishioners were among his great qualities as a priest, but he was at his best, as in this instance, when he was made to feel he was needed.

Hopkins has dealt compassionately with the blacksmith's past. The impression we are given here is of a handsome high-spirited young giant who took delight in the play of his muscles, using force more than finesse, but enjoying for years strenuous labour which the slight physique of the poet could not have endured for an hour. Tools flung down in *random* disarray could be snatched up again with a careless stride when wanted. While *grim* suggests 'grimy' (a dialect sense), its prime meaning, going back to *Beowulf*, is 'cruel, fierce', like a monster breathing fire, something which only a brave man could confront. The forge was no place for weaklings, as *peers* measured their powers against each other's in the skill and speed of their work: with the largest horses they sometimes worked in pairs. The iron was brought to white heat by furnace and bellows and moulded by heavy blows to the shape of the hoof. Holding with one hand the bent foot of the horse against his slightly raised knee, the farrier had to nail on the hot shoe with the other, often supporting part of the animal's weight as it leant comfortably on him. The magnificent Shires and Clydesdales used for pulling heavy brewers' drays stood nearly six feet high at the shoulders (sixteen to eighteen 'hands'). Only unusual natural strength could cope with the farrier's trade.

The sonnet finishes in a brilliant climax. The verb *fettle*, which scholars once mistook in this poem for a stray fifteenth-century archaism, was still in current dialect use throughout Britain in all sorts of contexts – to fix, to clean, to grind or file a piece of rough metal, to groom or adorn. The repeated 'ay' sounds ('great grey dray') ring out like blows on the anvil. *Sandal* used to be a technical word for a type of horseshoe, though this could scarcely be guessed from our dictionaries. The phrase 'his bright and battering sandal' sweeps us out from the grim Vulcan's cave of the smithy to witness the proud horse in indomitable stately action, its shoes glinting in the sunlight, and the blows of its metalled hooves resounding on the cobblestones.

The structure of the sonnet is worth observing. It concentrates in turn upon the wasting away of the body (ll. 1–4) and the awakening of the soul (5–8). The development of mutual affection between the priest and a patient weak as a child (9–11) leads to the dramatic flashback of the last three lines. Beginning with a life's ending (worn out but peaceful), it terminates with the farrier at the meridian of his great muscular power. Of the various poems based by Hopkins on his professional contacts this is by far the most artistically balanced, and in no other portrait of man or woman are we given such varied glimpses of a vivid life history.

No. 54 Brothers Dated at Hampstead, August 1880.

This simple narrative poem, drawn from his own professional experience, occasioned Hopkins and his first editor much uncertainty. In August 1879, while still in his Oxford parish, he had told Bridges that he hoped to enclose a little scene which had touched him at Mount St Mary's school the year before. Because the incident it related was rather slight – an older boy's nervous absorption in his younger brother's role in a school play – Hopkins aimed at a simplicity of style very different from the complexities of such other Oxford poems as 'Henry Purcell' or even 'The Candle Indoors' (Nos 45–6). Wordsworth had headed one section of his works 'Poems founded on the Affections', the first of which was 'The Brothers', reprinted from *Lyrical Ballads*. Just as Hopkins in 'Andromeda' (No. 50) had emulated Miltonic plainness and severity, so here he set out to achieve something of Wordsworth's pathos, 'inimitable and unapproachable' though he felt that to be: 'pathos has a point as precise as jest has and its happiness "lies ever in the ear of him that hears, not in the mouth of him that makes"' (*Letters*, p. 86).

He began writing it in stanzas, but he could not satisfy himself and thought of abandoning the subject. No copy of this earliest version has survived. A year later, recuperating in Hampstead with his family from the strain of his Liverpool duties, it fortunately occurred to him to drop the stanza-form in favour of three-stress lines of Sprung Rhythm rhymed in couplets. He probably handed a copy to Bridges while still on holiday in London, but in response to his criticisms began revising it in September (*Letters*, p. 106). However, between his two poetic advisers, Bridges and Dixon, he found just those differences in personal reactions to pathos which he had anticipated, and even as late as 1884 he was still carrying out modifications in an effort to satisfy both of them and himself.

In all Jesuit schools much importance was attached to the production of plays, particularly at Christmas and Shrovetide. As Shrove Tuesday precedes the austerities of Lent it has long been a traditional time for comedies and relaxation, though Shrovetide plays were not permitted at Stonyhurst until 1850. Percy Fitzgerald in his *Stonyhurst Memories* (London, 1895), devotes several chapters to dramatic activities in that famous school, mentioning the 'green-room' with its wealth of costumes for all periods, and the farces or Shakespearian tragedies they performed. As no female parts were allowed, in Sheridan's *The Rivals* Captain Absolute had to conduct his complicated wooing and intrigues through Lydia's brother! At Mount St Mary's Hopkins notes that in *Macbeth* (presented at Christmas with a Prologue from his own pen so ingenious that it was misunderstood) Lady Macbeth had to be transmuted into Macbeth's younger brother Fergus (*Further Letters*, p. 149).

Father Francis Keegan's researches into the background of this poem reveal that very probably the play was 'A Model Kingdom', and the brothers were Henry and James Broadbent, Henry being the elder, as Hopkins has him (born 1866), and James a year younger. Reproductions of the playbill and an obviously earlier photograph of the Broadbent brothers are given in *All My Eyes See* (pp. 50–1), along with a view of the hall in which the school plays used to be performed. The playbill conceals the authorship of the piece, but if we consult the lists of plays produced at

Stonyhurst (*The Stonyhurst Magazine* for June 1888, Vol. iii, pp. 181–4), we discover that it was an anonymous expansion of a burlesque on eighteenth-century drama written by Henry Carey (of 'Sally in our Alley' fame). This was first acted in 1734 under the impossible name of its king – 'a sovereign worth a crown' – (pardonably misspelt in the Jesuit versions): 'Chrononhoton-thologos: the Most Tragical Tragedy that ever was Tragediz'd by any company of Tragedians'. The Jesuit version had appeared at Stonyhurst as a Shrovetide play in 1851 and 1875, but Mount St Mary's was three years ahead of its rival school in staging the expanded burlesque, 'A Model Kingdom'. If young Harry made the hall ring when he at last appeared (l. 33), that was surely just right for his role as herald to the King of Queerroumania. (For later details of Father Keegan's discoveries see *Hopkins Quarterly*, Vol. VI, No. 1, Spring 1979, pp. 11–34.)

Readers may be confused by the way John in the early part of the poem is replaced by Jack, almost as though the poet had forgotten what name he had selected. It is no consolation to observe that both forms are used as rhymes. Teachers usually differentiate two Johns or two Henrys by decreeing that one of each pair will in future be referred to as Jack and Harry. But in the original draft, lines 24–5 seemed to pit John against Jack: 'He hung by John's success./Now Jack was brass-bold'. The older brother is 'Henry' at first: one could argue a case for the change to the pet-form Harry when he became 'heart-forsook' in line 31 (where the first draft made the switch-over), but when lines 31 and 35 differ (as in all later versions), one must assume that Hopkins was embarrassed at repeating the name.

A number of the revisions which he sent Bridges or Dixon in 1881 are scarcely improvements. It is hard to accept, 'Why, a part was picked for John' (l. 7) as having only three stresses, though the text as printed could also be misread as Sprung tetrameters frequently enough, e.g. in lines 1, 5, 11, 19, 23, 25, 28, 30, 32 and 40. The climax when the young actor at last appears on stage is inadequately rendered by another revision, 'Eh, how all rung' (l. 33). The critical points for the management of the pathos are lines 17–21 and 35–37. With the second of these passages he had no hesitations, but the first gave considerable trouble. 'The boy writhed on love's rack/And all his thoughts were Jack' was his earliest attempt. The rack (and its rhyme Jack) persisted through all revisions, but the next line hesitated through such mutations as 'The lad's thoughts beat on Jack', the lad was 'all wrapped in Jack', or (an alien note) was 'All jeoparded in Jack'. The image of the diver in line 20 catches the pantomime of a rather nervous swimmer preparing to plunge, as well as a boy tense with waiting.

The moral in the last six lines is meditative rather than didactic, its reflections based on the contrasting experiences to which he had been exposed since he had left the school. In the drink-sodden selfishness of the Liverpool slums, after looking daily 'with sorrow and loathing' at the 'base and besotted figures and features of the Liverpool crowd', he had come to feel how 'inveterate' human nature was, its evil since the Fall deep-seated and endemic (*Letters*, pp. 110, 127). The memory of the kind elder brother reassured him that unselfish concern can also be a natural human heritage. Homely, swift and quite successful in what it set out to achieve, the narrative ends with a lyrical cadence similar to the one in 'Binsey Poplars' (No. 43), but opposite in mood.

No. 55 Spring and Fall: *to a young child* Written at Rose Hill, Lydiate, Lancashire, 7 September 1880. The plainchant music which he tried to compose for it (*Letters*, p. 119) has not survived.

If the true incident in 'Brothers' had been hard to formulate in verse, the next poem, 'not founded on any real incident', shaped itself so easily that Hopkins felt able to send Bridges a copy within three days of its birth (*Letters*, p. 109). It is an exquisite lyric which came to him as he was walking back to the train from Rose Hill, a Catholic country house with a chapel and farm near Lydiate – a village half-way between Liverpool and Southport. Once a week one of the priests went out from St Francis Xavier's, spent the night there, said mass before breakfast in the private chapel, and returned by train to the city (*Further Letters,* pp. 155–7; *Correspondence*, p. 42). Hopkins was (to his great relief – except in winter) often sent out there to celebrate mass, enabling him to escape from the press of houses and people in the city. Even at the end of the century Lydiate had a population of only a thousand.

The inclusion of 'Spring' in the title invites us to recognize the young girl with her 'fresh thoughts' as a symbol of that season, representing something of the 'Innocent mind and Mayday in girl and boy' which Hopkins had praised in his earlier sonnet ('Spring',

No. 33, l. 13). She certainly seems to be in harmony with nature, though the perpetual Spring which 'earth's sweet being' enjoyed in Eden has become merely seasonal, the Fall of man having been accompanied by the year's fall which strips trees bare. Margaret also reminds us of the child, fresh as a light dawn mist, sketched in the opening stanza of 'Morning, Midday, and Evening Sacrifice' (No. 49); but if she is weeping her heart out, it is not for any tarnishing 'gold-wisp' of her own, but in sympathy with the trees whose golden tresses are being dispersed. For them the generous heart of the little lass is sparing both sighs and tears, and not from any consciously selfish motive. In 'Spring' (No. 33) the 'glassy peartree *leaves* and *blooms*' while we watch it, but here Golden-grove is 'unleaving': the process is being reversed.

Critics have naturally been tempted to enquire into particular sources for both the names, Margaret and Goldengrove. Grover Smith and David DeLaura have found some possible models for Margaret among the works of George Eliot and Mrs Gaskell (*English Language Notes*, Vol. 1, No. 1, 1963, p. 43; *Victorian Poetry*, Vol. 14, No. 4, 1976, p. 341). Others have written about the beautiful estate called 'Goldengrove' a few miles from St Beuno's College (e.g. Peter Milward, *Landscape and Inscape*, pp. 70–1), and of another Goldengrove in South Wales which was the home of Jeremy Taylor, and known to the poet through its use as the title of a book in the Hopkins family library (*Hopkins Research Bulletin*, No. 6, 1975, p. 19). These parallels may be enriching, but I agree with Father Milward that the Goldengrove of this poem is to be found in no gazetteer. It is 'Goldwood' from a child's secret sketchmap, part of her Earthly Paradise. Margaret represents the stage in a child's development when for the first time she becomes dimly aware of nature's Intimations of Mortality. As yet her mouth cannot explain her grief since her mind has not yet fathomed it, but her heart has felt the sorrow of the falling leaves and her spirit has intuitively responded (ll. 12, 13). The phrase 'ghost guessed' is another indirect reminder of death – spirit can be separated from body.

Margaret is pictured as alone in her grief: the poet addresses her only in his thoughts with a sophistication of analysis beyond the comprehension of a child. As her experience of the 'things of man' widens, like the maidens in 'The Leaden Echo' (No. 59) she will become increasingly convinced that there is no device 'to keep/

Back beauty, keep it, beauty, beauty, beauty, . . . from vanishing away', and her tears will spring from a more self-involved despair.

The eighth line, the most beautiful in this lyric and among the most appealing in all Hopkins's poetry, originally ran 'Though forests low and leafmeal lie'. The revision of 1884 owes its mysterious magic to words invented to supply a previously un-realized need: 'Though worlds of wanwood leafmeal lie'. This is the adult view of late autumn. Instead of the young child's secretly prized Goldengrove we are shown a universal decay: to east and west stretch unnamed 'worlds' of faded leaves and bleak-bare branches; the foliage that was once a living green is lying on the ground crumbled into meal, or piled up in ditches as leaf-mould. From Virgil's *Aeneid* (vi. 309) to Shelley's 'Ode to the West Wind', the fallen leaves of the forest had been interpreted as a ghostly image of the powerless spirits of the dead. The older Margaret will weep at the Fall as she does in her childhood now; she will then be weeping for herself just as she really is now; but with a colder heart will have come a clearer mind so that she will be consciously identifying her own fate with the withering in Nature.

In a sermon preached the month after he wrote this poem Hopkins itemized some of the sorrows which have made of God's providence 'a shattered frame and a broken web' – 'cold, want, weakness, hunger, disease, death' (*Sermons*, p. 90). In later meditation notes he identified the origin of these evils in the efforts made by Satan, the old serpent of Genesis and the dragon of the Apocalypse (chap. 12), to sweep away the woman (who in some ways symbolizes for Hopkins the human race) by means of a flood of water. This river he interprets as the 'law of decay and consumption in inanimate nature, death in the vegetable and animal world, moral death and original sin in the world of man' (*Sermons*, pp. 197–200). Because of the Fall of man (implicit in the poem's title), a thousand springs of sorrow well up from this one great underground stream.

The rhythm of the opening line (a trochaic tetrameter) is often mangled in spite of the stress marks. The name should not be pronounced 'Már-grit', but (with a half-foot pause after it) be spread over the time value of four syllables. Sprung Rhythm, of course, permits the poet to absorb into the weight of the stress any slack or unaccented syllable which he cares to omit. The fas-

cinating variety of the lyric's rhythms will repay examination. The
full trochaic tetrameter is found only in lines 2, 4, 6 and 15. Where
the last (slack) syllable of one line is dropped, the rhythm of the
next line tends to become iambic, the two adjacent lines forming
one unit through 'overreaving'. This process is variously illustrated
by lines 7 and 8, 11 and 12, 13 and 14. The time-value of the
omitted second (slack) syllable is absorbed into the first syllable in
lines 3 and 5, leaving the first foot monosyllabic; the second foot is
a lengthened monosyllable in lines 1 and 11 – and so on. But this is
the merest simplification of an intricate process which contributes
in subtle ways to the little lyric's unique inscape. The only sense of
strain may occur with the second couplet, where the syntax is
artistically bent to the shape of the metre. In straightened form it
seems rather prosaic: 'You with your fresh thoughts can care for
leaves, can you, like the things of man?' Finally, what a touch of
genius it was to introduce the coping-stone of a triplet into the
middle of the poem, three couplets before and three after it. This
yields the lyric a central climax, followed by a thoughtful pause
and the feeling of a new direction.

No. 56 Inversnaid Composed during a brief visit to Loch Lomond,
28 September 1881.

Water exerted a special fascination upon Hopkins. Three of his
poems are about rivers and streams – 'Epithalamion' (No. 159)
about the tree-banked rock-strewn Hodder at Stonyhurst,
'Penmaen Pool' (No. 30) on a sandy lagoon in a broad tidal
estuary, and this musical piece celebrating a wild Scottish burn.
Inversnaid is the name of a tiny hamlet on Loch Lomond in the
heart of the long untamed Rob Roy country: it also names the
waterfall where the stream called Arklet Water cascades down
into the lake. Splendid coloured photographs of the stream and a
discussion of the poem will be found in *Landscape and Inscape*
(Milward and Schoder, pp. 75ff).

Hopkins had been stationed for eight weeks in Glasgow,
supplying the place of a priest on leave. Before going south again
he was allowed two days in which to see some more of Scotland
(*Letters*, p. 136). He travelled by steamer up Loch Lomond to
Inversnaid, where he spent a few hours before making the return
trip. Recalling the occasion six years later he wrote: 'The day was

dark and partly hid the lake, yet it did not altogether disfigure it but gave a pensive or solemn beauty which left a deep impression on me' (*Further Letters*, 288). The poet must have climbed up the winding woodland path beside the cascading mouth of the stream (st. 1), past the 'boiling pots' in its rocky middle course (st. 2), and up to the heathy, bracken-covered braes near Loch Arklet (st. 3). The poem, by following the course of his own visit, thus begins with the most impressive part of the burn, the waterfall which is all most visitors ever see of it, and retreats further and further to the less frequented wilder hillsides near its source.

The opening stanza shows us that this is no friendly conversational Tennysonian brook, sparkling its pleasant way through villages and under man-made bridges. Over the Inversnaid Falls rush the peat-brown waters of Loch Arklet, after dropping some five hundred feet in a hurried mile of ever-steepening rock-bed to the comparative placidity of Loch Lomond. The word *darksome* hints at the difficulty of coming to terms with this sombre torrent. If *horseback* reminds us momentarily of the gleaming brown of a freshly groomed pony, the idea of tame subservience is quickly removed by the next line: this is a wild horse, hooves reverberating in his mad descent over break-neck stones and boulders. He bears some affinity with the frantic Tartar horse on which Byron's Mazeppa was bound: 'And on he foam'd – away! – away! – ' . . . 'Torrents less rapid and less rash'. The lather from his foaming flanks rushes under cooping overhangs and, combed into fluted grooves by rocky ridges, falls at last peacefully into its destined lake.

Higher up, away from the noise of the cascades, spray like steam boils from a water-worn cauldron (st. 2), a smooth pit of blackened rock. On the surface of its impenetrable depths a foam-cap, hollowed by the breeze, circles and circles; the poet fancies that a melancholy man staring down at it might be hypnotized into a death-plunge. *Twindles* was not to be found in the standard dictionaries of Hopkins's time, but it existed in dialect, and he must often have heard it as a noun in Lancashire used for twins. As a verb it could (like its simpler form 'to twin') be applied either to doubling or dividing in half, both of which processes we can observe in the foam on a pool.

Another Lancashire word introduces the third stanza, *Degged*, meaning sprinkled. In this upper part of its course the brook only *treads*, moving with a more deliberate pace between the rounded limbs of the braes. These hillsides, from which it draws its water, vary in colour with the angle of light catching the dew. The slopes are dense with Scottish heather, their flowering stems tough as wire. The bracken or fern dries out after a hot summer into russet-brown flakes like woodcutters' *flitches* – thin vertical slices from a tree-trunk. Here and there a rowan or mountain-ash overhangs the stream, ornamented in autumn with bead-like orange or scarlet berries.

The last stanza reminds us that the nineteenth century had already glimpsed the spectre of a world population so swollen that every usable surface would be occupied by houses or cultivated fields. John Stuart Mill could foresee the possibility of a world whose wealth and population would have so expanded that escape from the presence of humanity would be impossible:

> Solitude, in the sense of being often alone, is essential to any depth of meditation or of character; and solitude in the presence of natural beauty and grandeur, is the cradle of thoughts and aspirations which are not only good for the individual, but which society could ill do without. Nor is there much satisfaction in contemplating the world with nothing left to the spontaneous activity of nature; with every rood of land brought into cultivation which is capable of growing food for human beings; every flowery waste or natural pasture ploughed up, all quadrupeds or birds which are not domesticated for man's use exterminated as his rivals for food, every hedgerow or superfluous tree rooted out, and scarcely a place left where a wild shrub or flower could grow without being eradicated as a weed in the name of improved agriculture.
>
> (*Principles of Political Economy*, 1848, Vol. ii, p. 311)

Mill argues with the cold polysyllables of a commission report. Hopkins, basically different in his philosophy, reacts emotionally in this lyrical plea for 'the weeds and the wilderness'. When the Wordsworths and Coleridge had visited Inversnaid in 1803 under arduous conditions there was only a ferryman's hut close to the falls, and as they toiled on foot towards the head of the stream the absence of any houses gave the scene 'a character of unusual wildness and desolation' (Dorothy Wordsworth's *Journal*, 26 and 28 August 1803). But the success of Wordsworth's poem 'To a Highland Girl' mentioning the lonely waterfall helped to establish a hotel there, which referred to the poem in its advertisements along with lawn tennis and billiards. By Hopkins's time there were coaches meeting the steamers at Inversnaid to convey tourists to

Loch Katrine and the Trossachs along a road which had been built close to the course of the stream. Its wild beauty seemed seriously threatened.

Among the musical qualities of this fine poem are the variations in momentum shown as possible in Sprung Rhythm, which can equate seven deliberate syllables in one line (l. 1) with twelve more hasty in another (l. 12). All the available vowel sounds are mingled and echoed with a most artistic judgment. And if familiarity with the lyric has blinded us to the rarity of the special words which combine with typical Hopkinsian inventions to give the poem its character, half-an-hour's defeated search for parallels among the concordances of his more voluminous contemporaries will set us right.

No. 57 As kingfishers catch fire, dragonflies draw flame Undated. Probably written at St Beuno's College during 1877.

This sonnet contains the most striking poetic illustrations of Hopkins's Scotist theory of the inscapes to be found among natural and man-made things; yet he seems never to have reached the stage of writing out a fair copy of it for others to enjoy. The sole surviving MS is a single sheet with many corrections, the pencil version in some cases overlaid by emendations in ink. It is undated, and was believed to belong to his year as a Tertian (1881–2). But my discovery that the varying physical layouts of his sonnets (indenting and line-spacing) indicate his changing practice has enabled us to assign 'As kingfishers catch fire' to his last wonderfully productive year at St Beuno's. The handwriting matches other 1876–7 poems: it was probably written about the same time as 'The Starlight Night' (No. 32).

The octave contains superbly worded examples of how we recognize things in an instant by a characteristic flash of colour or the individual *timbre* of a note. The metaphor of men questioning each thing with a 'Who are you?', and receiving a ready response is even clearer in an earlier version: 'as every string taxed tells and bell's/Bow knocked-on answers and calls clear its name'. Each one gives out again the special quality given to it by its maker. The kingfisher's azure back and wings (and sometimes its red breast) scintillate fire as the sun's rays catch it: both Ruskin and Richard Jefferies praised it as unequalled for colour among the birds in the

British Isles. The dragonfly jets flame like a blow-pipe, unmis-
takably itself. Pebbles represent the inanimate objects of the
mineral kingdom ('earth' in the old classification of the elements)
from which (as St Thomas remarked) 'nothing emanates save by
the action of one thing on another' (*Phil. Texts*, ed. Thomas Gilby,
No. 497). Hopkins evokes from boyhood the memory of tossing
little stones down the shaft of a well and listening to their musical
notes, each one distinctive.

Medieval Catholic philosophers, and their followers in the
seventeenth and eighteenth centuries, believed that every created
thing was fashioned by the supreme Goodness to occupy a link in a
great Chain of Being which stretched from nothingness up to God
Himself, and that each separate creature exhibited one minute
facet of the indivisible perfection of the Godhead. This idea can be
traced back to Plato's *Timaeus* (29ff, etc.). St Thomas Aquinas
emphasized God's desire for variety in the universe.

If someone asked why God had created stones as well as higher
beings, St Thomas answered: 'Although an angel, considered
absolutely, is better than a stone, nevertheless two natures are
better than one only; and therefore a universe containing angels
and other things is better than one containing angels only; since
the perfection of the universe is attained essentially in proportion
to the diversity of natures in it, whereby the divers grades of
goodness are filled, and not in proportion to the multiplication of
individuals of a single nature' (I *Sent. dist.* 44, q. 1, a 2, quoted in A.
O. Lovejoy. *The Great Chain of Being*, Harvard University Press,
1936, p. 77).

Hopkins illustrates and expands these ideas (*Sermons*, p. 239):
'The birds sing to him, the thunder speaks of his terror, the lion is
like his strength, the sea is like his greatness, the honey like his
sweetness; they are something like him, they make him known,
they tell of him, they give him glory . . .'. We might compare
Psalm 148. By expressing itself each creature and object below
man is fulfilling the purpose of its being, revealing its particular
inscape, and so flashing to us brief glimpses of the Creator.
Hopkins parallels the world with a harp which God plays on
(*Sermons*, p. 239). Here each *tucked* string (l. 3, a current dialect
word for 'plucked') vibrates at the pitch to which it has been
stretched. This image is derived from the familiar view of the
universe as an orchestra of numerous different instruments.

The 'bow' of the bell (though not recorded under that name in the fourteen-volume *Oxford English Dictionary* and its 1972 Supplement) is the 'sound-bow', a thickened part of the rim which strikes against the loosely hanging 'tongue' or clapper as the bell is swung into chime on her axis (Milward, *Commentary on the Sonnets of G.M.H.*, p. 85). The bow may therefore be said, literally, to 'find tongue' as well as, figuratively, finding her own true voice. Each individual bell has been tuned to a precise set of harmonics by the bell-maker, and matched in tone with the other members of her belfry. Anyone with a musical ear quickly learns to identify the clock-bells and church peals in his neighbourhood by their different tonal 'colours'. Hopkins associated the bells of Mitton near Stonyhurst with orange (*Journals*, p. 218), and as an undergraduate had enjoyed the 'much music of our Oxford bells' ('Richard', ii, No. 107).

But for man, as the sestet informs us, this simple ideal of self-expression is insufficient. Man was, in a special moral sense, modelled on God, and so ought to reflect back to God the image of Christ, Who is God made man; yet, as Fr Boyle observes, 'the self becomes more the self when it becomes Christ' (*Metaphor in Hopkins*, p. 103). St Ignatius in his *Spiritual Exercises* had stressed how 'all good things and gifts descend from above, as for example my limited power comes from the supreme and infinite power on high, and in the same way justice, goodness, pity, mercy, etc., just as the rays descend from the sun and the waters from the spring' (quoted *Sermons*, pp. 193–4). Of the Christian's armour, the '*cuirass* of justice' seemed to Hopkins the most important, since it covered nearly the whole body, particularly the heart, though unfortunately not the head (*Sermons*, p. 234). So he concluded, justice was the 'whole duty of man'. The man 'made just', or forgiven his sins through the grace of Christ, *justices* (l. 9), acts with Christlike justice or goodness. If he keeps hold of the grace given him, all his goings, his everyday acts, will be gracious, pleasing to God. 'When a man is in God's grace and free from mortal sin, then everything that he does, so long as there is no sin in it, gives God glory . . . To lift up the hands in prayer gives God glory, but a man with a dungfork in his hand, a woman with a sloppail, give him glory too' (*Sermons*, pp. 240–1).

St Catherine of Siena wrote to a newly ordained priest: 'Christ has no body now on earth but yours. No hands but yours. No feet but yours. Yours are the eyes through which His compassion must look out on the world. Yours are the feet with which He must go about doing good. Yours are the hands through which He must bless the world now.' This famous passage may well have been in the poet's mind, because the draft of the last lines of the poem runs: 'Christ comes in ten thousand places,/Lives in limbs, and looks through eyes not his/With lovely yearning'. The final version involves the concept of a star actor taking over the part of an insufficient stumbling amateur – in fact, all the parts. We might think of a radio play so inadequate in rehearsal that the producer is driven to playing all the roles over the air. If the lifting and sustaining grace on God's side is met with action, 'correspondence', at the human end the man can then say (to quote one of Hopkins's picturesque notes), 'That is Christ playing at me and me playing at Christ, only that it is no play but truth' (*Sermons*, p. 154). Christians can be assimilated into Christ, and assume His features through grace. It was T. S. Eliot who wrote: 'After the kingfisher's wing/Has answered light to light, and is silent, the light is still/At the still point of the turning world' ('Burnt Norton', IV). Hopkins has conducted us from the kingfisher's reflected sunlight to the Father of lights Himself.

This sonnet beautifully illustrates, through the musical echoes in its lines, his assertion that the sound of a thing conveys the heart of its meaning. The word *tucked* in line 3 imitates the pluck of the taut string (an improvement on the earlier reading 'taxed' – cross-questioned, as it were). The bell's gradually quickening chime seems to be caught by the more rapid return of the second rhyming word: 'each *hung* bell's/Bow *swung* finds *tongue* to fling out broad its name'. For a discussion of the allied subject suggested by the octave – the onomatopoeic theory of the origin of human language – see my Writers and Critics *Hopkins*, p. 83.

No. 58 Ribblesdale Begun at Stonyhurst in 1882 and completed by June 1883. A sonnet in regular rhythm.

Although on his first arrival at Stonyhurst in September 1870 Hopkins had missed the luxuriant woods of Surrey around Manresa House, finding the Lancashire scenery 'very bare and bleak' (*Further Letters*, p. 234), on his return for a third spell in 1882, also from Manresa, he described it as a 'noble . . . landscape, Pendle Hill, Ribblesdale, the fells, and all around, bleakish but solemn and beautiful' (*Letters*, p. 151). In between these two periods at Stonyhurst, when he went to St Beuno's in 1874, his deep response to the instress of Wales was partly because in certain lights the view from the ridge above the Welsh College 'was so like Ribblesdale from the fells that you might have thought you were there' (*Journals*, p. 261). This sonnet, he told Bridges, was in fact meant as a companion-piece to 'In the Valley of the Elwy' (No. 34), the sestet of which praised the *lovely* Welsh landscape while regretting the incomplete development of the creature, Man, who inhabited it.

The artistic success of 'Ribblesdale' arises largely from the contradictory forces which are poised against each other. If we were to end our reading at the beginning of line 8, with 'and thus bids reel/Thy river', the dominating impression would be one of beauty (*sweet, sweet, lovely*) and submission; *throng* is a dialect word for 'closely packed' and *louchèd* means 'bent-backed'. Next, we would be struck by the immemorial age of the landscape, and also by the absence of change implied by the fact that the Creator who dealt the dale down 'thus' (i.e. who made it look like this) is still dealing it down thus in the present. The moorland scene in the octave has some affinity with the description of Egdon Heath in the opening chapter of Hardy's *The Return of the Native* (1878), a novel which Hopkins recommended to Bridges with admiration in 1886 and may already at this time have known (*Letters*, p. 239). Hardy speaks of the sombre patiently-enduring Egdon Heath, 'from prehistoric times as unaltered as the stars overhead. . . . The sea changed, the fields changed, the rivers, the villages, and the people changed, yet Egdon remained'. 'Civilization was its enemy.'

Hopkins added in Latin an epigraph from the Vulgate of Romans 8: 19–20. Dr Weymouth tries to catch the personification in the Greek original: 'For all creation, gazing eagerly as if with outstretched neck, is waiting and longing to see the manifestation of the sons of God. For the Creation fell into subjection to failure and unreality (not of its own choice, but by the will of Him who so subjected it).' Bishop Challoner, commenting on the rather obscure Douay translation, says that the reference is to the 'corporeal creation made for the use and service of man; and, by occasion of his sin, made subject to . . . a perpetual instability, tending to corruption, and other defects.' Both from this passage and from the poem we catch what Hopkins called 'the pathos of nature and landscape', of which he was himself increasingly aware and which he found also in the works of Wordsworth and Canon Dixon (*Correspondence*, p. 3).

The subjection of the earth to imperfection was an action of God resulting from the actions of Man – his Fall – but in the sonnet the agent in the second quatrain seems to be primarily if not exclusively the Creator. 'Deal' is a word Hopkins often assigned to God, e.g. in the 'Wreck', stanza 28 and *Sermons*, p. 232: God 'dealing me out my life, my voice, my breath, my being'. It is interesting to note that the origin of the word 'dale' was believed by some earlier philologists to be the same as 'deal'.

We must now confront the *volta* or turn of the sonnet (prepared for in the epigraph), contained in the last clause of the octave, 'and o'er gives all to rack or wrong'. It was, of course, God who cleft the earth with rivers (Hab. 3: 8, 9), but by giving man the earth as his inheritance and subsequently cursing the ground because of his sin, the Creator has delivered this heritage to an often ungrateful and destructive tenant. The capitalizing of *Earth* in lines 1 and 9 indicates that Ribblesdale is being treated as representative of inarticulate Nature as a whole. In the notes on the *Spiritual Exercises* made during his tertianship Hopkins had differentiated between the tribute to God paid on the one hand by the brute or inanimate creation unconsciously ('they give him glory, but they do not know they do', since if they can think at all it is mainly about food), and on the other hand by the prayers and work of men and women, who were 'made to give, and mean to give, God glory' (*Sermons*, pp. 238–41). Man alone has the aesthetic eye, the heart with which to respond, and the tongue to formulate praise, but though he has endearing qualities he is also obstinate. Hopkins deliberately describes men in animal terms: 'dogged' can impute either the bad or good qualities of a dog to a person. Here it may refer to his sullen obstinacy.

The image of man as a spendthrift heir stripping an estate which has descended to him recalls some of Pope's thumb-nail sketches of eighteenth-century land-owners (Epistles to Bathurst and Burlington). In a strain reminiscent of 'God's Grandeur' (No. 31), Hopkins, much more deeply affected than Pope, argues that disregard for the world of Nature frequently goes hand-in-hand with disregard for the spiritual world. In the clause 'And none reck of world after', *none* is a common dialect adverb recorded from over twenty counties and meaning 'by no means, in no degree'. The heir cares not a straw for the life hereafter: so far from laying up treasure in heaven he is preoccupied with squandering the treasures on earth. And because the condition of our environment is a reflection of the moral health or impairment of man, as we look sensitively at Nature, though she may not herself be able to feel care (l. 3), we may through empathy experience an infinite patient suffering. The last sentence might be paraphrased: 'Ah, for earth's heir (so bound on his own crooked ways and tied to his intentions) to strip bare the rich round world so wastefully and to care not a jot for an after-world, this is what brings to the Earth's face furrows of deep care and affectionate concern'.

No. 59 The Leaden Echo and the Golden Echo Begun at Hampstead, August 1880, not completed until 13 October 1882 at Stonyhurst.

This was intended to be part of a play on which Hopkins worked over a span of ten years without completing it, 'St. Winefred's Well' (No. 152 – see notes, p. 224 for legend). As it was to be sung by a chorus of St Winefred's Maidens (*Letters*, pp. 106, 153–8), whom the beheaded saint gathered about her after she had been restored to life, it was probably meant to provide a moral *finale*. But the surviving fragments of the play do not deal with the problem of 'beauty that must die', and we can only conjecture how Hopkins intended to integrate the chorus with the action. He could have made the impermanence of physical beauty the moving current of Winefred's dialogue with Beuno when she told him her desire to devote her life to Christ. A more direct link could have been established if Hopkins had planned as the final act or scene St Winefred's ceremonious dedication of her virginity to God. Alban Butler, to whose account of St Winefred Hopkins refers, draws attention to two early virgin martyrs who cut off their hair as a sign of the consecration of their chastity – Synletica and Justina (*Lives of the Saints*, *sub* 6 January, 11 September, and Controversial Index under 'Virginity').

Winefred's 'shining hair' shimmered like the tresses of a water-fall as her head rolled down the bank (No. 152, Act II, ll. 18–21). In the 'Echoes', hair is one of the chief marks of beauty ('Leaden Echo', l. 1, 'bow . . . braid . . . lace'; l. 4, 'stealing messengers of grey'; l. 11, 'hoar hair'; 'Golden Echo', see esp. ll. 14–15, 20–1, and the apt analogy in 22–3 of the 'heavyheaded' golden locks of grain). In the allusion of the final two lines to beauty being kept in the heavens, we may even detect a spiritualizing of the classical legend of Berenice's hair, which she is said to have dedicated in the temple of Aphrodite for the safe return of her husband from war, and which was then eternally preserved in the constellation of Coma Berenices (Catullus, 66). When Hopkins was holidaying at home in Hampstead in August 1880 he wrote 'some dozen lines or less' of the play (*Letters*, p. 124). That these were from the song and were shown to Bridges (who was still then living in London) seems probable from Hopkins's comment early next month in a letter to him (p. 106): 'You shall also see the *Leaden Echo* when finished. The reason, I suppose, why you feel it carry the reader along with it is that it is dramatic and meant to be popular.' But he did not manage to complete the 'Echoes' or send him a copy till October 1882 (*Letters*, pp. 153–8).

We can find a suitable epigraph for this chorus in John 12: 24–5: 'a grain of wheat must fall into the ground and die, or else it remains nothing more than a grain of wheat; but if it dies, then it yields rich fruit. He who loves his life will lose it; he who is an enemy to his own life in this world will keep it, so as to live eternally' (Knox). The Greek word translated 'keep' is *phulasso*, which has those overtones of 'guard, preserve, hold securely in a safe place' with which Hopkins infuses the first line. Along with the image of keeping beauty *in*, an unwilling captive, is the imagery of keeping *out* the encroachments of age – 'frowning . . . Down', 'waving off', 'To keep at bay'. Neither action is possible, and the 'Golden Echo' propounds the only effective alternative, a refusal to allow 'dangerously sweet' beauty to preoccupy attention, its wearer freely returning it instead to the giver. As St James says, all gifts worth having come from above (chap. 1: 17), and therefore the poet sends them 'high as that' again ('Golden Echo', l. 31).

The imaginative adjective, '*Tall* sun's tingeing' (l. 5) combines height with the Shakespearian sense of prowess in battle. Another evocative description is of the *wimpledwater-dimpled* face (l. 10 – the autograph has only one hyphen), the cupid's-bow ripples in running water suggestive of Elizabethan wimples. Compounds such as *gaygear* (l. 15, which modern overtones must not be allowed to spoil for us) have an Anglo-Saxon type of vigour about

them. In line 26 ('so fagged, so fashed, so cogged, so cumbered')
colloquial and dialect words mingle with the literary/Biblical
cumbered (Luke 10: 40, A.V.); *fagged* (wearied) also retained in
country parlance the otherwise obsolete sense found in Hopkins's
reference to primroses enclosed in a letter, 'wilted' (*Further
Letters*, p. 118); *fashed* is Scottish (*Journals*, p. 5); but *cogged*
presents problems. To gloss it as 'deceived, cheated' makes it
odd-man-out among the other participles. I hazard that it may be a
variant of the dialect word *cagged* (grieved, vexed), very close in
some county pronunciations (see my *Hopkins*, p. 122), but Milroy
plausibly connects it with the cog (wedge or skid) fastened in front
of a cart's wheel to brake its descent down a steep hill (*Language
of Hopkins*, p. 235).

In claiming that 'not a hair is . . . lost' (l. 20) Hopkins was
quoting Luke 21: 18. Catholic teaching on the resurrection of the
body is absolutely clear that the individual will receive back his
earthly body, but glorified, subject neither to decay nor pain and
fatigue. St Thomas Aquinas devoted a long section of his *Summa
Theologica* (Supplement, Q. 69–70, etc.) to a detailed exposition
of the Resurrection.

Echo poems, which date back to Ovid's account of Narcissus
and Echo (*Metamorphoses* iii. 379–99), had been popular in the
seventeenth century. Sidney in the *Arcadia* introduces an eclogue
between himself and Echo, contriving to sing on a higher note
those syllables or words which he wants Echo to repeat. Thus
when he asks 'In what state was I then, when I took this deadly
disease?' Echo answers 'Ease' (*Poems of Sir Philip Sidney*, ed. W.
Ringler, pp. 63, 402). But the device quickly becomes trite, and
Hopkins allows only one mechanical echo, *despair, Spare!*,
bridging the two sections. The choruses were meant to be sung,
however, and though Hopkins has left us no score we must
imagine antiphonal effects between sections of the choir, the
phrases being passed from one to another as the voices combine or
separate. Hopkins told Canon Dixon in October 1886 'I never did
anything more musical' (*Correspondence*, p. 149). Sturge Moore,
with complacent impercipience, eliminated the melodious echoes
by reducing Hopkins's 547 words to 204 (*Criterion*, IX, 1930,
pp. 599–603). Bridges upset Hopkins by declaring that the rhythm
reminded him of Walt Whitman's free verse, a charge which
Hopkins was at some pains to refute (*Letters*, pp. 154–8).

No. 60 The Blessed Virgin compared to the Air we Breathe Written in May 1883 at Stonyhurst to be hung near the statue of the Blessed Virgin, along with other poems in various languages. See notes on 'The May Magnificat', No. 42.

Hopkins did not expect Bridges to like this poem: it was a 'compromise with popular taste', and particularly Catholic in sentiment; but to his surprise Bridges described it to Dixon as 'admirable' and Patmore singled it out as 'exquisite', one of the few poems he could enjoy without effort in the whole album of Hopkins's verse which he had just been sent (*Letters*, pp. 179, 182, 186, 190–2, 195; *Correspondence*, pp. 108, 110; *Further Letters*, p. 353). Hopkins considered some of the other pieces written at the college in honour of Mary 'far-fetched, for people gravitate to us from odd quarters'. The Virgin has down the ages been represented by innumerable images, such as Noah's dove, the Ark of the Covenant, Star of the Sea, the Sheep that bore the Lamb of God and the Church's Diadem. Here Hopkins develops with skill some metaphors for Mary in various famous hymns in the Divine Office – 'the portal of heaven' or 'the gateway through which light arose over the earth': in having given birth to the Light of the World she is like the air which transmits sunshine and acts as intermediary between earth and heaven. Mary's traditional colour, blue, favoured the image, which Hopkins had already used in a sermon on 5 October 1879 (*Sermons*, p. 29).

The opening line hints at Mary's superiority over the powers ascribed by the ancient Greeks to such divinities as Gaea, the Earth Mother: the Blessed Virgin mothers even mother-earth (cf. ll. 26–8). *Wild*, which Yvor Winters found 'very curiously in discord with the subject of Mary' (*Function of Criticism*, p. 148), is repeated in *wild web* (l. 38) and *air wild* (l. 124): the adjective, as elsewhere in Hopkins, indicates the freedom with which a being expresses its own nature – e.g. the handsome heart of the lad 'wild and self-instressed' (No. 47, l. 7), or the *wild rash* waters of St Winefred's Well, eloquent of that saint (No. 152, part C, l. 15). Just as Mary embraced and nurtured Christ, so does the air nestle every hair and snowflake, nourishing even the least significant living creature. In claiming that Mary 'mothers each new grace/ That does now reach our race' (ll. 22–3), Hopkins was alluding to the belief, common from at least St Bernard's time, that Christ has chosen to route His gifts through her as Mediatrix of all Graces.

The Latinic structure of lines 40–1, if rearranged to bring out its prime meaning, would become: 'Since God has let her prayers dispense His providence'. But it also manages to suggest that her prayers *are* His providence. Line 32 shows the glory of God as reaching mankind both *through* and *from* Mary. The poet safeguards himself in line 46 by not claiming to understand the mystery fully, and by emphasizing that the grace she brings is Christ Himself. Vatican Council II (1962–5) warned Catholics not to carry devotion to Our Lady to extremes, reminding them of the unique position of Christ as mediator: through Him men may have direct access to God (Vatican Decrees on the Church, viii. 56).

Other passages allude to Mary's role as the spiritual mother of mankind, the second Eve, helping to undo the Fall: 'She, wild web, wondrous robe,/Mantles the guilty globe' (ll. 38–9), cleansing its pollutions, and bringing to the *deathdance* in our blood the spiritual oxygen we need (l. 52). But what men breathe in is Christ (ll. 67–8).

A rather obscure sentence beginning in line 56, and interrupted by the parenthesis 'Though much the mystery how' (l. 57), argues that just as Christ in Mary's womb took flesh, growing in bodily size, so now He takes 'fresh and fresh/ . . . spirit', new Christs being born all round the world as divine vitality reaches Christians through the Blessed Virgin. The point is clarified in the sestet of No. 57, 'As kingfishers catch fire' – what Charles Williams (editor of the Second Edition of Hopkins's poems) liked to call 'coinherence'.

The verse-paragraph in lines 73 to 102 attempts a poetic science. The sky is 'sapphire-shot' (a shimmering blue like shot silk), 'Charged' (loaded with colour), and 'steepèd' (soaked in dye); yet it transmits the sun's beams without altering their colour (cf. *Sermons*, p. 29), or if it does add soft bloom to the aloof and lofty mountains, they are all the more beautiful for it (ll. 90–3). The experience of astronauts has confirmed the optical theories of lines 94–102: the earth's atmosphere scatters the sun's rays into a beautiful azure pool above us, and mitigates their blinding power. Travellers in space see the sky as black, the sun as a pulsing ball of flame, surrounded by a thicker array of stars than are visible through the atmosphere. Quartz-fret is a gem cut into a pattern which reflects piercing points of light.

In the next paragraph (ll. 103–13) the spiritual counterpart is developed: God, the solar *daystar* (as in 2 Peter 1: 19), the blinding Sun of Righteousness (much less approachable in Old Testament times), took through Mary visible flesh like our own. Mary may be said to sift the glory of God through her fingers (ll. 75–8, 110–13; cf. *Journals*, p. 154). In the final section the poet contrasts Mary's immaculate life with the sin-scarred world, and he longs for her spiritual embrace. The imagery of the last line, 'Fold home, fast fold thy child', reflects a serene confidence which was soon to be replaced in his Dublin days by conscientious anxiety over the 'two folds' of right and wrong.

The curious metre of the poem, iambic trimeter, was one he had met in Dixon's poem 'Nature and Man' (*Selected Poems*, pp. 116–20): the idea in its opening lines is reflected in Hopkins's lines 90–3: 'Blue in the mists all day/The hills slept far away'. The rhythm mutates at times into two dactyls (e.g. l. 19, 'Dwindled to infancy'; l. 24, 'Mary Immaculate'; l. 65, 'Bethlem or Nazareth'), reminding us of Thomas Hood's 'The Bridge of Sighs'. Further variety is given by the infusion of triplets into the regular couplet formation (e.g. ll. 1–6, 17–19, 28–33).

Father Alfred Thomas points out that this poem proved so attractive that it was the only one of considerable length by Hopkins to be included in several collections before Bridges published the First Edition of his poems in 1918 (*The Book Collector*, vol. 20, 1971, pp. 103–4). More recently it was quoted in a collection of articles, *The Blessed Virgin Mary: Essays by Anglican Writers*, edited by E. L. Mascall and H. S. Box (1963). But readers have tended to dismiss it rather as Bernard Bergonzi does (*Gerard Manley Hopkins*, p. 107): 'an idiosyncratic and baroque treatment of a conventional topic'. Though it risks a Greek or Latin syntax at times by separating adjective and noun with an interposing parenthesis, rhythmically it seems spontaneous. As Patmore ponderously remarked, Hopkins had 'attained to move almost unconsciously' in what appeared to that conservative critic to be his 'self-imposed shackles' (*Further Letters*, p. 353).

No. 61 Spelt from Sibyl's Leaves Started at University College, Dublin, in October 1884. A second page of drafts, written in November/December, carried the poem up to line 10. The finished poem was not sent to Bridges until two years later.

This extraordinarily weighty sonnet, half a line of which may carry as many syllables as a common iambic pentameter, and as many ideas as some simpler poems, cannot be adequately treated in a short article. Selective emphases only are offered here (see note at the end for more detailed treatments).

It opens after sunset. Where Milton in *Paradise Lost* (iv. 598) had ushered in man's first evening of bliss in Eden with only one adjective (*still*), Hopkins needs seven for the ominous onset of what seems, to begin with, the last evening before Chaos takes total repossession of the universe. The evening which 'strains to be[become] . . . night' is *earnest* (solemn); *earthless* ('wholly independent of the earth' – his impression of the Northern Lights, which seem like evening preoccupied with the day of judgment – *Journals*, p. 200); *equal* (impartial, balancing day and night, uniform in appearance); *attuneable* (all its elements in harmony with each other); *vaulty* (arched like a burial crypt); *voluminous* (immense, like an enormous 'volume' or scroll encircling the earth). The dots which follow mark a pause equal to a foot in length. The Latin root of *stupendous* suggests a reaction of numbness and fear (cf. the cognate 'stupefy') rather than ad-miration of size; evening is stretching its great coils to envelop everything as though it were the primal undifferentiated night out of which every variety of form in the universe was originally born (*womb-of-all*), and the home to which they will have to return (cf. *Paradise Lost*, ii. 894–911). Though the noun *hearse* was the name of several objects, all imply imminent entombment. One less well known, which may contribute overtones in this context, is a canopied frame mounted above the cathedral tomb of a dis-tinguished person, and on special occasions lit with scores of little tapers like stars. Norman White interestingly connects *hearse* with the Holy Week service *Tenebrae* in the Roman Church, during which the only light is provided by candles on a triangular frame called a *hearse*: these are extinguished one by one during the service to symbolize the darkness which spread over the land during Christ's Crucifixion (*English Studies*, Amsterdam, Vol. 49, 1968, pp. 546–7).

Such daylight as has survived is doomed to *waste* away (l. 4) – a verb which imparts a note of regret over receding vitality: the yellow after-glow of sunset, diffused as though through the horn casing of an old lantern, fades because the great dome of the sky, which has wound it to the west, continues its slow westward revolution. The 'wild hollow hoarlight hung to the height' has probably been best explained by David Levy (in an unpublished Queen's thesis on Hopkins and astronomy) as the zodiacal light, a nebulous luminosity like a conical tent faintly lit from inside, sometimes seen after sunset hanging from near the zenith down to the west in the plane of the ecliptic (see *Journals*, p. 199). (Any amateur astronomer will reject the older interpretations of *hornlight* as the crescent moon and *hoarlight* as the stars on the convincing grounds that both of these grow brighter in the gathering dark.) Only as daylight vanishes do the forerunners of the starry hosts appear.

The poem might have been more simplistically unified if Hopkins had shrouded the sky with impenetrable clouds. But the slackening of tension he allows us is more typical of the minor alleviations which sustain us through even grim periods. And the noble stars illuminate only the heavens, and though they bend over the earth in apparent sympathy they are no substitute for the sun. 'Home by starlight and Jupiter', reads an entry in his journal of a visit to Devon, 'stumbling down steep dark lanes' (*Journals*, p. 153), while a meditation note written in Ireland discriminates a spark or star, which we can see but not see with, from 'a light shed on our way and a happiness spread over our life' (*Sermons*, p. 262).

Shapelessness afflicts earth as all the sharply-edged inscapes of nature around him dissolve into an indistinguishable mass, their selving crushed out of them, *pashed* like fruit which has rotted or been pounded into a pulp. We may compare in passing the reversal of 'creation' which some present astronomers envisage: they predict that the universe, in which galaxies are now still separating themselves from each other in violent expansion, is destined to contract itself again into the same chaotic fireball of formless radiation out of which they believe it exploded billions of years ago. It is perhaps symbolic that the parts of this sonnet merge into each other, quatrains and tercets melting at the edges, and the octave flowing into the sestet in line 7: 'Heart, you round me right/With . . .'. The message with which his conscience *rounds* him (i.e. reproaches him in a whisper) occupies the rest of the poem. It leads into the *oracle* promised by the title and asked for in line 10, but instead of the scattered leaves of a book on which the ancient Sibyl of Cumae scribbled her enigmatic prophecies, the leaves from which this warning derives are the only clearly demarcated remnants of the dappled Nature Hopkins had so admired – tree-leaves overhead, cruel as the beaks of flying dragons, etched against a steel-grey *tool-smooth* sky like damascene work on a menacing sword. (Shakespeare, we may remind ourselves, uses *tool* for a weapon of war, e.g. in the opening scene of *Romeo and Juliet*.) Nature is now degraded to a sinful *black*, in contrast with an imagined white of perfection, here represented only by the *bleak* light of heaven.

The mood changes in line 10 to acceptance. The poet in a lofty moral appraisal takes into reckoning only the ultimate criteria of the great Day of Judgment (called *Dies Irae* in the famous requiem hymn from which the title of this poem derives: 'That day of wrath . . . to which David and the Sibyl bear testimony'). Though to the aesthetic imagination of artists, as he had long ago realized (*Journals*, p. 83), life is a source of infinitely varied coloured skeins from which they may weave their tapestries, the moralist is colour-blind, recognizing only the stains of sin, and sorting the fibres of daily actions into dark and light, wrong and right. Christ, while promising to be the Good Shepherd to all who followed Him, depicted Judgment Day as a separating out of the sheep from the goats (i.e. those who looked after themselves only, unconcerned with love and justice), who were destined to everlasting punishment (Matt. 25: 31–46). The just man will anticipate Judgment Day, being constantly aware of the moral imperatives, of the contest in his own mind between the urge towards the ideal and the drag towards harmful pleasure. The last line reads like evidence from his own tortures of conscience. Unlike the pangs of a victim on the rack, these terrible tearing pains come not from any external levering of the screw but from his spasms of self-reproach, as he probes his exposed soul and unsheathed nerves, right and wrong wrestling endlessly in his own mind in exhausting struggle. Projecting his mind into the torments of the damned, Hopkins once wrote 'The keener the consciousness the greater the pain; . . . the higher the nature the greater the penalty' (*Sermons*, p. 138). Some critics feel driven to Fulweiler's extreme statement that it is 'impossible to distinguish between his vision of a world stripped of everything but moral choice and hell itself' (*Letters from the Darkling Plain*, p. 153).

Yet Hopkins's comments when he sent the newly completed poem to Bridges show that he had not applied this Sibylline oracle to his life with the extremity Fulweiler suggests, or guiltily emptied his world of all music and art. He remained a poet as well as a priest. His letters to Bridges are preoccupied with the *performance* rather than the message of the sonnet. Remarking upon the 'effects almost musical' which he had attempted and the careful timing of all its phrases, he said that to realize these qualities the poem needed to be 'almost sung'. Pointedly classifying 'all my verse' as 'living art', he demanded that it be given 'loud, leisurely, poetical (not rhetorical) recitation, with long rests, long dwells on the rhyme and other marked syllables' (*Letters*, pp. 245–6). Acoustically at any rate, self must on no account be 'steepèd and pashed' in self!

The poem with its eight-foot lines is seldom given a performance which Hopkins would have approved. The worst sufferers are the pause in line 1 represented by dots (a full bar in length) and the monosyllabic sprung feet, which require the same time as a trochee and extra weight. Among them are (1. 2) *tíme's vást* — two separate feet; (1. 5) *Fíre*; (1. 6) *páshed*; (1. 7) the second *dís*; (1. 8) the first *Óur* and *whélms, whélms*. Trochees and dactyls interplay. Even the seemingly eccentric shifting of emphasis in line 6 produces a calculated effect: the stress on *in* which reduces the *self* on either side of it to at most a medium stress reminds us that all individuality has been broken down in the confused pulp of dusk. In line 14, however, the poet's metrical marking seems less satisfactory: 'thóughts agáinst thoughts ín groans grínd'. Most readers will want a stress upon *groans*.

[For a more detailed exposition with references to many other commentaries, see my article in *The Malahat Review*, No. 26, April 1973, pp. 218–28; also my chapter in *A Festschrift for Edgar Ronald Seary*, ed. A. A. Macdonald *et al.*, Memorial University of Newfoundland, 1975, pp. 151–69, which traces sources such as Virgil's *Aeneid* vi and discusses the evolution of the drafts.]

No. 62 To what serves Mortal Beauty? A sonnet in alexandrines, written during a retreat at Clongowes, Ireland, 23 August 1885, along with the next sonnet, '(The Soldier)'.

The question with which Hopkins launches this poem, though it
concerns beauty, is a matter of ethics, not aesthetics. And 'mortal
beauty', while primarily a reference to the beauty of mortals, does
not exclude the other beautiful but transitory creations which
Keats in his 'Ode on Melancholy' embraced as 'beauty that must
die'. Down the ages Christian theologians have been caught
between their admiration for numerous evidences of God's perfection scattered through the world (including God's 'image'
discernible in human individuals) and the scriptural warning 'Love
not the world, nor those things which are in the world' (1 John
2: 15). St Augustine of Hippo drew a famous distinction between
using a thing as a means to some end beyond it and *enjoying* it,
that is, dwelling with satisfaction on it for its own sake. Only God,
he said, is to be enjoyed; the beauties of this world can seduce our
love away from Him. 'We have wandered far from God; and if we
wish to return to our Father's home, we must make use of this
world rather than enjoying it, that . . . by means of what is material
and temporal we may attain to what is spiritual and eternal' (*On
Christian Doctrine*, 1.4.4).

The practical problem which Hopkins confronts is how we can
best use mortal beauty. Ascetics had decided that the temptations
of the flesh carried so much risk that it was wise to cut themselves
off from the pleasures of human society and the good things of this
life. At first Hopkins seems to be agreeing with them. His opening
sentence has hardly begun – it runs to the middle of line 3 – before
it is disrupted by a troubled aside about the dangerous way in which
human beauty can set leaping the 'tame blood' (this phrase from a
draft images emotions which had been previously brought under
discipline). Attempting to enlarge upon physical perfection in
looks and bearing, however, the poet becomes allusive to the edge
of obscurity ('the O-seal-that-so feature' . . .). Among earlier
versions is a simpler description, 'face feature-perfect'. He
imagines a movement more stirring than that of a soldier or dancer
stepping out to some magnificent Purcell air. Purcell's music struck
Hopkins as 'something necessary and eternal' (*Correspondence*, p.
13), and in his sonnet to Henry Purcell (No. 45) he alludes in
passing to the 'proud fire' which his compositions could kindle in
the listener. But here the people Hopkins is admiring express
through their gracefulness a heavenly, unheard music, to which
Purcell's 'air of angels' is only an earthly approximation.

The relationship between external beauty and interior goodness which he proceeds to expound is familiar to Catholic theology and Renaissance philosophy. One of its best known formulations falls towards the end of Castiglione's *The Courtier*, in a passage from which W. B. Yeats quoted twice, in *A Vision* (London, 1937, p. 293), and his private *Memoirs* (1972, p. 157). Castiglione makes one of his characters declare that beauty is a holy thing, and that it is very seldom that an evil soul dwells in a beautiful body. 'And therefore is the outward beauty a true sign of the inward goodness, and in bodies this comeliness is imprinted more or less (as it were) for a mark of the soul, whereby she is outwardly known. . . . Therefore Beauty is the true monument and spoil of the victory of the soul, when she with heavenly influence beareth rule over . . . gross nature' (Hoby's translation). Hopkins had discussed the same doctrine in a letter to Coventry Patmore of 24 September 1883, using instead of 'imprinted' the metaphor of a signet-seal pressed into wax. Sometimes, he admitted, the 'wax' of the body was too cold or too molten to receive the clear impress of the soul. In an earlier letter to Bridges (22–5 October 1879) he had set out the three levels of beauty. At the base, fascinating but dangerous, comes beauty of the body, next beauty of mind, and at the summit, beauty of character (the *grace* to which he alludes at the close of this sonnet).

Recognizing in all beauty the evidence of divine beauty, Hopkins tried to respond positively but with reserve, allowing his mind to warm in admiration of the pleasant good sights that exist around us (ll. 3–4). The face of someone completely absorbed in doing a job well can reveal at a mere glance the genuine personality beneath; but 'staring [him] out of countenance' (to quote a draft of l. 5) would make him self-conscious and obscure that transparent revelation.

An apt example of the right reaction to physical beauty occupies lines 6–8 – the famous story of how Father Gregory (later Pope Gregory the Great) encountered some handsome English slaves about 587 AD. By then the Christianized Celts had been driven to the fringes of Britain by the invading Angles, worshippers of 'stocks and stones' (cf. l. 8), as Gregory remarked in one of his letters. But for their beauty, Gregory might not have stopped to enquire where they came from or have then determined to send Augustine (later Archbishop of Canterbury) to convert them to

the worship of the supreme Man among the 'World's loveliest —
men's selves'. Bede sets down the 'tradition of our ancestors' as to
why Gregory took

> such interest in the salvation of our nation. It is reported, that some
> merchants, having just arrived at Rome on a certain day, exposed
> many things for sale in the market-place, and abundance of people
> resorted thither to buy: Gregory himself went with the rest, and,
> among other things, some boys were set to sale, their bodies white,
> their countenances beautiful, and their hair very fine. Having viewed
> them, he asked, as is said, from what country or nation they were
> brought? and was told, from the island of Britain, whose inhabitants
> were of such personal appearance. He again inquired whether those
> islanders were Christians, or still involved in the errors of paganism?
> and was informed that they were pagans. Then fetching a deep sigh
> from the bottom of his heart, 'Alas! what pity', said he, 'that the author
> of darkness is possessed of men of such fair countenances; and that
> being remarkable for such graceful aspects, their minds should be void
> of inward grace.' He therefore again asked, what was the name of that
> nation? and was answered, that they were called Angles. 'Right', said
> he 'for they have an Angelic face, and it becomes such to be co-heirs
> with the Angels in heaven . . .'. [*Ecclesiastical History of England*,
> II. 1, trans. John Stevens, ed. J. A. Giles, London, 1849, p. 67.]

This is for Hopkins an instance of how handsomeness is to be met—
with an acknowledgement of its divine origin, and a wish for that
lower beauty (and indeed for all men and women) to be enriched
with the higher beauty of spiritual grace (ll. 13–14). 'To meet', as
Wendell Johnson reflects, 'is not to hold; to own – that is, to avow
or accept – the gift of beauty is not at all to own in the sense of
possessing it' (*Gerard Manley Hopkins*, p. 142).

The poet's own biography produces other examples. Whenever
he was moved by the 'instress and charm' of nature (as when he first
came to Wales) he felt the urge to work as a priest for the highest
good of those who were surrounded by it (*Journals*, 258). And the
expression of respect for a fine physique was most characteristically followed by a prayer for spiritual grace in its possessor (e.g.
'Eurydice', No. 41, ll. 73–120, and 'The Bugler', No. 48, ll. 16–20).

No. 63 (The Soldier) The sole autograph, an untitled draft with
many cancelled variants, is dated Clongowes, August 1885. Hopkins had then just returned to Ireland from a month in London and
other parts of England.

This much misunderstood sonnet is not a patriotic effusion in honour of British soldiers and sailors, a product of Victorian fervour for the Empire. On the contrary, the octave somewhat laboriously analyses the self-congratulatory sources of the man in the street's pride in men of the army and navy, while the sestet tries to substitute the concept of the Christian warrior. And it was written when the English public wanted prosperous peace rather than Imperial glory.

The year 1885 was a gloomy one for Hopkins, not only because of his serious nervous depression, but also because of the apparent incompetence of the British Government in managing affairs at home and abroad. Tennyson and Swinburne shared his misgivings. In January (as he recorded in his Dublin Notebook) came the fall of Khartoum. The *Pall Mall Gazette* (to which Hopkins had access) in April 1885 published foreboding articles on the weakness of the royal navy. Tennyson was roused into publishing in *The Times* (23 April) a poem on 'The Fleet', which Cardinal Manning declared 'ought to be set to music and sung perpetually as a National song in every town of the Empire'. (*Tennyson, A Memoir*, by Hallam, Lord Tennyson, London, 1906, pp. 681, 686, 691). Hopkins agreed with Baillie that Gladstone, who seemed to be negotiating the surrender of the Empire, deserved to be beheaded on Tower Hill, but, as himself a 'great patriot', he was still more concerned because the English electorate did not seem to mind (*Further Letters*, p. 257; *Letters*, pp. 131, 210). With hindsight we can understand Gladstone's policies with more detached wisdom.

This sonnet, which deals with sailors as well as soldiers, contrasts the imperfect and sentimental civilian view of men in the fighting services (mere 'outscapes' of them) with the way Christ looked on them: 'we all, seeing of' (l. 1) is pitted against 'Christ . . . seeing' (l. 11).

The use of the partitive genitive, 'seeing *of* a soldier', emphasizes how limited our seeing is, noting only the soldier's red uniform, the sailors tarpaulin storm-proof jacket from which they drew their nickname 'tars'. As a priest who had regularly visited the crowded Cowley Barracks and heard confessions, Hopkins knew how seldom the noble 'regimental red' corresponded in peacetime with noble behaviour (No. 48, 'The Bugler's First Communion', ll. 9, 41–3). In English we use the word *brave* for mere showy uniform as well as courageous conduct. The public, though almost indifferent to the conditions under which servicemen worked and relaxed, loved patriotic songs (e.g. 'Rule Britannia!' and 'The British Grenadiers') and learned patriotic poems by heart. They had inherited concepts of military courage from such works as Cicero's *On Duty* (which Hopkins expounded to his Irish students), and willingly deceived themselves into thinking that the men of the army and navy individually deserved the reputation won through Britain's past victories. Hopkins brooded throughout the 'eighties on the disgrace of Majuba, when (in the story as he heard it) 'our gallant fellows' ran away from a handful of Boers (see *Further Letters*, pp. 293, 443–4; *Letters*, pp. 128, 131–2).

In the sestet, Hopkins draws upon many New Testament passages in which parallels are established between the way of Christ and the fortitude and sacrifice of a soldier. 'This is the greatest love a man can shew, that he should lay down his life for his friends', said Christ (John 15: 13, Knox). The Jesuits took pride in their willingness to carry their share of hardship like good soldiers of Christ their Captain (2 Timothy 2: 3). The Book of Revelation (19: 11–16) foretells the coming again of Christ at the head of a great army of conquest (l. 14). The nineteenth century is full of stories of almost superhuman exertions by Britain's Indian, Egyptian and English troops in marching to the relief of besieged towns or defending them against attacks which would have been followed by the indiscriminate slaughter of the inhabitants. Hopkins depicts Christ as regarding these actions not as a proof of the *man*liness of the British soldier – which is how the proud heart of a *man* conceives them (ll. 3, 4) – but as evidence of the divine flame in him. The justice displayed by the just man (No. 57, 'As kingfishers catch fire', sestet) and the courage shown by the soldier or sailor should equally be credited to Christ rather than to human nature (ll. 10–13). The Supreme Commander to whom Hopkins directs us is not Queen Victoria, ruler of the British Empire, but 'Christ our King'.

Though this sonnet is not one of Hopkins's better poems, it is more subtle than may appear on the surface, and only when it has been misinterpreted, I think, can it be dismissed as childish and exhibiting extreme instability of judgment (John Robinson, *In Extremity*, 1978, pp. 96–7).

THE DARK SONNETS, or SONNETS OF DESOLATION

Robert Bridges prefaced his notes to the First Edition of *The Poems of Gerard Manley Hopkins* with a lordly criticism of his stylistic faults, concentrating upon flaws among unmentioned triumphs. But he ended with warm praise for a number of sonnets found among the Jesuit's papers after his death and therefore known as 'posthumous'.

These sonnets (Nos 63–9, 75, 149, 150 and 153) do not form a unified group: they include '(The Soldier)' and '(Ashboughs)' which contain none of that 'terrible pathos' which Canon Dixon had recognized in some earlier poems (*Correspondence*, p. 80), and which led Bridges to choose for the most poignant of them the rather risky title of 'terrible . . . sonnets'. Dr W. H. Gardner preferred to call them 'sonnets of "desolation"' (*Study* ii. p. 330), deriving the name from *The Spiritual Exercises of St Ignatius*. He felt they were 'seven or eight' in number. If we think of them as Hopkins's 'Dark Sonnets' we must admit that their gloom shades from the intense emotional blackness of 'I wake and feel the fell of dark, not day' to others in which the eastern horizon becomes an encouraging 'brown brink', or where he remembers how trudging miles can be suddenly transformed into lightfooted ones by a smile from above, as when 'skies/Betweenpie mountains'. That complaint of sterility in spring, 'Thou art indeed just, Lord', though not posthumous, surely belongs among them. To some critics '(Carrion Comfort)' and 'Patience', by ending in consolation, exclude themselves from the list. So they might, but my memory of them is dominated by such phrases as 'these last strands of man/In me', 'me frantic to avoid thee and flee', 'O thou terrible', and 'We hear our hearts grate on themselves: it kills/To bruise them dearer'.

Another sonnet which invites inclusion, though not posthumous, is 'Spelt from Sibyl's Leaves' which Fulweiler (*Letters from the Darkling Plain*, p. 146) treats as 'the poetic prelude to Hopkins' . . . sonnets of desolation' and 'perhaps the most terrible of all' – though (as I have shown) by the time he had completed it Hopkins was able to comment with artistic detachment on the correct way in which it should be performed. There is, in fact, no agreed list of these 'Dark Sonnets', or title which will cover with equal warrant more than a few of them. Even to arrange a central seven in a series of lessening discouragement is to invite challenge, and I do so with an open invitation to the reader to devise his own grading: 'I wake and feel', 'No worst', 'To seem the stranger', 'Thou art indeed just', 'My own heart', '(Carrion Comfort)' and 'Patience'. Moreover our reactions may vary from time to time as we emphasize this ingredient or that. Nor should we imagine that their chronology can be settled by regarding them as a brightening sequence from the midnight of despair to the relief of a dawn survivor – nor, as some would prefer, the reverse. This is as alluring and inconclusive a pastime as the renumbering of Shakespeare's sonnets.

The dating of the sonnets is still largely problematical because of missing evidence. Hopkins dated only one of my seven; though some exist in draft form, we cannot date those from their handwriting because he is then apparently revising poems composed or begun much earlier (cf. *Letters*, p. 262); and moreover when he mentions these sonnets in his letters he omits to identify them. Thus in May 1885 he lamented his loss of poetic capacity, finding himself unable to go on with anything; then added 'I have after long silence written two sonnets, which I am touching: if ever anything was written in blood one of these was' (*Letters*, p. 219). The phrase 'written in blood' indicates the painful exertion with which that unnamed poem was written, word by reluctant word, and (through an association with compacts signed in blood) the truthfulness of the self-revelations.

There are critics whose canons of interpretation forbid them to read any poem as basically autobiographical: they regard the Dark Sonnets as powerful projections of imagined moods cast into traditional or experimental forms, no more personal than the love-spurned cries of Elizabethan sonneteers. But Hopkins's frequent declarations that a writer should be 'in earnest' and not use a 'theme for trying style on' (*Letters*, p. 225, etc.) should modify this attitude. He expected a reader to derive 'greater interest and edification' from his *Deutschland* ode through knowing that 'what refers to myself in the poem is all strictly and literally true and did all occur; nothing is added for poetical padding' (*Letters*, p. 47).

The desperate emotions in the Dark Sonnets are mirrored in his letters from Ireland. In private meditation notes, torn from him in anguish shortly before his final illness (*Sermons*, pp. 261–3), as he looks back on the period during which those sonnets were written he uses imagery which parallels one poem after another. He pictures himself 'dazzled by a spark or star in the dark, seeing it but not seeing by it', and lacking a light shed on his way (cf. 'Spelt from Sibyl's Leaves', No. 61, ll. 4–10). In the midst of 'hopelessness', he clings forlornly to 'hope . . . of happiness hereafter' – cf. '(Carrion Comfort)', No. 64, ll. 1–4. Trapped and bound in a 'wretched life' he exclaims 'I wish then for death' (cf. 'No worst', No. 65, ll. 12–14). He declares that all his undertakings miscarry (cf. 'To seem the stranger', No. 66, ll. 11–13). How can there be peace, he asks, for a mind in which 'something bitter distills' (cf. 'I wake', No. 67, ll. 9, 10)? He struggles to accept what is good in his lot, but laments that God will not give him at present 'bodily energy and cheerful spirits' (cf. 'My own heart', No. 69). He compares himself to a 'straining eunuch' and he tries to reconcile himself to the scriptural statement 'Thou art indeed just, Lord' (see No. 74, ll. 1, 13). All these parallels do not encourage us to treat the Dark Sonnets as no more than masterly poetic exercises.

The two sonnets which best qualify for the title 'written in blood' are 'No worst' and 'I wake and feel the fell of dark, not day'. Neither can be certainly dated, but drafts of the second poem occur above the beginnings of another sonnet, the fragment 'Strike, churl' (No. 154). The handwriting is compatible with May 1885, when we know that a hailstorm, such as is alluded to in the fragment, occurred (*Further Letters*, p. 171). 'No worst' culminates in the bleak comfort offered by sleep, but as if to justify his forebodings that worse griefs might follow, 'I wake and feel' records the invasion of even the dark hours by nightmares more wearing than the pain-shot endurances of day. Moreover, his most recent traumas have there infected his memories of the past: 'where I say/Hours I mean years, mean life' (ll. 5, 6). The sonnet ends in a comparison of his state with those of the damned, so ambiguously worded that not all scholars can agree as to which of the two he felt was worse off than the other. We happen to have more surviving evidence of the difficulty with which he formulated his thoughts with 'I wake' than we do with 'No worst': he had to dip into his veins constantly to pen its last few lines. The solemn asseveration of truth also associated with something signed in blood is claimed in the second quatrain: 'With witness I speak this'. Pens can be metaphorically dipped in *blood* or *gall*, both of which figure in the sonnet. If we are to choose from 'I wake' and

'No worst', the one more likely to have been 'written in blood', we may also argue that the miseries of self-contempt (absent from 'No worst') would have made 'I wake and feel' the more agonizing of the two to complete. But readers may be persuaded by Norman White's preference for 'No worst' (*English Studies*, Amsterdam, April 1972, pp. 123–5); both sonnets, as he reasons, are certainly better candidates than '(Carrion Comfort)', which Bridges concluded must be the one referred to.

One further statement throws a little light on the posthumous sonnets. In September 1885 Hopkins told Bridges with unfounded optimism 'I shall shortly have some sonnets to send you, five or more. ~~Three~~ [cancelled and replaced by] Four of these came like inspirations unbidden and against my will'. This hardly corresponds with Bridges's subsequent picture of his friend at work on these unidentified sonnets, learning how to 'castigate his art into a more reserved style', but it does support the attribution of the majority of the dark sonnets to 1885/86. 'Thou art indeed just, Lord', dated by Hopkins himself 17 March 1889, shows a return of spiritual aridity some four years after the earliest sonnets of desolation. In between came periods of comparative poetic elation. Yet the poems which issued out of the scorching turmoil of these last years have eclipsed in their appeal to modern readers nearly all the products of his more serene years. 'The poems face despair but without ever wholly succumbing to it' observes Bergonzi; 'there is a saving energy in them which we do not find in the complaints of weakness and lassitude in Hopkins's letters' (*Gerard Manley Hopkins*, p. 133).

Many aggravating causes of his nervous prostration can be identified, though they do not together account for the acuteness of his misery: the open disrespect with which his students treated him; the slave labour every few months of marking miles of uninspired translations and barren facts from students in other colleges of the Royal University ('that bodiless examination booth' as Dr Oliver Gogarty called it, where in 1885 the Matriculation and Arts examinations produced 631 failures to 1,213 passes); the active sympathy shown those rebelling against England by Irish Catholic priests and bishops — all these certainly warred against bodily, mental and spiritual health. Hopkins told Bridges that 'my fits of sadness, though they do not affect my judgment, resemble madness' (17 May 1885; *Letters,* p. 216). He wrote to Baillie: 'The melancholy I have all my life been subject to has become of late years not indeed more intense in its fits but rather more distributed, constant, and crippling' (*Further Letters,* p. 256).

But in the Dark Sonnets his main concern, never mentioned in his correspondence, is that God has moved beyond earshot, or remains incomprehensibly deaf to his prayers and vows. 'Comforter, where, where is your comforting?' he calls, unanswered (No. 65, l. 3). 'And my lament/Is cries countless, cries like dead letters sent/To dearest him that lives alas! away' (No. 67, ll. 6–8). He complains that 'dark heaven's baffling ban/Bars' his best inspirations from developing (No. 66, l. 12), and his condition is like that of the lost (No. 67, l. 13).

The Spiritual Exercises, under 'Rules for the Discernment of Spirits', describes Spiritual Desolation as the opposite of Spiritual Consolation in which occurs 'increase of hope, faith, and charity, and all interior joy, which calls and attracts man to heavenly things', rendering his soul 'quiet and tranquil in its Creator and Lord' (ed. Father John Morris, 1887). Though desolation may be sent as a trial, it is not to be regarded as a Christian's normal state, but as a desert tract through which his road temporarily runs. Some have regarded Hopkins's experience as the Dark Night of the Soul known to saintly mystics. Though this may err on the positive side, it is a preferable explanation to its opposite against which Dr Cotter wisely warns us (*Inscape*, pp. 225–6): 'The modern association of personal guilt with mental illness parallels the older superstition of physical suffering as a consequence of sin. No moral evil, as Job protested of himself, need be involved in Hopkins's anguished isolation and melancholia.' What emerges in poem after poem is his refusal to give way to his depression, or to believe that God is dead; just as in letter after letter during the same period we find his astonishing mind busying itself with some recondite enquiry or exhilarated by some new insight. Even in the darkest hour he orientates himself towards the dawn.

No. 64 (Carrion Comfort) Composed about August 1885 and revised September 1887.

This is a troublesome sonnet to analyse, for reasons associated with its success in replicating some of the drawn-out miseries from which it arose. The sestet is an epilogue which looks back upon two seemingly incompatible and distinct phases in a year of darkness now safely past: valiant resistance to adversity personified as a divine wrestler (ll. 12–14), and filial submission to that same suffering imaged as strokès of purifying punishment (ll. 9–11). Because the fact that he 'kissed the rod' was the crucial step which led to the gradual recovery of vigour and satisfaction, we may assume that the chronological sequence of these phases has been reversed. Further confusion arises when we see that the opening quatrains refer to two other and different crises in his year-long night, also probably in reverse order. Neither is alluded to in the sestet.

Since the octave at first sight gives no glimpse of the protagonist resisting anything other than Despair, his sense of triumph when the experience is over is not prepared for in any obvious way. Yet the successive drafts of the sonnet's last three lines show the poet increasing his emphasis upon the disparity between the contestants.

The last half of the sestet, indeed, raises two points of doubt: was the protagonist courageous, foolhardy or even perhaps sacrilegious in struggling against his divine Adversary? And which of the two combatants more fully deserves our respect? Going back to the beginning of the sonnet to settle these conundrums in a second reading we find little to guide us. In fact in the first quatrain it would seem that the fight is already over. That there has been a struggle we assume from the sheer exhaustion of a man apparently left for dead on a night-shrouded battlefield: only the dogged will to survive can prevent him from becoming food for the carrion vultures. He has resolution enough to reject the relief from his pain offered by Despair (disguised as a comforting rescuer) – a dulling opiate which will carry him quietly to death, unravelling the sinews of life. Despair corresponds with Job's tempter, the Enemy of man, who is permitted if not encouraged by God to test His servant and who is therefore in a sense a divine assailant (Job 1: 6–12; 2: 1–7). Only if we can interpret the struggle against Despair as a wrestling with God does this quatrain blend with lines 12–14. Job, bereft of all those he loved, his possessions and his health, refused to 'curse [renounce] God and die' (2: 9). Hopkins in a 'deep fit of nervous prostration' thought he might be dying (*Letters*, p. 193): this sonnet gives glimpses of the unspectacular but desperate exertion of his fighting spirit which saved him from a mental and physical breakdown (cf. 'St. Alphonsus Rodriguez', No. 73, ll. 6–8).

The second quatrain dramatizes the spiritual bewilderment found in many poems Hopkins wrote in his Irish period – as to why Christ has to make existence so miserable for someone devoted to Him (cf. Nos 65, l. 3; 66, l. 12; 67, l. 9; 74, ll. 1–7). In place of a sympathetic Paraclete 'who comforts, who cheers, who encourages, who persuades, who exhorts, who stirs up', as he had described Him to a Liverpool congregation (*Sermons*, p. 70), comes a nightmare vision of a monstrous animal with lionlimbs who pins him to the ground. Is this threatening beast the Devil or Christ? Both figure as lions in the Bible. His eyes seem to consume the man's flesh, exposing the bruised skeleton beneath, and his breath is as hot as the stormy east wind of Palestine which brought Job's home crashing down on his children (Job 1: 19). It is no coincidence that this sultry wind from the desert is often used as an image of the breath of God (e.g. Exodus 14: 21; 15: 8). The breath of the beast fans the flames like bellows, but the word *fan* is the hinge which connects octave with sestet while facilitating the abrupt swing in direction at line 9. The destructive gale turns into a winnowing wind, the huddled, terrified protagonist becomes *heaped* threshings, thrown against the breeze by the shallow scoop or *fan* he had described in his meditation notes (*Sermons*, p. 267). The husks and chaff are blown away, and the grain piles up *sheer and clear*.

The answer, unassailably sound in theology, here falls on most ears, I think, as too facile, as though the poet's mind had assented to it while his emotions remained convinced that (at least in his own case) exhausting trials had left him almost unserviceable. 'Take it that weakness, ill health, every cross is a help', he instructed his soul in June 1884 (*Sermons*, p. 256). But nearly five years later he attributed his sense of academic and spiritual futility in Ireland to God's refusal to give him 'bodily energy and cheerful spirits' (*Sermons*, p. 262).

The cross-currents in the sonnet, the gaps which we are left to fill as best we can, the questions posed but not satisfied, suggest that emotionally Hopkins had not reached as assured an understanding of his own problem of suffering as the retrospective epilogue professes. The darkness he had experienced was not yet entirely *done*.

No. 65 'No worst, there is none.' As the only surviving MS is undated, there is no direct evidence when this sonnet was written. I assign it conjecturally to the winter of 1884–5.

The explicit and inherent images in the Sonnets of Desolation stem from Hopkins's struggle to find (in a phrase made famous by T. S. Eliot) 'objective correlatives' for his mental experiences – metaphors and terms so redolent of humanity's contests and trials that sensitive readers would find involuntary echoes of his emotions aroused in them if they let his lines simply reverberate. The more profoundly they shared a common heritage with the poet the more readily they would resonate with him. A direct account of the poet's crisis, such as Yvor Winters demanded, would be comparatively dilute, prosaic and ineffective. (See his lecture on 'The Poetry of Gerard Manley Hopkins', in *The Function of Criticism*, London, 1962, pp. 107–8.)

'Worst! No worst, O there is none', runs an earlier draft, in obvious allusion to some previous statement. We recall, among numerous prototypes, the speech of Moloch in 'Paradise Lost' to his fellow-sufferers in hell, 'what can be worse/Than to dwell here . . .?' and Belial's retort, 'Is this then worst,/Thus sitting, thus consulting, thus in arms?' when, as he points out, their punishing fires could be heated sevenfold (ii. 85–6, 163–73). Further back in time is Edgar's hopeful exclamation in *King Lear* (a play which enriches many lines in this sonnet): 'To be worst,/The lowest and most dejected thing of fortune,/Stands still in esperance, lives not in fear' – an assessment of his state quickly discredited when his blinded father is led past. Edgar is driven to Hopkins's conclusion: 'Who is't can say "I am at the worst"?/I am worse then e'er I was . . ./And worse I may be yet' (Act IV, Scene i. ll. 2–4, 25–8, Pope's emendation). Other echoes of *King Lear* in this sonnet are pointed out by such commentators as Gardner and Milward.

'Pitched past pitch of grief' is a phrase which may relate either to *pangs* as does the equivalent phrase in earlier versions, or to *me*, understood after *wring*. 'Pitched past pitch' associates together such danger-fraught experiences as the pitching of a ship into a sea-chasm so deep that its crew gives up hope of its ever struggling out again; mountaineers on a steep pitch of rock which traps them above an overhang; a fleeing bird driven by a pursuing hawk beyond the highest altitude or pitch to which the shape and muscles of its wings enable it to climb without utter exhaustion; an unnatural high-pitched cry of terror. To these the verb *Pitched* adds a sense of violent flinging or rejection.

The word *pangs* reminds us of some of the highest levels of pain experienced by human beings – a woman in difficult childbirth, or a soldier dying of wounds; *schooled* personifies the pangs into professionally trained torturers. Familiarity with pain makes sensitive personalities suffer more with each attack – in nurses of this type successive exposures to stress are known to worsen their reactions because they brood on their experiences.

If the fifth line had come down to us with *lacunae* where we now read *herds* and *huddle*, it is doubtful if editorial ingenuity would ever have hit upon these unpredictably evocative words. We can only guess at some of the experiences in life and art which may have converged into 'My cries heave, herds-long' by thinking of some examples which help us to interpret it. The melancholy sound of a lowing herd is associated with man's sorrow in two famous elegies, Gray's and *In Memoriam*. Greater poignancy is added by the frieze among the Elgin Marbles where a lowing herd of oxen are being led to sacrificial slaughter by priests. Hopkins as a schoolboy (much in love with Keats's poetry) had used his knowledge of the Parthenon friezes in his 'Escorial' (st. 7; *Poems*, p. 245). In Dublin, he tells us, he felt at times that the institution of which he was a part 'drags me on with the collar round my neck', an unwilling victim, enslaved in the cause of a political enemy (*Sermons*, pp. 262–3). But with 'My cries heave, herd's-long; huddle' the emphasis falls rather on distress than sacrifice.

But *herds-long* also prepares us for the gradual widening of focus as the *My* of line 5 expands into the *our* of line 11. The protagonist is only one in a host of indistinguishable sufferers exposed to the blast, *huddled* together metaphorically like cattle in a storm through their common misery. The references to *world-sorrow* and an *age-old anvil* point to St Paul's awareness of a universe sharing the individual Christian's groans as he waits for his body to be ransomed from slavery: 'Up to the present . . . the whole created universe groans in all its parts as if in the pangs of childbirth' (Romans 8: 22–3, New English Bible). Sorrow (as Hopkins said his weeping Margaret would one day discover) has only one ultimate spring (No. 55, l. 11). The anvil on which the heart is beaten is as ancient as the high precipitous mountains to which Vulcan the smith orders his servants Might and Force to rivet Prometheus (Aeschylus, *Prometheus Bound,* ll. 1–6). Hopkins as a student had translated part of this play into verse (No. 160).

The sestet introduces one of the most telling images in modern poetry: 'O the mind, mind has mountains; cliffs of fall/Frightful, sheer, no-man-fathomed'. The world's mountains have been conquered one by one in the last century, an index of man's spiritual aspiration, but never before, I think, have so many found themselves on the brink of mental precipices. The cliffs may be below us, but to have climbed high is no consolation if we feel we are clinging with gradually failing strength to a crumbling ledge above an abyss. Hopkins disclosed to Dr Bridges in September 1885 that during the preceding months his 'spirits were so crushed that madness seemed to be making approaches' (*Letters,* p. 222). Some who have never trembled on so precarious a height would in current jargon dismiss his miseries as '*merely* psychological'.

It is certainly tempting to parallel Hopkins's situation, hanging on the cliff, with the archetypal figure of Prometheus, riveted to the mountain face in agony because he had given mankind fire and hope and the arts. Sister Mary Humiliata has demonstrated how much the imagery of this sonnet owes to Aeschylus's play (*PMLA*, Vol. 70, 1955, pp. 58–68). But we must not press the resemblances too far. There is a world of difference between the hero Prometheus and a man who, lost on the mountains, has slipped to the brink of disaster. Prometheus would rather be hurled into black Tartarus than hang immovably in torment; moreover, he is condemned by his immortality to endure everlasting pain, but mortals have at least death to hope for. Or like climbers overtaken by darkness on an inhospitable rocky face, they may creep into some shallow cave to bivouac, losing consciousness for a while in fitful or exhausted sleep. To sleep, even to death itself as the end of this seemingly counter-productive torment, the final lines of the sonnet look forward in a desperate flight from pain.

No. 66 'To seem the stranger lies my lot' The sole autograph is undated. The allusion to his being 'in Ireland now' suggests that it may have been written during the first half of his Irish period, probably 1885–6.

In the depression caused by his unsatisfying work in Ireland Hopkins carried out a highly critical reappraisal of his whole career since the academic triumph of his First at Oxford. In another sonnet he characterized his entire life as long-stretching rough-roaded 'black hoürs' (No. 67, ll. 1–6); here he emphasizes his continual loneliness. It was not merely that he felt himself always 'among strangers' (for nearly everywhere he went he developed an affection for the people around him) but that he seemed '*the* stranger' to others. In each new environment he was liable to be treated by his Superiors as the one man who could most easily be spared, and so be moved on before he could become thoroughly familiar to the people: he was too often 'the new Father' – as it were among stepsons and stepdaughters.

In this sonnet he sets out the three 'removes' or stages in a journey away from those he had known and loved best. The first block in communication (ll. 1–4) had been his conversion to the minority religion, Catholicism. Though it brought his mind peace, it parted him in sympathy from his own family, who were Anglicans, in just the way Christ had predicted (Matt. 10: 34–7; see also *Further Letters,* pp. 94–6). As a priest when conversing with people Hopkins was always primarily conscious of whether they shared his religion or not (*Further Letters,* p. 245). Yet with people from old Catholic families, as a convert he would be aware that they were often more at ease in their religion than he was, so many basic attitudes stem from early childhood.

The second gap in communication, due to his development of a strange and difficult poetic style and rhythm, is almost invariably misread: it occupies lines 5–8 and 11–14. He considered that a great work of art by an Englishman was 'like a great battle won by England', being praised even by those who hated her; but to achieve this action in her honour a work must become widely known (*Letters,* p. 231). The creative thoughts which he tried to put into poetry, however, had not been understood by Englishmen – even his fellow Catholics: 'The Wreck of the Deutschland' and 'The Loss of the Eurydice', designed to help England recover her spiritual honour by returning to the true Faith, had both been thought too odd to publish by *The Month* and so remained unheard. Instead of entering the battle for England's honour by producing stimulating works which would redound to the national credit, he had been wearied by continual rejection, first of his poems and later his articles. Others were busy fighting, while he was perforce idle, a mere bystander (ll. 7–8).

The third remove was to Ireland, which since 1860 had been a separate Jesuit Province. Whereas in England he knew most of his fellow Jesuits through having trained or worked alongside them, in Ireland he was the only member of the English community in a sort of exile (Boyd Litzinger, *Hopkins Quarterly,* Vol. I, No. 1, April 1974, pp. 41–2). Englishmen were then rather unwelcome to the Irish population at large. Though Hopkins had made friends in Ireland as elsewhere, he was still to them 'the English Father'.

The sonnet ends with a great cry of frustration as he thinks of the many inspirations for poems or learned articles which had come to nothing, owing to a state of mind and body brought about either by God for some unfathomable purpose or by the Enemy of Mankind. He was forced to hoard his messages like someone who has found gold coins which no one will accept, or like a prophet whose warnings are simply ignored. No wonder inspiration dried up. In a letter to Bridges in October 1886, for example, he announced with characteristic enthusiasm that he had 'made a great and solid discovery about Pindar', but when he thought of securing its publication, remembering his faltering health and continual disappointments he ended, 'But all my world is scaffolding' (*Letters,* p. 229). The allusion with which this sonnet sadly terminates is perhaps to Christ's story of the man who set out to build a tower, laid the foundations — and then ran out of funds; he was mocked by everyone who saw the aborted enterprise: 'This man *began* to build and was not able to finish' (Luke 14: 28–30). A 'lonely began' is different from a 'beginner'; in no sense was Hopkins at an elementary level. Whatever the subject he explored – art, music, philology, prosody, Greek textual cruces – he tended to emerge with some penetratingly original ideas. Being regarded by colleagues as a strange man, he was seldom encouraged to proceed with them or helped into having them printed. But though lonely during his lifetime, he has been a seminal influence on English literature in this century. (For an excellent analysis of the economical style of this poem, see Schneider, *Dragon in the Gate,* pp. 190–2.)

No. 67 'I wake and feel the fell of dark' Undated sonnet, discovered among Hopkins's papers after his death. It was probably written before May 1885.

The letters which Hopkins wrote from Dublin contain many references to 'work, worry, and languishment of body and mind' . . . to being 'continually jaded and harassed', to 'a fagged mind and a continual anxiety' (*Letters,* pp. 216, 221; *Correspondence,* p. 139). Some private meditation notes, which should be dated January 1889 (*Sermons,* pp. 261–2), refer in more revealing detail to a state betrayed also in this sonnet. He uses terms which suggest his wearily plodding round an endless circle: 'I began to enter on that course of loathing and hopelessness which I have so often felt before, which made me fear madness and led me to give up the practice of meditation . . . and here it is again . . . being tired I nodded and woke with a start. What is my wretched life? Five wasted years almost have passed in Ireland. . . . The body cannot rest when it is in pain nor the mind be at peace as long as something bitter distills in it and it aches.' Capable only of 'a barren submission to God's will', he finds himself alone 'in the dark'.

'I wake and feel the fell of dark, not day': to the modern reader that strangely effective phrase, 'the fell of dark', might suggest the *fell* of a mountain, a high moorland waste on which he has wandered, torn with self-disgust, or the miseries of the *fell* (terrible, unsparing) night when a man is feverish with worry. For all the homophones of *fell* see my Writers and Critics *Hopkins*, pp. 88–90. He may also vaguely (and correctly) connect *fell* with *fall*: a *fell* is a prostrating blow. To Hopkins's classical ear it would also anticipate the keyword in the sestet, for another *fell* comes from the Latin for gall. But most important, to a Catholic theologian who knew the Vulgate Bible and St Augustine, yet another *fell*, a skin or hide (from the Greek word *pellis*) would take him back to the ejection of Adam and Eve from Paradise. Psalm 103: 2 (A.V., 104) speaks of the heavens being stretched out like a curtain or tent or pavilion; the Latin Vulgate uses the word *pellis*. St Augustine connects this with the skins with which God clothed fallen Man: their sin had brought death into the world, symbolized by the skins of animals sacrificed in atonement. The heavens, says Augustine, conceal the light of God from sinful mankind (*Confessions*, Bk. 7. xix, Bk. 13. xv). Hopkins certainly makes us feel as though an oppressive weight has been thrown on him, as in the plague of Egypt – a darkness that could be *felt* (Exodus 10: 21).

The plague of spiritual darkness spreads over the protagonist in this poem: it colours time, for the hours become *black hoùrs*, and it disfigures the past as the hours are reinterpreted as *years*, sullying the whole of his life, every part of it viewed in searing retrospect as a failure. This provides the most obvious interpretation of the *sights* and *ways* of line 3. The ordeal of the night lies in retraversing the past, as many sensitive poets have done – Yeats, Edward Thomas, Eliot – unable to forgive themselves for well-meant blunders. Note how the scale of both time and place is suddenly enlarged as his cries are converted into unanswered letters. A shout for assistance assumes that someone may be within earshot; its success or failure is immediately apparent. But weeks and months of slowly blighted hope follow the sending of an unanswered letter on its indefinite journey. The letters are called *dead* the moment they leave the writer's hand, not merely by a striking anticipation or prolepsis, but because their address is wrong. In his dark night, the victim cannot even properly direct his prayers for relief. Yet the second quatrain does not state that for Hopkins God is dead. On the contrary he specifically implies that *He lives* (l. 8) – but unreachably somewhere else.

The main imagery of the octave is of travel – the nightmare journey of a man lost in the dark. The indescribable sights owe their horror, not as in Dante's *Inferno* to the torments of other people, but to the fact that they are inside his own mind. The darkness is in the dome of his spiritual skull (where in a further sonnet he gropes like a blind man fumbling in his self-dark). In another meditation note he speaks of the unprofitable minor hell in which 'we act over to ourselves again and again the very scene which costs us shame' (*Sermons*, p. 138). We may compare Yeats's intense play *Purgatory,* misnamed since it foresees no purging of guilt. In contrast to the 'ways you went!' – the heart's stumbling search for an exit route – we read of the lover's journey: he it is who has gone 'away', and no amount of plodding pursuit enables the neglected suitor to overtake him. Undelivered letters are sometimes returned by the Post Office marked simply 'Gone away'.

In the sestet the imagery becomes medical. During severe jaundice, the gall or bile whose function is to help us digest nourishment seems instead to permeate the whole system, flooding into the blood and the lymph, staining the tissues and skin and the eyes until the victim feels 'I *am* gall'. Allusions to the inescapable burden of the Fall and original sin are to be found in *curse* as well as in *sweating*: 'through thy act', said God to Adam, 'the ground is under a curse. . . . thou shalt earn thy bread with the sweat of thy brow' (Gen. 3: 17, 19, Knox). But instead of being nourished by bread he is being nauseated by a *dull dough* soured by *selfyeast* and bile, and the *sweating* points to a feverish spiritual hepatitis, a homeopathic purgatory on earth.

The diet, like the darkness, is not due to any conscious choice on his part. He is not a prodigal son, but a dutiful if imperfect one whom the father he loves has apparently deserted without explanation. 'How impossible it is to search into His decrees or trace His footsteps' said Paul (Romans 11: 33, Weymouth). Because Hopkins the priest cannot fathom the reasons behind his long-drawn debilitating trials, he says 'God would have me taste His *deep* bitter decree'. Here he uses *deep* in the same way as the psalmist does *high*: 'Such knowledge is beyond my understanding, so high that I cannot reach it' (Ps. 139: 6, New English). Hopkins changed *deep* to *just*, but this implied that the speaker was a rebel rightly sentenced, so he changed it back again to *deep decree* – an 'inexplicable' verdict against him.

This sonnet ends somewhat enigmatically, perhaps because he could not decide whether it was more painful to be an outlaw aware that he is being justly punished, or to be a loyal citizen summarily imprisoned on an unknown charge, and left to languish unheard. He first wrote: 'I see/The lost are like it, and their loss to be/Their sweating selves as I am mine, but worse'. The syntax no doubt intends 'the lost are like it . . . but worse'. The punctuation here suggests that the damned share with him the crucial lack of a remade self, but that they are worse — presumably because their state is a permanent hell, his a temporary hell on earth. Yet a nagging ambiguity obtrudes: the last part of the sentence might linger in the mind and be interpreted out of its grammatical context: 'I am mine, but worse'. He therefore moved 'as I am mine' to the beginning of the line. The shifting of clauses in his revision is less important than the change from *loss* to *scourge*: 'their loss to be . . .' means that for a man to be no more than his unregenerate self is to be lost. But 'their scourge to be . . .' is different: scourging can be an indication of acceptance if it is administered on earth rather than after death. Such a consolation, however, can be purely theoretical to the patient who feels critically ill.

The *fell of dark* remains in this poem unalleviated, and it seems to me very likely that this was the sonnet described by the poet as 'written in blood' (*Letters*, p. 219; see above, pp. 170–2).

No. 68 'Patience, hard thing!' The only autograph is undated, but probably belongs to 1885–6.

The opening quatrain of this sonnet makes little sense if we equate a prayer for patience with the common sort of situation in which a man, under severe provocation, says to himself 'Don't let me lose my temper! I must have patience!' The last thing that man wants is an exhausting conflict and a wounded self-image: he is trying to keep tensions down. In a sense, therefore, John Robinson is right when he glosses the phrase *wants war*: 'the quality of patience is never required where there is excitement. No one engaged in active warfare ever needs it . . . but only those whose lives and whose jobs are dull' (*In Extremity*, p. 147). But this overlooks the derivation of patience from the Latin *patior*, I suffer, and the prime definition of it: 'The suffering of afflictions, pain, toil, calamity, provocation, or other evil, with a calm, unruffled temper' (*Imperial Dictionary*, 1859; Webster, 1864). That is the true theological virtue of patience: when a man asks for this, he is by corollary inviting 'afflictions, pain, toil' and so forth – he may well be said to be asking for a continuance of the conflicts in which he is already being buffeted. In an earlier sonnet (No. 51, 'Peace') Hopkins had complained that his prayer for Peace had brought him only a fledgling substitute, Patience. Patience was 'a virtue that Hopkins needed often', says Fr Boyle, gathering successive passages from his letters and poems (*Metaphor in Hopkins*, pp. 116–17). Here the poet puts in a *bid* for a stock of Patience, knowing that the upset price of it is willingness to suffer. His letters during 1885–6 often express the conviction that his condition is not likely to improve. By accepting as an apparently inevitable situation the circumstances which time and again blocked him from completing a scholarly undertaking and publishing it he was crushing one aspect of his self – his professional respect and his belief in the need to educate the public and enrich the nation – but simultaneously being strengthened in grace.

As in a Shakespearian soliloquy, the imagery is constantly changing. The second quatrain makes an implicit antithesis between the *rare* virtue and the common plant called Patience (a type of dock). Thomas Fuller remarked that 'Patience grows not in every garden' (Gnomologia, 1732). The true Patience demands a particularly harsh soil in which to flourish, but once it has struck root it spreads like ivy over ruins, hiding wrecked attempts from sight. The word *wrecked* (combined perhaps with 'unruffled' in the definition of patience) converts the creeper into a lazy groundswell concealing a sunken ship: the purple berries of the ivy bask like bathers floating among the gently surging leaves.

But, as the sestet makes clear, this placid surface conceals from others the continuing pain below. The civil war goes on, one set of qualities and desires suffering almost mortal injuries in conflict with more austere aspirations. The timbers of the ruined structure of line 7 now seem to be living stems, split by the storms, grating against each other in the hostile gusts of life, bent out of their natural wilful shape in order to satisfy the divine gardener. In contrast the final image springs from the fact that ivy flowers attract bees by their nectar. Honey used to be 'distilled' in the older sense of being squeezed out of the combs by pressure.

But the last tercet does not, I believe, necessarily imply that the poet had in his present trials reached a state beyond very fragmentary consolation. It seems rather to be an attempt to carry out the instructions in the *Spiritual Exercises*: 'Let him who is in desolation strive to remain in patience, a virtue contrary to the troubles which harass him; and let him think that he will shortly be consoled' ('Rules for the Discernment of Spirits', viii, Father Morris's edn, 1887). The distiller of delicious kindness, still living, alas! away, is apparently patiently waiting, like Perseus hovering invisible above pang-morselled Andromeda, for the ordeal to reach its climax (Nos 67, l. 8 and 50, 'Andromeda', ll. 10–14). The ways along which Patience travels with its spiritual sweetness may be known mainly from past experience or the records of the saints. There is not much sign of these laden honeycombs in Hopkins's correspondence or meditations of this period. Instead the predominant impression they leave on us is rather of the heart grating against itself, the final state in 'Spelt from Sibyl's Leaves' (No. 61, l. 14).

Despite the upward turn forced by an act of will upon the last three lines, few poems seem to me so full of the 'terrible pathos' which Canon Dixon found even in Hopkins's earlier work (*Correspondence,* p. 80). This is surely one of the 'Dark Sonnets', although it represents a great advance upon the blackest of them because instead of the horror-sodden 'ways you *went*' – the tracks worn by an agonized mind, dwelt on in retrospect (No. 67, l. 3) – here we have the attention focussed forward on the route along which in God's 'good' time will arrive the ability to surmount frustrations, the Patience 'that *comes* those ways we know'.

No. 69 'My own heart let me more have pity on' Undated, but attributable to 1885–6.

Writing in April 1885 about a friend's death which he suspected to have been suicide, Hopkins epitomized him as 'a selftormentor' (*Further Letters,* p. 254). The description fitted his own psychological state in Dublin: in several sonnets (e.g. at the end of 'Spelt from Sibyl's Leaves') Hopkins had recognized himself as his own inquisitor. At other times, it is true, he had attributed his agonies to an external Fury or a nightmarish Being whom he addresses as 'thou terrible' (No. 64, '[Carrion Comfort]', l. 5; 65, 'No worst', ll. 3, 7). Here he remembers something he had known as an undergraduate, that a man may have 'duties to himself', and that when we objectify ourselves, try to see ourselves from the outside, 'self-love becomes the reverse of selfishness and self-respect of self-conceit' (*Journals,* p. 124). If meditating on past sins in the first week of the Spiritual Exercises 'numbs and kills the heart' it ceases to be a cleansing process, producing instead a helpless loathing. During his Tertianship Hopkins had recognized that this self-scrutiny should not be merely torturing: 'we may pity ourselves . . . that such a thing as sin should ever have got hold of us. This pure pity and disavowal of our past selves is the state of mind of one whose sins are perfectly forgiven' (*Sermons,* pp. 134–5, 262–3). John Pick quotes and discusses Father D'Arcy's acute analysis of Hopkins's over-scrupulousness, attributable partly to the fact that he was a convert and brought with him the unbending rectitude practised by High Anglicans in Victorian times (*Priest*

and Poet, pp. 109–13). If we are commanded to love our neighbour as ourselves, hating ourselves makes a bad model.

The first quatrain contrasts the new regime ('let/Me live . . .')
with the unkind, uncharitable regimen of the immediate past ('not
live . . .'): the echoing three-fold *torment* is exactly right for the
bitter cycles of self-accusation which madden consciousness without providing any forward drive.

The poet addresses himself (or parts of himself) as *heart, self,*
and *soul*. The 'I/me' varies in its identity and angle of vision. In
the first two statements (down to *charitable*) this 'I' seems to be
sympathetic but somewhat detached, almost a repentant task-
master who has just realized that his ruthless discipline has been
counter-productive. But he is soon identified with his victim, and
precipitated into the torture-chamber of the mind (ll. 3, 4), into a
prison cell devoid of light and furnishings (ll. 5, 6). In more
modern terms we may think of a typical Samuel Beckett situation,
or a dissociation room designed to bereave a man of all his own
resources. Hopkins uses two powerful images, opposite in scope,
to reinforce his sense of exhausted isolation, yet each carries with
it a new awareness that his self-imposed poverty is surrounded by
abundance. Why should he reduce himself to the predicament of a
blind man by groping around the cramping darkness of his own
lowest self, an unlit cellar, when he could struggle up into the
daylight, to 'the heart's cheering', and watch for the clouds to lift
and the heavens to smile? After this claustrophobic image comes
an equally alienating situation, that of a lone survivor from
disaster at sea, surrounded by a hostile waste of undrinkable water
when his whole body is one raging thirst. The vividness of his need
(as Father Boyle finely remarks) is shown by the comparison not to
a thirsty man but to thirst itself (*Metaphor in Hopkins*, p. 147). If
there is a reminiscence here of the Ancient Mariner, as seems
probable, we may remind ourselves that the mariner had to show
pity himself before the saints took pity on him. We are aware
today that restoration to health may depend on an intricate
co-working of miraculous drugs from outside and the personality's
own store of 'Self-heal'. This Hopkins argues in spiritual terms in
his fascinating account of the parts played by the external yet
internal factor of God's grace and the 'sigh of aspiration' from an
imperfect or injured spirit which opens the way from inside for
that grace to enter.

In the sestet the *I* ascends (as in Eliot's *Burnt Norton*) above the inveterate scars, a kindly counsellor to the overwrought *Jackself*, who has been dulled by the proverbial 'all work' and no joy. *Jackself* also provides a link with the octave since Jack is a rather condescending name for a sailor. Another application of the term Jack is to a common labourer; the poet is still living 'in drudgery, day-labouring-out life's age' as in a sonnet written a decade earlier (No. 39, 'The Caged Skylark'). *Jackself* therefore leads on naturally to *jaded* (we recall 'The jading and jar of the cart' in 'The Wreck', st. 27). His own packs of bloodhounds have been making a carrion-feast of his sad self: but they can be called off for a while. Instead of cultivating only the rare-rooted Patience (No. 68, l. 5) he must allow more than a grudging crevice in the rock to Comfort, relying upon God to send his roots rain (No. 74, l. 14). To root out all impulses as sinful may destroy wheat as well as poppies. What sparse joy he had recently experienced was stolen (No. 64, l. 11), but if space is left for it, joy will spring up and grow to a *size* God will Himself determine (cf. No. 111, 'Stephen and Barberie', l. 6).

In the final image, the sky itself seems to smile as the thunder clouds part to reveal a curve of vivid blue which the poet associated with the blessings of Mary (No. 60, ll. 73ff). The skies '*Betweenpie* mountains' (extraordinary but expressive verb): the darkness of the mountains and of the clouds may remain, but they are made into pied beauty by the bright sunlight between them. Even one *lovely mile* will enable him to face the rest of the valley of the shadow with a more springy step. The cheerful prospect with which this poem ends seems less brittle than in the preceding sonnet; pity may provide happiness a little more tangible than everlasting patience can do.

No. 70. Tom's Garland Begun at Dromore (County Down), September 1887, but probably not completed until December. See *Letters*, pp. 261–74: Hopkins pointed out that it was semi-satirical (p. 266). The two codas are each introduced by a half-line, as in Milton's caudated sonnet 'On the New Forcers of Conscience'.

It is almost impossible in these democratic days to realize the apprehensions with which otherwise liberal-minded Victorians viewed the proletariat. Even much later both Yeats and Eliot listened with alarm to reports of the Bolshevik revolution, and have had their forebodings laughed at in retrospect. Some impression of the fears rampant around the time this poem was composed is to be found in an unexpected source, a pamphlet on unemployment called *Men versus Machinery* published in 1888 by H. Halliday Sparling, who helped William Morris edit his Socialist paper called *The Commonweal*.

> A million of starving people, with another million on the verge of starvation, represent a potential of destructive force to measure which no dynamometer has yet been made, but which will, if suddenly liberated, assuredly and absolutely destroy any vestige of nineteenth century civilisation so-called; will destroy it more completely than time has destroyed the traces of the society of Nineveh, of Babylon, Greece and Rome, or even Mexico.

The Times during 1886 and the following year was sprinkled with reports of unemployment, depressed trade, riots, strikes, and mass demonstrations, culminating in a gigantic socialist meeting in Trafalgar Square in August 1887 and Bloody Sunday on 13 November. Although Cardinal Manning had shown great statesmanship and foresight in his pronouncements upon labour relations and his efforts to obtain relief for the unemployed, in general Church organs denounced Socialism as basically destructive of values cherished in Christian and civilized countries. The Papal Encyclical of 1885, *Immortale Dei*, stated that 'whosoever possesses the right to rule derives it from no other source than God, the Supreme Ruler of all', and attacked the new socialist doctrine that all men were equals in practical affairs and entitled to govern themselves.

Before he had come into close contact with the lowest strata of society in the great cities of Liverpool and Glasgow, Hopkins had expressed more open sympathy for them than is obvious in this poem. Writing to Bridges in his famous 'Communist' letter of 1871 (*Letters*, pp. 27–8), he had even condoned their threats. 'They profess that they do not care what they wreck and burn, the old civilisation and order must be destroyed. This is a dreadful look out but what has the old civilisation done for them?' Alluding to the confiscation of the Church's wealth under Henry VIII, Hopkins viewed English society as founded on wrecking, but the poor 'got none of the spoils, they came in for nothing but harm from it then and thereafter'. The immense wealth accumulated during the

Industrial Revolution had only 'made their condition worse' despite their major contribution to creating this plenty.

As Hopkins worked on the poem, it became increasingly complicated and elliptical. Yet he was astounded when his friends could not understand it and had to ask him for a translation. This is given in *Letters*, pp. 272–4, and reproduced in the notes to the Fourth Edition of the *Poems*, pp. 291–2. Who but Hopkins would call circles of steel studs on a boot-sole a *garland*, and, pushing his joke still further, incorporate this in the title? Two years later W. S. Gilbert in *The Gondoliers* was to set London laughing at the king who was so profoundly sympathetic that he 'to the top of every tree/Promoted everybody'. Hopkins has some fun by first presenting society upside down, as socialists might view it (and as Eliot does in the last section of the *Waste Land*). Instead of the Queen's golden crown at the top, we would then find the navvy's boot-protectors (l. 1).

Dragging his feet on the flinty trudge homeward, the navvy strikes sparks (l. 3): it would seem that it is Tom who first *piles pick*, followed by Dick, his *bootfellow* (work-mate). Because the navvy is the foot of the social structure, his boots receive humorous emphasis throughout: even his rôle in society could be symbolized by the low arc in which his boot swings (ll. 5, 8). But underlying the whole sonnet, lighthearted though some portions may seem, is the serious Pauline argument in I Corinthians 12 that the Church, like the human body, needs all the diversified gifts of its specialized limbs and organs; the head cannot inform the feet that it can do without them nor can it deprive them of the honour in which they should be held (vs. 21–3). Hopkins had preached eloquently in Liverpool on the mutual responsibilities of various ranks or estates in a commonwealth (*Sermons*, pp. 58–9).

In British parliamentary practice, the sovereign is only the titular head, as Hopkins very well knew. He makes few allusions to the queen in his letters; in his spiritual writings references to the status of the king in a commonwealth are based on the New Testament (e.g. *Sermons*, pp. 161–5). But in correspondence with Bridges, Dixon, Baillie and Patmore he frequently expressed his belief that the real ruler, Gladstone, was betraying the honour of his country (e.g. *Letters*, pp. 210, 300; *Correspondence*, p. 136; *Further Letters*, pp. 171, 257, 293). It is true that since July 1886 Gladstone had ceased to be prime minister, but a year later

Hopkins referred to him as the 'Grand Old Mischief-maker loose,
like the Devil, for a little while and meddling and marring all the
fiercer for his hurry' (*Letters*, p. 257). The conscious model for this
sonnet was the Italian type of mocking or burlesque poem
introduced by Francesco Berni (*Letters*, p. 266), and it is easy
enough to recognize the 'rollic' which Hopkins gave the portrait of
the navvy. But I feel its presence too in the references to the *lordly
head* among the stars, wearing as he explained in his translation,
'an enormous hat or skull cap, the vault of heaven'. This can
hardly be mistaken for a deferential allusion.

The basic argument of the poem begins in line 8: with its tangles
straightened it means 'If all had bread, I would not much mind
inequalities of status in the Commonwealth': *lacklevel* is a spirited
substitute for 'hierarchy' – coined in an era when the destitute
unemployed were being spoken of as 'lackalls'. At one extreme
within the membership of society was the ruler, in theory under
heaven's direct guidance, though Henry VIII and his Protestant
successors had in Catholic opinion robbed God's Church of its
possessions and had not shared them with the poor (*Letters*, p. 28).
The ruler's contribution to the country is *mind* (l. 13), though
obviously not enough of it in Hopkins's estimation. The
navvies were contributing *mainstrength* in such quantities as to
spoil the face of England, which they were being employed to
'trench, tunnel, blast, and in other ways disfigure, "mammock"'
(*Letters*, p. 273). In return they received their steel-shod
boots, symbolic of a comparatively care-free well-clothed
existence.

Lines 12–20 allude to the people who for one reason or another
remain outside these mutual arrangements – unsatisfactory
though these clearly are. The head is garlanded with gold: it seems
to me impossible to miss the poet's irony in 'gold go garlanded/
With, *perilous*, O no' (ll. 13–14, my italics): which we could
loosely paraphrase as 'How could the rulers expose such men to
the temptations of riches?' Contributing neither mind nor muscle,
they are *nó way sped* (benefited), crowned with neither gold nor
steel, neither *glory* nor *earth's ease* nor anything else (*all*, l. 16). In
contrast with their utterly destitute state the healthy labourer (as
the poet remarked in his gloss) might be said to enjoy 'ease of
mind, absence of care'. The workless, treated as an outcast
(*Undenizened*), finds no place for himself in the whole world; he is

a nobody. But the members of society allow him one great 'privilege': he may *share care* with those whose responsibilities fill their minds with thousands of thorny worries! The last two lines show the stages by which unemployment ravages morale. If a man's reaction is despair, this leads to apathy in which he ceases to try, devolving into *Hangdog dull*; but if his frustrations lead to rage, he will grow into something worse, a creature who preys upon society, a *Manwolf*, of which the age has produced packs.

Although I do not feel, with John Robinson, that the last couplet is 'journalistic in its sensationalist generalisations' (*In Extremity*, p. 100), the poem seems to me among his least successful sonnets. Sentences have had their units displaced from their natural syntactical position, with a rhetorical skill which would be admirable in Latin or Greek. But as the English words are not inflected, their relationships become conjectural. Lines 12–17 suffer the most. 'But no way sped,/Nor mind nor main-strength', for example, assumes that the reader possesses the power of divination – or the poet's own 'crib'. Hopkins was right when he conceded to Bridges that 'It is plain that I must go no farther on this road: if you and he [Canon Dixon] cannot understand me who will?' But by the end of the letter he was already wavering: 'I think that it is a very pregnant sonnet and in point of execution very highly wrought. Too much so [for the intelligence of his audience?], I am afraid' (*Letters*, pp. 272, 274). The subject of the poem might have been highly topical, but its experimental, rollicking, burlesque tone adds ambiguities of interpretation to its crossword puzzle grammar.

No. 71 Harry Ploughman Written at Dromore, County Down, September 1887. See the notes to the Fourth Edition for the intricate metrical marks and the poet's anxiety that it should be heard rather than read silently. A facsimile of the autograph in MS *A*, in which Bridges has inserted revisions made by Hopkins, faces page 262 in *Letters*.

An experience recorded by Dom Wulstan Phillipson (*Downside Review*, L1, No. 146, April 1933, p. 339) may possibly have stimulated the writing of this poem. Hopkins, fascinated by an Irish ploughman at work, was allowed to experience the strenuous process for himself.

Ploughing in 'The Windhover' is a symbol of the Christian priesthood. But in this sonnet Hopkins aimed at nothing more than a 'direct picture of a ploughman, without afterthought'. He hoped that someone listening to the sonnet being recited (perhaps with a chorus coming in on the half-lines or 'burden-lines') would receive a 'vivid picture' of Harry Ploughman before his mind's eye. When Bridges indicated that he found difficulties in understanding the poem, Hopkins assumed that the trouble must be syntactic. 'Dividing a compound word by a clause sandwiched into it was a desperate deed, I feel, and I do not feel that it was an unquestionable success' (*Letters*, pp. 262–5). This is normally taken as a reference to his compound-splitting (*tmesis*) in line 15: 'See his wind-lilylocks-laced'. But 'windlaced' in line 14 prepares us well enough for its echo with variation in the next line, so this is not a major cause of obscurity. Hopkins must have been writing loosely, or referring to a discarded version, since no surviving draft has a whole clause, or even a phrase, sandwiched between elements of a compound word. The line with which Bridges was having special difficulty is more likely to have been in the last tercet, when syntactic ingenuity seems designed to baffle even the close student, let alone the listener to whose ear the work was directed.

A further source of obscurity is the deployment of words at whose meaning one can still only guess after the resources of scholarship have been exercised. Before we attempt a running paraphrase of the portrait, we might look at a few examples. In line 1, the ploughman's arms are shown as 'breathed round' with a 'broth of goldish flue' – the fine blond hairs are like fur. The word *flue*, marked by contemporary dictionaries as obsolete, was still used in dialect for soft down, fur or hair. But *broth* is a puzzle. A 'broth of a boy' may be an Irish form of commendation; the context, however, calls for something visual. The *Imperial Dictionary*, 1859, notes under *broth* that 'In *America*, the word is often applied to foaming water'. But does foam *breathe*, or remind us of light hair on an arm? Could Hopkins have assimilated the word with the dialect *brough* (rhyming with Scottish *loch*) defined by the *Whitby Glossary* of 1855 as 'the halo round the moon, when it shines through a mist or haze'? This would be quite good for a misty down on a sunlit arm. But Wedgwood's *Dictionary of English Etymology*, 1859 (a copy of the work was in Stonyhurst, e.g.), under *broth* quotes as cognate the Irish *bruth*, strength,

heat. Significantly, that word is also applied to the nap or down of
cloth. The following year Hopkins mentions to his mother that he
is 'making a collection of Irish words and phrases for the great
English Dialect Dictionary' and is in correspondence with the
editor (*Further Letters*, p. 184). In line 7, *curded* gives pause, but
as a doublet of *curdled* it could mean 'rose like a swell of water'.
Among other problems are *crossbridle* (l. 14), possibly connected
with the bridling movement of a head, and *frowning* (l. 17), which
must define, not the appearance of his feet, but the wrinkles in his
boots (*broad . . . bluff hide*). Other verbal conundrums we will
tackle in passing.

The first part of this most unsonnet-like sonnet (the octave almost
loses its shape when the burden-lines break each quatrain differently) shows the ploughman braced for action, every set of muscles
ready to perform their intricate part in guiding the plough-ship on
its turbulent journey. They are categorized as though an artist was
examining the body as a marvellous piece of mechanism. The
tough arms, like willow withes, seem continuations of the plough's
wooden handles or stilts. The sudden switch to the beauty of the
golden down anticipates the combination of 'Churlsgrace' and
'child of Amansstrength' in line 16 (cf. No. 38, l. 10, 'as a stallion
stalwart' yet 'very-violet-sweet'). The ploughman is not yet full
grown, nor is he well fleshed, as we might deduce from *rack of ribs*
(though *rack* is a technical term for the human ribcage). The
scooped flank is hollowed by the taut thigh muscles below the hip.
The path of stress next flows like a liquid to the thigh muscles,
plaited like rope or a twisting streamlet. The legs rotate backwards
from the knee like spokes from a hub or *nave*. The swell of the
lower leg is caught by *barrelled*. The half-line adds in no particular
sequence other essential parts, *Head*, *foot*, *shoulder*. All these are
like sailors ready to hoist the anchor and sails, each with a specific
task to be performed under the captain's eye. Every member is
braced, waiting for Harry's shout of command to the (invisible)
horses whose sudden lurch into action will tax their co-ordinated
skills.

Muscles invite comparison with water (as in the common
attribution of 'rippling' to both). Such unity as the poem has issues
from the words which compare sinews to a flowing liquid and the
plough to a ship, or which carry overtones of either: *broth*, water
ribs (*Journals*, p. 67) and *ribs* of a ship, *barrelled*, *steered*, *crew*,

liquid waist, wallowing, furls, fountain. In line 7 the thigh muscles
rise in smooth swells or are sucked under like the current in a
brook.

The sestet (l. 12) shows the sudden transformation from
potential to actuality as the horses heave into motion. To keep the
furrow straight in spite of clods of earth and the uneven surface,
the ploughman's straining back, elbows and waist have to absorb
and resist the deflections. The verb *quail* may not only indicate this
pliant yielding to sudden pressures but perhaps suggest the
forward reaching of arms and back – like a quail running with
outstretched neck. The rest of the sonnet appears to be devoted to
two fountains – the ploughman's blond curls of hair, which the
wind lifts and blows sideways or allows to cascade from his crown
like water blown as it drops from basin to basin; and the curling
ringlets of gleaming earth, cut and shot out by coulter and
ploughshare. The word *cragiron* can be felt more readily than
defined. Meanwhile the feet seem to run races beside the clods and
ploughshare, laced up in broad stout boots, creased like a
frowning forehead.

Most readers feel that Hopkins has defeated his intention of
producing a strong and vivid effect by the excessive elaboration of
each detail. They might agree with Day Lewis when he says, 'If
Harry *is* a monumental figure, then I get only a fly's eye view of it,
a series of blinding close-ups, as if I were crawling laboriously from
limb to limb over the surface of a corrugated, undemonstrative
statue' (*The Poetic Image*, London 1947, p. 126).

**No. 72 That Nature is a Heraclitean Fire and of the comfort of the
Resurrection** Composed in Dublin, 26 July 1888, on a 'windy
bright day' preceded and followed by floods of rain – a 'pre-
posterous summer' (see *Correspondence*, p. 157).

The theories which Heraclitus of Ephesus held about the
universe some five hundred years BC were obscure even to the
Greek philosophers who followed him, and they present more
serious riddles to us because from his work have survived only
enigmatic and provocative quotations. Yet his Fragments
stimulated three of our leading modern poets: Hopkins, Yeats and
Eliot. We are not sure whether he believed in four elements as his
predecessors had, or only three (omitting air); but we do know
that to Heraclitus fire was the substrate or underlying matter of the

universe. He appears to have used the term not only for physical
flames, but as symbolizing the process of change which characterized all things. His Fire at times even seems a being with
intelligence, the substance of the pure soul. In interpreting this
poem we need not trouble ourselves as to whether the Stoics were
right in attributing to Heraclitus a belief that the world was
periodically destroyed by fire (l. 20), since Hopkins was not
limiting his thought to one Presocratic teacher. He told Bridges
that in the poem 'a great deal of early Greek philosophical thought
was distilled' – though his own passionate observation of, and
empathy with, nature had flavoured what he called the 'liquor of
the distillation' (*Letters*, p. 291).

The elegaic tone of the sonnet up to line 16 may be paralleled in
the famous 'Lament for Bion', formerly attributed to the Greek
bucolic poet Moschus, and praised by Hopkins in a schoolboy
letter (*Further Letters*, p. 6): the writer contrasts the mallows and
fresh green herbs in the garden, which die and spring up again,
with the fate of men, so tall and strong and intelligent, who are
buried in a hole in the earth from which they never arise (ll.
99–107). Innumerable elegaic poems, down to Tennyson's *In
Memoriam*, had echoed the lament, but seldom with either
Hopkins's sense of zest for inanimate nature nor his pity for the
brevity of man's *firedint* – brave thoughts struck from the ironstone
of adversity, briefly lighting the mental world around him.

Heraclitus alludes to a constant exchange of state occurring in
the elements, a downward movement causing Fire to transmute
itself into Sea (Water) (cf. ll. 10–13), which in turn condenses into
Earth; and an upward return movement in which the Earth
rarefies into Water, and that again separates out into clouds of
moisture and the Fire of which even the sun and the stars are
made. Hopkins depicts the upward cycle in Nature: sun-fire and
wind are drying the storm-flooded ground. But the only path of
Man visible to the observing eye is a downward one.

In the first two lines the clouds mushroom up from the soaked
earth and take flight, jostling each other on an aerial road like
tipsy revellers. Rays of light, intermingled with a cordage of
branchy shadows from mast-high elms, dart down walls roughcast
or whitewashed. The *bright* breeze (a combination of air and fire)
hurls itself in playful rough-and-tumble on the earth. It sponges
water from (*parches*) the spreading mud which edges pools and

wheeltracks, turning it into earth again in three stages – *dough, crust, dust*; it dries and crumbles away the bootprints left by an army of labourers, sweeping away Man's hallmarks on the ground.

The images of violence which recur in these lines mirror Heraclitus's belief that strife was the father of all things – a saying in which W. B. Yeats delighted. But nature's wounds heal rapidly. Cloud-bushes torn from the earth in tufts soon join together again in *gay-gangs* (a very Anglo-Saxon touch). Sunbeams are sharp as splinters (*shivelights*); they whiplash the wall and pierce shadows like a spear, but the result is lovely as lace. The high-spirited schoolboy vigour of the wind is exercised '*Delightfully*'. Whatever nature's bonfire burns up is presently recreated.

The three codas which lengthen this sonnet also invite the postponement of the 'turn' beyond the normal octave. Hopkins has allowed himself only one extra line before this *volta*, but his sonnet is in three contrasted portions, not two. Five lines and two half-lines (10 to 16) lament the brevity of man's fame after death. Though Man is the most beautiful and distinctive form of the Heraclitean fire, he vanishes like a mere spark made when flint is struck upon rock. On the downward path his fire seems to be overwhelmed by the sea. It is a delusion for men to think of the illumination they spread as being like the eternal stars – which were to Heraclitus fire in its purest form, beyond the reach of drowning water.

The imagery of the Resurrection as a *beacon* (lighthouse) is just possibly a reminiscence of a cryptic Fragment of Heraclitus (31) which speaks of the sea as becoming half earth and half 'burner' (lightning or fire). At the Day of Judgment our bodies will be transformed (as Christ's human frame was at the resurrection) into 'immortal diamond'. No one, however, would have described Christ's earthly body with the disparagements Hopkins heaps on his own body – Jack of all work, a bad joke, a piece of broken pottery, an ill-matched piece of cloth (or in Elizabethan parlance a fool), a jagged fragment of splintered wood. Yet it had in common with Christ the divine soul, the immortal diamond which alone will survive even a world-fire.

The sonnet is one of the best executed and most judiciously poised of his Dublin poems. Though it seems as spontaneous as the descriptions in his Welsh nature sonnets, here all the details subserve the total purpose with a more disciplined subjection. The vocabulary blends into unity homely dialect words (*squandering, shive*), his own poetic compounds (*rutpeel, firedint*), and such Romance words as that polysyllabic and seemingly unpoetic product of legal Latin, *residuary*: combined with the simple and undignified *worm*, this shrugs off our mortal remains as laughably negligible. Rhythmically the sonnet's range is equally superb. Using alexandrines instead of pentameters, and Sprung Rhythm instead of iambs, with liberally added outrides, Hopkins moves from the excitement of the opening passage to the evident effort of the recurrent monosyllables in *dough, crust, dust* (l. 7), or the ponderous rolling waves of 'Both are in an unfathomable, all is in an enormous dark/Drowned' (ll. 12, 13). The poem deserves the high praise it has evoked.

No. 73 *In honour of* **St Alphonsus Rodriguez** *Laybrother of the Society of Jesus* Written in Dublin, during September/October 1888.

'Why should we honour those that die upon the field of battle?' mused W. B. Yeats. 'A man may show as reckless a courage in entering into the abyss of himself.' Yeats could hardly have been aware that the relative meritoriousness of external and internal victories had been argued by such Church Fathers as St Jerome, Gregory the Great, St Augustine and St Thomas Aquinas. The question arose in considering whether martyrs who had faced physical violence were more deserving of a special crown than those whose warfare was spiritual. Gregory emphasizes the claims of the latter: 'Although persecution has ceased to offer the opportunity, yet the peace we enjoy is not without its martyrdom; since even if we no longer yield the life of the body to the sword, yet do we slay fleshly desires in the soul with the sword of the spirit' (*Hom.* iii *in Ev.*). St Thomas, however, reasons that 'Just as pleasures of touch . . . hold the chief place among all pleasures both internal and external, so pains of touch surpass all other pains. Consequently an aureole is due to the difficulty of suffering pains of touch, for instance, from blows and so forth, rather than to the difficulty of bearing internal sufferings' (*Summa Theologica*, Suppl. Q, 96, Art. 6).

In 1888 Brother Alphonsus Rodriguez (? 1533–1617), the lay-brother who had been hall porter for some forty years at the Jesuit College of Montesion in Palma, Majorca, had just been canon-ized, and for the celebration of his first Feast Day (October 30) Jesuits in other provinces were asked to send tributes. Hopkins composed 'to order' (i.e. in response to a general or specific request from his superior) a sonnet close enough to the traditional form and metre (unlike all those he had recently penned) to be acceptable to such colleagues as Father Matthew Russell. He sent a draft to Bridges on October 3 with a request for his opinion. The buoyancy of the letter seems to indicate that he was in excellent spirits: 'And please do not put it aside "for further neglect" but answer smart. It has to go to Majorca. Call in the Canon [Dixon], have a consultation, sit, and send result by return – or soon' (*Letters*, pp. 292–3, 296–7).

Hopkins had probably heard readings from *The Life of Blessed Alphonsus Rodriguez* by Brother Henry Foley both before its publication, when he was a novice in 1868, and in the year it was published, 1873 (Thomas, *Hopkins the Jesuit*, pp. 218, 233). As a Jesuit Alphonsus had spent forty-six unadventurous years within the placid walls of a single college on a beautiful and temperate island. But Foley, drawing on the extensive spiritual writings left by Rodriguez (who must not be confused with another Alphonsus Rodriguez, author of *The Practice of Christian and Religious Perfection*), related with what struggles he maintained purity in mind and body. In order to increase his sanctity 'Almighty God made him pass through the trial of the worst and fiercest temp-tations . . . During the space of seven years God permitted the devils to pursue a most unrelenting and cruel war against his body to overcome his chastity . . . with the most horrid and impure forms, gestures, and actions . . . he was reduced to such terrible straits, pain, and weakness from the violence of his efforts to resist them, that he must have died, if God had not put his enemies to flight.' Rodriguez disciplined his eyes never to look man or woman in the face. It may in fact have been from him that Hopkins copied the penance described in his *Journals*, p. 190, of foregoing observation of nature for six months. At any rate Hopkins approached this sonnet in St Alphonsus's honour with great sympathy and insight.

The octave takes us back to medieval chivalry and King Arthur.

Some terms remind us of Spenser: *exploit* (which Bridges thought 'flat') and *galled* (shorn of ornamentation). Disfigurements become badges of honour, and the hero (long retired from the field) may leave them to testify to his victories. Bridges thought the end of line 1, 'so we say', an anti-climax, not realizing that Hopkins intended it to be just that: 'I mean "This is what we commonly say, but we are wrong"' (*Letters*, p. 297). The proofs of valour are not so easy to gauge: there are also heroes, Hopkins argues, who struggle against spiritual forces and keep on fighting to the end, though cheered by no crowds and encouraged by no trumpets since there are no flashing swords to watch and fine steel armour to admire. The Godhead provides analogies for *both* types of fighter contrasted in the sonnet. Christ (ll. 1–5) is the model of those who have undergone physical wounds, scars which now pay eloquent tribute to His victory over sin and death. But the present actions of God the Father, who is ceaselessly hewing out mountains, continents and the very earth itself, go unobserved: the weapons He wields are not recognized as His by materialistic man. With 'trickling increment' (a phrase obviously related to the oozing drops growing to impressive evidence in 'God's Grandeur') He creates the veins of beauty in flowers as small and hidden as a violet.

   Some of the most picturesque imagery occurs in drafts of the sestet, where Hopkins parallels the quiet achievements of God in the world (he may have been remembering the limestone mountains of Majorca and its marble quarries) and in the saint. Hopkins restlessly changed his metaphors. At first the Lord is seen as a blacksmith or foundryman: 'God that moulds mountain . . .'. Presently this becomes 'that quarries mountain, continent/Carves'; and (in the version sent to Bridges, which his critic thought 'cheeky'), 'Yet God the mountain-mason, continent-/Quarrier, earthwright'. Slightly uneasy himself over imagery which he later defended as often 'applied to God Almighty . . . in the Scriptures and the Fathers' (*Letters*, p. 296), Hopkins added a footnote alternative: 'Or, against singularity, we may try this: "Yet God that mountain and that continent,/Earth, all, builds"'. But, as he later admitted, two divine activities were here somewhat confused. The 'trickling increment' covered His building *up* of living organisms, but geologically speaking mountains and continents 'are made what now we see them by trickling *de*crements, by detrition, weathering, and the like' (p. 296). Eventually he sacrificed such vivid metaphors as *earthsmith* in favour of an expressive simplicity: 'God (that hews mountain and continent,/ Earth, all, out . . .)' – a reading which supposes a giant but unseen axe shaping the hills, and which (as he remembered from his meagre Hebrew) had in its favour the fact that the verb translated in the Old Testament scores of times as *create* is sometimes used for *hew* or *cut down* (Joshua 17: 15, 18).

After reading 'Harry Ploughman' (No. 71) and 'Tom's Garland' (No. 70) written the previous year, Bridges had warned Hopkins that he was becoming too obscure to follow, a fault the critic attributed to lack of sufficient poetry reading. But Hopkins replied that the 'effect of studying masterpieces is to make me admire and do otherwise', and what he lacked 'to be more intelligible, smoother, and less singular, is an audience' (*Letters*, pp. 290–1). This fascinating sonnet bears out his argument, for while writing it he was assured of an audience in Dublin and in Majorca which, however select, was far larger than any he had recently enjoyed.

No. 74 'Thou art indeed just, Lord' Written in Dublin, 17 March 1889.

Plato would not have approved of his sonnet. In the *Laws* he makes his mouthpiece, the Athenian, affirm 'if I were a lawgiver, I would exercise a censorship over the poets, and I would punish them if they said that the wicked are happy, or that injustice is profitable' (662). He argues that 'you cannot make men like what is not pleasant, and therefore you must make them believe that the just is pleasant' (663). On the other hand, T. S. Eliot commended *In Memoriam* because it avoided pious insincerity (which Plato seems to advocate and which Eliot finds typical of too much religious verse). 'Its faith is a poor thing, but its doubt is a very intense experience' (*Selected Essays*, 1951, p. 336). No one could fail to feel the tensions in this Hopkins sonnet as the poet tries to reconcile his urgent emotional judgments with what he has been taught and has himself preached.

The epigraph from Jeremiah 12: 1 sets the tone and imagery of the sonnet, and is partially paraphrased in the first two lines. Dr James Moffat renders it vigorously: 'Thou art always in the right, Eternal One, when I complain to thee; yet I would argue this with thee – Why do bad men prosper? why are scoundrels secure and serene? 2. Thou plantest them and they take root, they flourish, yes, and they bear fruit!' The prophet then condemns their hypocritical lip-service to God, and urges that the Lord should 'drag them away like sheep to the slaughter' – a malediction in which Hopkins does not follow him.

Other conscientious religious men have joined in the lament that self-pleasers too often 'get away with it'. The Psalmist's report that he had 'seen the wicked in great power, and spreading himself like a green bay tree' (Ps. 37: 5) is better known than its sequel, that the next time he looked for him the prosperous villain had disappeared. Milton assigns some eloquent passages of doubt to the chorus in *Samson Agonistes*. 'Just are the ways of God,' they piously chant, but presently they are quoting the opinions of many 'who doubt his ways not just' since He seems always ready to exempt Himself from His own laws (ll. 293ff, and 667–704). This concept goes back to the ancient Greeks. In an unpublished high school classical notebook (B 2), on Aeschylus's *Prometheus Desmotes*, lines 189–90, Hopkins translates Prometheus's denunciation of Zeus as a harsh god, 'one who holds justice in his own hands', or 'who has a justice of his own', 'is just in his way' – actually an expression of 'abhorrence of his injustice'. (See No. 160 for earlier passage.)

In this sonnet the Jesuit's opening sentence is a little obscure. How are we to paraphrase 'but, sir, so what I plead is just'? The earliest version was forthright: 'but, sir, what I shall speak is just'; after changing this in favour of the final version as we print it he went back to 'these words I speak are just'. The enigmatic phrase 'so what I' figures in several drafts. The usage might seem to be best covered by definition 26 under 'so' in the *OED*: 'so (that), in limiting sense: On condition that, provided that, so long as, if only'. Sir Thomas Browne, for example, wrote: 'Ulysses cared not how meanly he lived, so he might find a noble Tomb after Death'. Hopkins would then be asserting that God will be just in his arguments but only if the poet's pleas are just also. This might be in line with Psalm 17: 35–6 (Douay), 'the Lord will reward me according to my justice: . . . With the holy, thou wilt be holy; and with the perverse thou wilt be perverted'; or as Moffat translates it (18: 25–6), 'To the kind thou provest kind, and true to the true, to the pure thou provest pure, and treacherous to the treacherous'. However, an alternative reading of 'but, sir, so what I plead is just' would rearrange the words to run 'but, sir, so is what I plead (just)', or 'so too what I plead is just'.

The reference to just pleading does not consign the imagery to the law-court, for the notions of enmity and friendship in line 5 would there be out of place. The overall relationship is more that of patron and protégé, or master and servant, or great landowner and tenant: George Herbert had used all these metaphors to reflect aspects of the bond between God and man. The *sir* (ll. 2 and 9) is at once respectful and yet a trifle distant – though in his beautiful hymn 'Thee, God, I come from' (No. 155, ll. 14, 20) he uses both 'Father' and 'Sir' as compatible terms addressed to God. (We may compare Auden, who begins his prayer in 'Petition' with 'Sir, no man's enemy'. . . .) In the present sonnet, the reversal of the natural justice we expect seems to be subtly mirrored in the reversed (trochaic) rhythms of lines 3 and 4 (indicated in the MSS by counterpoint symbols): 'Whý do sínners' ways prosper? and why must/Dísappóintment all I endeavour end?'

Some of the frustrations in his spiritual, professional and literary life, systematically thwarted by a hostile 'friend', are set out in a very frank private cross-examination of his personal situation at this time, recorded during a retreat at Tullabeg, January 1889 (misdated 1888 in his MS). Though his own allegiance as a soldier of Christ and the Church was unshaken, he felt that the Catholic Church in Ireland, the Irish Jesuits and even the college in which he taught had been partly captured by the enemy, and 'against my will my pains, laborious and distasteful, like prisoners made to serve the enemies' gunners, go to help on' a partly unlawful cause. 'Yet it seems to me that I could lead this life well enough if I had bodily energy and cheerful spirits. However these God will not give me.' These bitter thoughts led, not to pride in himself as worthy of better opportunities, but to self-loathing in which he could only cry out the epigraph to this poem '*Justus es, Domine* . . .'. 'All my undertakings miscarry: I am like a straining eunuch. I wish then for death: yet if I died now I should die imperfect, no master of myself' (*Sermons,* pp. 261–2).

The *volta* or turn in this Miltonic sonnet is not at the end of the octave. In fact most of the sestet develops a picture of luxuriating nature curiously linked to the success spoken of in the octave, of those who serve only their own pleasures, while the toiling poet enjoys none: 'Oh, the sots and thralls of lust/Do in spare hours more thrive than I that spend,/Sir, life upon thy cause. See, banks and brakes . . .' – all this might seem part of the same argument, and lines 9–12 might appear metaphors for prospering sinners. We would, of course, be entirely wrong to read into the poem a conscious equating of spring life with lust, especially as versions of the sestet speak of the spring foliage as 'broidered by thee', and in view of the final appeal to the 'lord of life' to send his own roots rain.

The *fresh wind* which he lacks hints at the absence of poetic inspiration (cf. No. 76). 'Time's eunuch' introduces a metaphor within a metaphor, parallel to a bird too listless even to make a nest, let alone hatch out offspring. Oriental nations in Biblical times frequently emasculated their captives: we therefore have a contrast between the 'slave(s) of lust' in line 7 (the reading of three early versions) and himself, a slave to God (cf. a draft of ll. 8–9: 'I that bend/Ever to bear thy yoke'). Like Paul, who described himself as 'a slave of Jesus Christ' in all his epistles, Hopkins ended a long account of his literary and scholarly enterprises which had been for one reason or another frustrated by telling Bridges: 'Nothing comes: I am a eunuch – but it is for the kingdom of heaven's sake' (*Letters*, p. 270).

The hard-hitting second quatrain recalls the bafflement of the Dark Sonnets of 1885–6. In contrast with 'Hurrahing in Harvest', No. 38 ('what looks, what lips yet gave you a/Rapturous love's greeting of realer, of rounder replies?') this sonnet might be entitled 'Bitterness in Spring'. It is ironic that one of his most enduring poems should be based on the conviction that no work of his would ever endure.

No. 75 'The shepherd's brow' Written in Dublin, 3 April 1889.

The mention of a shepherd in the first line may easily prove a misleading introduction to the argument. As we discover in line 5 ('But man—we . . .'), the second quatrain obviously contrasts the human race with beings discussed in the opening quatrain. The shepherd is cited as a symbol for men who recognize *God's* grandeur when it flames out and who *do* 'reck his rod' (cf. No. 31, ll. 1–4). It was a group of shepherds leading a simple natural life, 'awake in the fields, keeping night-watches over their flock' (Luke 2: 8, Knox) that witnessed the glory of the Lord when Christ was born in Bethlehem, and who were filled with fear and joy. Pastors are so called because they are spiritual shepherds, owning the divine majesty and glory. The stress in the first two lines is meant to fall on God although He is not named; He is the Lord of the 'lightning and lashed rod' ('Wreck', st. 2).

Next in the traditional chain of being come the angels. Hopkins chooses to cite those angels who rebelled, pitting their might against the divine authority, because men also frequently feel they have divine power and make similar unsuccessful attempts, leading to laments that they have been tragically mistreated. But the proud angels, giants though they were in comparison with puny men, were flung from heaven into torments terrible enough to justify their groans – unlike the wails to which men give utterance at the slightest discomfort (cf. ll. 12–14). Milton had described how Satan, leader of the fallen angels in hell, 'above the rest/In shape and gesture proudly eminent/Stood like a tower' ('Paradise Lost', i. 589–91). The least impressive among the angels is a veritable tower in comparison with the strongest man. The mention of towers naturally reminds us of the Tower of Babel which man resolved to erect to make his name famous, a challenge to God because its top was to reach to heaven (Gen. 11: 4). Milton makes Adam, when told that his descendants will try to construct this monument to their greatness, condemn the impious defiance of God, pointing out the folly of man's thinking he could survive in the upper air where he had no right to intrude: it would 'famish him of breath' ('Paradise Lost', xii, 43–78). Hopkins goes further in saying that man has difficulty enough drawing breath at ground level.

Mariani in a helpful footnote to 'Andromeda' threw out the suggestion that this sonnet might have been influenced by the Eiffel Tower then nearing completion (*Victorian Poetry*, Vol. 11, No. 1, Spring 1973, p. 42 n.). Reference to contemporary newspapers confirms his conjecture. The *Irish Times* of 3 April, the day on which the sonnet was written, had a sarcastic article on the Eiffel Tower which began: 'The restless Parisians have now got their new and huge toy complete to its top. . . . The modern Babel Tower has a flag flying from its summit at the full height of three hundred metres, or 984 feet. A salute of twenty-one shots was fired on Sunday afternoon from the cloud-capt turret in honour of the event. It has been two years in building . . . the disgrace and disfigurement to the beautiful city is a permanent eye-strain.' It had been planned to mark the centenary of the French Revolution which had overthrown the tyranny of State and Church, and newspaper articles pointed out how it dwarfed into insignificance the noble temple of God, Notre Dame Cathedral, whose towers were less than a quarter its height.

Man contrasts feebly even with his own ambitious towers – let alone with angels and God. Though priding himself upon differing from other mammals in walking upright, he is a mere air bladder surrounded by a score of fragile bony scaffolds (the full ribs): a precariously balanced skeleton whose natural posture in childhood is on all fours. The new-born baby is smacked to make its lungs work, and the aged draw breath with difficulty. At any stage in between life can be snuffed out with a rag stopping the breath, so that each aspiration should remind us of death (be a *memento mori*, l. 7). Yet we obituarize the loss of a man's tenuous existence as though it were a great tragedy – in hollow exaggeration of our self-importance, as futile as trying to produce profound and solemn organ tones from a fiddle. We soon lose our proud bearing if starved for a few days or stripped of clothes which cover parts we are ashamed of. Even the most publicized leader is as mortal as the commonest fellow, and, in mating with him, his wife uses the female endowment she shares with a woman of the streets.

Finally Hopkins turns to himself, and looking back on the compressed epics he had recently composed, sonnets of desolation in which each day's battle seemed to end for him in exhaustion like death (Nos 65, l. 14; 68, l. 9), he ridicules the storms of trouble he has generated in his mind or imagined himself suffering. As he feeds himself, the inverted caricature of a face which he glimpses in a spoon seems an apt image of the petty role he plays on earth's stage. The thought scales down the storms of complaint in his mind, his raging fires and feverish impatience.

Bridges detected in this sonnet something of the misanthropic and misogynous fits attributed to Swift, and (although the poem was complete and ran through four drafts to its polished final version) separated it from his 'serious' poems as a piece 'thrown off one day in a cynical mood' (Notes to Hopkins First Edition). In disagreeing with Bridges some critics have gone to the opposite extreme, finding no cynicism in it whatever. Yet the poem cannot be said to represent the whole truth about man, since it concentrates upon his body and views all men as equal, belittling the intellectual and spiritual qualities with which God has endowed outstanding philosophers, writers, heroes and saints down the ages. It does, however, provide a useful corrective to undue panegyrics. Many a gifted man (perhaps even Hopkins himself) might have led a happier existence, avoiding the violent switch-backs of depression and elation, if he had learned to laugh at himself good-humouredly more often.

No. 76 To R.B. [Robert Bridges]. Dated 22 April 1889, this is the last poem which Hopkins composed, seven weeks before his death.

This sonnet, inspired by his lack of inspiration and claiming that a poem has to mature through a nine-month if not a nine-year period, was sent to Robert Bridges, the poet to whom it was dedicated, a bare week after it had been written. In his letter Hopkins mentioned that he was ill: in fact the typhoid fever which was to carry him off on June 8th had already struck, though it had not yet been diagnosed (*Letters,* pp. 303–6).

It sets out in sexual imagery an idealized account of the conception and shaping of a poem. Its purpose was (in the words of the earliest surviving draft) to explain that his own 'withered world' knew 'no such bliss' as the 'rare rapture of an inspiration' and it ended roundly: 'Rebuke no more, but read my explanation'. Presumably then this particular sonnet did not spring from 'The fine delight that fathers thought', but (if we interpret the second line as an alternative urge to poetry) from the 'strong spur' of self-analysis and self-justification. Among the Dark Sonnets were four which, he said, 'came like inspirations unbidden and against my will' (*Letters,* p. 221); in their case ideas as searing as a 'blowpipe flame' certainly seem to have kindled a fire in his mind and to have produced poems which poured out like molten metal. The image may possibly have been suggested by medieval paint-ings in which the conception of Christ by the Virgin Mary was shown as occurring through a lancelike shaft of flame from a star entering her head (cf. Yeats, 'The Mother of God', ll. 1–2, 'a fallen flare/Through the hollow of an ear'). Hopkins treats his own inspiration as from God.

The poet's mind has to be impregnated from outside, but once this has taken place the poem is (somewhat simplistically) des-cribed as bound to become 'immortal song', its shaping in the womb of thought being a process of infallible instinct, 'never wrong'. (Would that editors, wrestling with uncancelled alternatives and poems in which the final revisions seem less happy than earlier ones, might claim a corresponding correctness of choice.)

The second quatrain extends the period of gestation from the nine months of the human foetus to the nine years during which Horace in *The Art of Poetry* recommended that the manuscript of a poem should be kept in the closet, after full consultation with critical, discriminating friends (ll. 386–9; cf. Pope, 'Epistle to Dr. Arbuthnot', ll. 40–6). Hopkins was prevented by illness and death from carrying out his precepts in this particular case. Bridges could make nothing of *combs* in line 6 (which as ordinarily interpreted seems the weakest line in the sonnet, though some have praised it without offering a satisfying reading). All four transitive verbs are original and striking, though each provokes queries: the mother/poet *wears* the child/poem (*OED*, para 8, 'To carry about with one in one's heart, mind, or memory'); *bears* it (carrying its weight, not giving birth to it?), *cares* [for] it and finally *combs* it. A letter of explication from Hopkins to Bridges could have cleared up our queries. Bridges, puzzling no sense out of *combs*, substituted *moulds* from another Hopkins poem (No. 60, l. 104). I have discussed his action in the Fourth Edition, pp. lii–iii, but may add here that Hopkins himself frequently urged changes of wording in Bridges's poems, and felt very strongly the necessity of some substitutions he recommended. Dr W. H. Gardner rightly restored the text, conjecturing that Hopkins might have used *combs* in the 'double sense of (1) unravel; put in order, as by combing, and (2) store, mature – as in a honeycomb; cf. No. 68: "Patience fills/His crisp combs . . ." ' (4th edn, p. 297). Dr R. Bremer has carefully examined all the uses of *combs* he could find in Hopkins's verse and prose (the three he omits do not affect his analysis): he concludes that the verb is here used in the sense given in the *OED*, paragraph 5, 'Of a wave: "To roll over, as the top of a wave; or to break with a white foam"' – a definition from Webster's *Dictionary* of 1828. But this usage is intransitive. Bremer stretches the sense therefore into 'filling to the crest, to the utmost' (*English Studies*, Vol. 51, No. 2, April 1970, pp. 144–8).

A possible alternative may be found in a letter from Hopkins to Dixon of October 1881 (*Correspondence*, p. 77), in which he alludes to the two images which he liked best in all Dixon's poetry.

One was 'the heart combed round with hair' (from 'Love's Consolation', *Selected Poems,* pp. 47–8). It ran:

>   of us some
> About our hearts meshed the loved hair with comb
> Of our great love, to twine and glisten there,
> And when 'twas stiffened in our life blood dear
> Then was it rent away; . . .

But perhaps the most direct interpretation would regard the four verbs of line 6 as charting the progress of the infant/poem from conception to its ninth year. The mother/poet carries the embryonic poem within his mind (*wears*); then he gives birth to the first lines on paper (*bears*); these he nourishes into growth (*cares*); finally, he polishes the poem into perfection (*combs*). The verb *cares,* used transitively to mean 'To take care of, tend', was an Irish idiom Hopkins himself contributed to the *English Dialect Dictionary*: his examples were 'To care a horse *or* a room'.

In line 7 the idea of the poet as a widow, doing her best to form the child left in her charge, is an interesting one, though textual editors are more aware of trial and error than of sure purpose among widows' drafts. What is important here is Hopkins's conviction that his state of mind would not preclude him from completing a poem if only he was given the 'one rapture of an inspiration'. He suggests that his lines have become 'laboured' (changed to *lagging*), because they lack 'The fire, the fall, the keenness, the creation' (one thinks of the 'blue-bleak embers' falling and lanced open in 'The Windhover', No. 36, ll. 13–14). That the final version of line 12 (much praised but not interpreted helpfully) owes something to the display flights and mating songs of birds in Spring, may be supported from another early reading: 'The wild wing, waft, cry, carol, and creation'. Bridges must certainly have been moved by his ailing friend's stark view of his own life, found in these working drafts after his death: 'This withered world of me, that breathes no bliss'. It is a pity that circumstances prevented a poem which has many beautiful phrases in it from being subjected to the maturing agencies of time and critical discussion.

Part Three FIRST EXPERIMENTS – THE APPRENTICE-POET

'Il Mystico' to 'St Thecla' (Nos 77–136)

This miscellany of unfinished poems, poetic fragments and other pieces finished but rather slight, belongs to Hopkins's pre-Jesuit days – with the possible exception of the last item in it (No. 136). It shows the wide range of experimentation through which the young poet trained himself for achievements in poetry and painting. In both fields careful observation was, in his day, a necessary preliminary. An analysis of these sixty numbers could occupy a hundred pages, but here we can look in detail only at the most ambitious poems. They show him cleverly playing 'the sedulous ape' with such diverse models as Milton and the Rossettis, Richard Garnett and Keats, Coventry Patmore, old ballads and, of course, Tennyson. New light will be thrown upon the character of his work in this section as we discover the various categories into which many of the remaining pieces fall, with briefer commentaries. A strictly chronological approach, though followed in the new edition of the Poetical Works, would confuse the general outlines of this analytic sketch.

No. 77 Il Mystico Sent to E. H. Coleridge, 3–6 September 1862 (*Further Letters,* pp. 8–14). Consciously modelled on Milton's 'Il Penseroso' and 'L'Allegro', it changes metre at l. 11, as he turns from abusive dismissal of sensual desires and welcomes spiritual ones. Seeking mystic union with the divine light through pre-dawn visions (ll. 11–40), he summons an angelic guide to appear. Aspirations for purity and insight are embodied (ll. 41–64) in Sir Galahad (cf. Tennyson's poem on that Arthurian visionary, a lifelong influence, as No. 48, l. 40, shows). The unswerving searchers of mysteries in the digression of ll. 48–52 are from Ezekiel 1. From mid-point, however, Hopkins's Romantic yearning for lonely heights (cf. No. 15) and delight in the countryside assert themselves, as he imagines himself lifted towards the upper clouds with a skylark (ll. 65–92). The gurgling rill of its singing is finely described – better than in No. 122 ('O what a silence'), and less obscurely than in the famous sonnet 'The Sea and the Skylark' (No. 35). But though the day-long drifting in *aether rare* suits the poet's profound preference for quiet and solitude, no lark could sustain that planing flight. The *silver rivulet* of song cascading to earth leads artistically to the last section (from l. 93), where the mystic, gazing up from the ground as sunset enriches a *silver shower* of rain, feels himself drawn upwards and absorbed into the luminous rainbow. Because Hopkins had not kept in check his ecstasy over natural beauty, his initial satisfaction with what he had written seems to have evaporated before he could finish and revise the poem. The poem breaks off with a rather unconvincing turn towards the concept of *pure souls*.

No. 80 Pilate Drafted ?May/June 1864, ending fair-copied in October: in octosyllabic rime royal, it reshapes some of the numerous legends about Pontius Pilate's fate after he delivered Christ to crucifixion. One tradition tells that he spent his last years in remorse among the rocky austerities and snow of the Swiss Mt Pilatus (the name of which is popularly derived from him), eventually drowning himself in a mountain tarn. His spectre is said to haunt the summit, causing its storms, and to be occasionally seen washing his hands as in a basin (st. 9). The poet shows him in a sort of Purgatorial state, impervious as a spirit to cold or heat, but suffering the pangs of isolation from God and man, from which he can only hope that Christ may at the Day of Judgment release him. Because of his efforts to save Jesus ('Sir! Christ! against this multitude I strain' – st. 8) he was thought by many to have some chance of salvation (st. 11). His immunity from physical pain makes the self-crucifixion he plans (last three sts) a symbolic attempt at atonement rather than a masochistic act. This idea could have been suggested to Hopkins by Clarkson Stanfield's dramatic engraving of 'Mount Pilate', with a wayside cross from which an almost lifesize figure hangs. It illustrated Scott's *Anne of*

Geierstein, a Waverley novel well known to the Hopkins family, where the legend of Pilate lends terrible force to a furious mountain storm.

No. 81 A Voice from the World Drafts run from about June 1864 to as late as June 1865. The young Hopkins, to our surprise, is more persuasive as a renounced lover in 'A Voice from the World' than as 'Il Mystico' (No. 77), for the poet-artist's pursuit of nature's inscapes is here disciplined. The model is Christina Rossetti's 'The Convent Threshold' (reprinted in Hopkins *Poems,* p. 346), which like almost all her treatments of love is unhappy and steeped in asceticism despite its erotic urges. Hopkins composes the man's protest, raised against her flight to the cloister in rejection of their guilty love – the precise situation is left romantically vague. He compares her parting letter crying 'Repent, repent' to the voice of the melancholy cuckoo which has survived alone into the winter, shaping 'Five notes or seven, late and few' (ll. 6, 7, 23). The tense setting and reversed repetition of the call impart a power altogether lacking in the plain naturalist's observation in No. 98 (xxxvii), 'When cuckoo calls and I may hear,/And thrice and four times and again'. He hints at the irreligious basis of their love (in a strongly Anglo-Catholic environment) by describing its springtime as 'scarce perceivèd Lent' (l. 11; cf. 'my Lent of lovelessness', *Journals,* p. 43). In the second section she seems as remote in her convent as a star almost beyond human sight, like the seventh sister in the Pleiades cluster. Most readers will find a convincing strength in the passionate pain of ll. 51–3, though ll. 64–7 strike us now as emotionally indulgent.

No. 118, 'But what indeed is ask'd of me?', may be a further fragment of this poem. What a pity that it was never completed. Careless handling of these tiny notebooks in bygone years has so smudged some pencilled pages that my repeated efforts to decipher them have still left some *lacunae.* (In No. 123, 'Mothers are doubtless happier for their babies', one word written on top of another defies confident transcription.)

No. 83 The Lover's Stars July 1864, imperfectly revised fragments which editors have tried to fit together into a poem. Hopkins described it as 'a trifle in something like Coventry Patmore's style'. He uses the metre of Patmore's *The Angel in the House* (2nd edn,

1858), parts of which he knew almost by heart (*Further Letters*, pp. 213, 298–9), but reverses the fortunes of the lovers. In Patmore the unsuccessful rival is the one whose ship takes him to the East for two years' service, while Honoria accepts the stay-at-home, who has tea with her in the breezy rose-garden and dances with her at the ball. But a writer of popular romances, playing Destiny, would bring the noble officer miraculously unscathed through every peril to win the lady on his return. The 'silver seed' (sts 3, 4) may represent the heroine's thoughts flitting lovingly after him abroad while his rivals think she is attending to their chatter. Sts 5–7 show 'Fate' dooming the unadventurous over-confident suitor to shattering rejection.

No. 109 The Queen's Crowning Entered in notebook about December 1864. Hopkins knew Coventry Patmore's anthology called *The Children's Garland from the Best Poets* (London, 1862), which contained eighteen old ballads, including 'Sweet William's Ghost', where the fetch of a dead man also seeks reunion with his living love. The metrical variations are particularly interesting, e.g. the trochaic opening.

No. 120 Continuation of Richard Garnet's Nix About 7 July 1865. The professor in Hopkins's dialogue 'On the Origin of Beauty' quotes Garnett's poem (reprinted Hopkins *Poems*, p. 351) from Patmore's *Children's Garland*; he praises its 'exquisite artifice' which makes it seem as natural as an old ballad (*Journals*, pp. 111–4). Hopkins's continuation provides the motive for the crafty water-spirit's theft of golden hair and blue eyes from the bride, now imprisoned in an undersea cave – she plans to rob her of her lover.

It is not surprising that a large proportion of the lines in this early miscellany of Hopkins's undergraduate poetry describe the appearances of nature. But less expected are the obscure cross-references in many 'fragments'. There seems to me to be a simple explanation for this, as well as for his failure to complete various dramatic works at which he toiled over many months.

The poetic activity which Hopkins enjoyed most even at this stage was identifying the exact shape of some individually distinctive beauty and the recapturing of this in words. Yet purely descriptive verse is in small demand. There is little scope for poems about the iridescence of 'The Peacock's Eye' (No. 86), or on such fanciful and outmoded themes as 'Love preparing to fly' (No. 87). Readers expect more human interest. But Hopkins was reserved, and not nearly as involved with the study of other people's characters and motives as he later became when a priest and confessor. Some of these pieces, therefore, which purport to be studies of a dramatic situation are simply products of his passion for verbalizing impressions, and the hints they contain of being fragments broken off some dynamic narrative poem or play are merely gestures, indications of what could be done with such details if he had the inclination.

Perhaps the most transparent example is 'Io' (No. 99), which Hopkins told Baillie was a 'fragment' (*Further Letters*, p. 221; cf. 252–3). If the original inspiration behind this leisurely portrait of a brown and cream Guernsey (?) had been the story of the unfortunate maiden transformed into a snow-white heifer by Zeus and later driven in frantic flight from the tormenting gadfly, Hopkins would not have chosen as model such a placid beast or emphasized its unsuitable colour. Nor would he have selected as metrical form for a vigorous narrative the last six lines of a Shakespearian sonnet, each stanza brought to a stop by its heroic couplet. Clearly he was practising for a career in painting and poetry by observing and verbalizing; identification with Io was an afterthought to make the exercise legitimate to his less artistic friends, who would not waste time on poeticized cows. (How astonished he would have been if he had known it would be printed in his collected poems a century later!) Hence the predominance of fragments – they came to a halt once his basic urge to describe had been satisfied; as he put it himself, 'though I finish nothing, I am not idle' (*Further Letters*, p. 214).

Many of the pieces can be most revealingly sorted into one of three categories. Take the action of the wind for illustration. No. 98 gathers together the simplest examples of sense impressions. In (i) the wind 'Runs his fingers through the wheat': a light breeze only grooves a grain-field here and there. The last line borrows *dusk* from 'The Lady of Shalott' (l. 11) to indicate the slight darkening of the heads as they dip before it. More elaborate is 'A Windy Day in Summer' (No. 78), showing how differently various trees are affected by a stronger wind – elms, willows, chestnuts, aspens – thus anticipating Hardy's opening to *Under the Greenwood Tree*. Wondering how he could use his studies of the wind, Hopkins in No. 98 (ii) and (iii) introduces undefined observers listening to the cooing of a contented wind or the laughter of a brisker one (cf. No. 160, ll. 1–3, a translation from Aeschylus's *Prometheus Desmotes*, a play in which Io also figures). Less successful is No. 90, 'Why if it be so', where a storm of wind and rain in which he had been caught near Bala (*Further Letters*, p. 212) is dissipated into Jacobean rhetoric to be kept in stock for some unwritten dramatic bluster.

No. 130, 'The earth and heaven, so little known', represents the next level of sophistication, where the wind is linked with the never-ceasing changes viewed from his tower by the unchanging philosopher – the country counterpart of 'The Alchemist in the City' (No. 15). The drive behind this fascinating poem issues out of profound concepts, e.g. from Plato's *Timaeus*, where the philosopher's eye is a sort of faulty analogue of the imperturbable *anima mundi* placed in the centre of the universe (34 b, 47). The poem also absorbs such 'words in search of a purpose' as *valve* (*Journals*, p. 65), here applied to a swallow/swift folding its pennoned tail as it comes to rest on a tower moulding. Yet the delight in description somewhat unbalances the original purpose; we have to wait for such poems as 'The Wreck of the Deutschland' (No. 28) and 'That Nature is a Heraclitean Fire' (No. 72) to find the action of the wind in contexts which it greatly enriches, and which in turn give it human importance.

The same categories (raw material for poetry, partially applied metaphors, and embodiment in full if not wholly appropriate settings) may be further illustrated from star images. No. 98 again proffers simple metaphors: in (xxiv) e.g. the night sky is a 'lantern/Pointed with piercèd lights'; (xxii), 'How looks the night?' tries to find for some products of the star-gazing he so enjoyed a dramatic setting such as a Shakespearian one he had minutely studied, where references to the 'patines of bright gold' and the heavenly harmonies of the spheres contributed to the idyllic love scene in the *Merchant of Venice* (see *Journals*, p. 11). A more animated use for the same idea of a crowded sky is (xxix), 'The stars were packed so close that night', the occasion alluded to being presumably as yet uncreated. But the fragment stayed in his mind, and some years later (1868), when a little journal in his school needed material, that stanza helped to generate 'The Elopement' (No. 135). But unlike Keats's 'Eve of St. Agnes' (one of the influences upon it), this hurried effort loses its tension because the sense impressions are not made ancilliary to the action. Hopkins was still an apprentice.

Sounds mingle with sights in No. 112, 'I hear a noise of waters' and No. 121, 'A noise of falls'. The lark's song, given too much attention in 'Il Mystico', recurs in No. 113, 'When eyes that cast about', and in No. 98 (xxviii) is found in company with the stars. In No. 122, 'O what a silence is this wilderness!', a vague human interest is added to two rather leisurely descriptive images.

The title given No. 79, 'A Fragment of Anything You Like' (the nucleus of which is the bewildered look of the moon when overtaken by daylight) indicates that the poet had at the moment only a general notion of how he could make suitable use of his discovery. The same title would fit a number of these fragments in which, for practice, he applies observations of nature to imaginary situations. Their enigmatic first lines sometimes 'refer back' to a context which probably never existed. ' – Yes for a time' (No. 101) demonstrates the art of using analogies to 'prove' either of two opposite contentions: a stage dialogue in this mode would soon empty a theatre. 'Boughs being pruned', No. 96 (vii), all in quotation marks, may have been pigeon-holed for a narrative poem in stanzas, and nobody need conjecture whose gain through loss is alluded to in line 7, 'Thus we shall profit . . .'. Prepared for some declamatory historical play, 'No, they are come' (No. 104) seems to lavish upon an invading army a series of metaphors, Biblical and Elizabethan. Still more enigmatically shorn of an intelligible story is No. 92, 'Glimmer'd along the square-cut steep', which begins with the tail-end of a sentence, and mingles sharp detail with an ominous and misty allegory. It is futile to ask ourselves who is threatened in No. 106 by 'The cold whip-adder unespied'. These are studio exercises. They are closely related to his patches of dramatic and narrative verse because both appear to have arisen from his wish to use his precise knowledge of the face of nature, either as artistic backgrounds or poetic metaphors for things which interested him less – imprecisely imagined characters and stock incidents from Renaissance drama. How seldom do these fragments analyse *human* faces. In No. 93 even the diapering 'loops of veins' seems to have come from an illuminated manuscript rather than a person, and his Donne-like vision of 'the men before the flood' dissolves after three lines.

Another favourite natural sight, already met in 'Il Mystico', was the rainbow. It figures in No. 84, 'During the eastering of untainted morns', among other moments of intensity (cf. No. 85, ' – Hill,/Heaven and every field, are still'). In No. 91, 'It was a hard thing to undo this knot', the scientific fact that the rainbow each man sees differs from his neighbour's is confusingly associated with the difficulty of opening some unspecified mental or spiritual knot. (A still slighter excuse is found in No. 108, where five lines showing exactly how the Pearl Underwing moth hides its rose wings below its grey ones in skilful camouflage are applied to rosy and sombre thoughts.) 'The rainbow' (No. 100) is a sort of crayon drawing in an artist's sketch-book, a necessary prelude to attempts at a full picture. Just such a rainbow passage in fact occurs in part iii of 'Richard' (No. 107). This was a pastoral poem in heroic couplets (cf. Keats's 'Endymion') at which he worked spasmodically from about the June of 1864 to July 1865. The moods of his shepherd Richard and poetic Sylvester obviously stirred his imagination less than the moods of the sky with its 'attuning stress' (an experience which as a mature poet he imbued with mysterious significance in 'Spelt from Sibyl's Leaves', No. 61, l. 1).

Like many other basically undramatic nineteenth-century poets, Hopkins felt that he *should* feel an urge towards drama (see *Further Letters*, p. 221). In his Jesuit days he repeatedly returned without much success to such projects as a play about St Winefred (see notes to Nos 59 and 152). In his tiny Oxford diaries unlinked passages from his dramatic 'Floris in Italy' (No. 102) recur between about August 1864 and September 1865, among a hundred pages of prose description and other poems. Though theatrically rather stale, and strongly reminiscent of Shakespeare and his successors, its blank verse contains closely observed details and happy turns of expression. 'Lodge his eyes fast' in line 20 of (i) applies to the eyelashes the technical word for crops laid flat by the wind, which is used literally in 'The Summer Malison' (No. 114). The *Journals* also prints the beginning of a comic scene from 'Floris' (pp. 42–3), though we have no proof that the mad scene with its un-Italian characters on pp. 44–5 was also meant for it.

The same doubt applies to the second passage of verse, No. 102 (ii), another reminiscence of Arthur's Britain, a subject which inspired him (cf. No. 77). But 'I am like a slip of comet' (No. 103) may well have been intended for 'Floris', to be put into the mouth of Giulia (a 'mere slip of a girl'?): the speech reflects a time before the discovery of Uranus (since Saturn is spoken of as the last planet). Even his fragmentary pieces should not be underestimated.

'Castara Victrix' (No. 125) offers some stilted conversation at 'the picnic or whatever we call it', perfunctorily placed between an account of 'dwarf and sourèd oaks' that 'Crept all along a hill' and an analysis of the reason a beautiful face weighs with the hero. We need not mourn the demise of this play: its best part might have been the melodious song, 'Who loves me here' (No. 124) assigned to Daphne, listed among the characters in *Journals*, p. 65. Songs he could manage better than dialogue or plot. 'Now I am minded to take pipe in hand' (No. 105) weaves poetic nature notes into an intricate lyrical pattern, perhaps too involved for a song: without its context the last four lines are obscure. But No. 110, 'Tomorrow meet you?' is surely another song for dramatic use. 'Stephen and Barberie' (No. 111), a projected narrative poem, survives only in fifteen melancholy lines.

In contrast with the ambitious Elizabethan pastiches and narrative poems come lively reminders that Thomas Hood was a family favourite. 'She schools the flighty pupils of her eyes' (No. 82) is full of puns, as are the two pieces 'By Mrs. Hopley' (No. 97). Mrs E. Duncan-Jones discovered that Thomas Hopley was a private school proprietor who in 1864 was sent to prison for causing the death of a pupil through severe discipline: his wife cheered his confinement with letters describing with what affection she and their children regarded him, only to sue for divorce the moment he was released (*TLS*, 10.10.68). Less congenial and careful are the satiric couplets on 'Miss Story's character' (No. 94), tossed off at the behest of Miss May: Hopkins and two Oxford friends, reading hard among the Welsh mountains for their forthcoming Moderations, found four (or three?) Miss Storys from Reading in the same lodging-house – 'a great advantage', said Hopkins, ' – but not to reading' (*Further Letters*, p. 213). Could Miss Story's 'dearest friend', so anxious to see that lady's character etched in verse, have been the poetess, 'Miss M.', to whom the third of the witty 'Seven Epigrams' in No. 96 is devoted? If so, Miss Story was amply revenged. Also personal and amusing is 'A Complaint' (No. 128), ostensibly from his sister Milicent, bewailing her forgotten birthday. We are reminded what a good ear Hopkins had for a catchy tune by the rhythm of No. 95, 'Did Helen steal my love from me?'. The middle verse – on Kate, we presume – he felt was 'bad' and did not record. Other little poems about people seem intended for children: 'As it fell upon a day' (No. 131), which runs like a nursery rhyme, and 'In the staring darkness' (No. 132). By contrast No. 134, 'Not kind! to freeze me with forecast', uses the metaphor of weather predictions for a situation which is not defined, but which sounds urgently personal: it may be connected with No. 13, 'Where art thou friend'.

Metrically these experiments show much variety. They include attempts at a much favoured verse form, the sonnet. 'Confirmed beauty' (No. 117) was copied into spaces in his diary above and below confession notes and casual memoranda, which split it into two seven-line parts. The gap should be closed up. At this stage he did not consistently subdivide his Miltonic sonnets, in which octave glides into sestet. Many changes in the printed format will be made in my fuller edition. Other sonnets ran out of energy prematurely. 'To Oxford' (No. 119) is two lines short: it was meant to companion the two sonnets in No. 12; the quatrain 'Bellisle' (No. 116) seems an earlier opening for it. 'When eyes that cast about the heights of heaven' (No. 113) breaks off once its purely descriptive treatment of the elusive lark is accomplished; we have only the first eleven lines of a Spenserian sonnet: the model has interlocking rhymes (*abab, bcbc, cdcd, ee*). His sonnet on 'Shakspere' (No. 126) suggests questions about the relationship between artist and saint which the missing sestet might have tried to answer: we have to turn to a much later fragment '(On a Piece of Music)', No. 148, for a partial solution.

The remaining poems to be considered are religious. 'O Death, Death, He is come' (No. 115) concerns Christ's descent into Hell (see notes to 'The Wreck', st. 33). As No. 127, 'Trees by their yield/Are known', falters to a stop, the poet seems about to argue in his own defence, which Hopkins does in a sonnet near the very close of his life, 'Thou art indeed just, Lord' (No. 74); some of the imagery is the same. 'Moonless darkness' (No. 129), written on Christmas Day, 1865, is a prayer for holiness which should be read

as a prelude to 'The Habit of Perfection' (No. 22), composed the
following month. The sixteen-line fragment of 'Summa' (No. 133)
belongs to the end of 1866. Hopkins intended 'to add a good deal
to it some day'; but anything more he drafted he apparently burned
with his other verses (*Letters*, pp. 15, 24), presumably realizing
that the summary treatise of his beliefs implied by the ambitious
title was inappropriate when his training as a religious had not
even begun. On the holocaust of his poetry see my *Hopkins*
(Writers and Critics), p. 13, and the further references there given.

The only autograph of 'St Thecla' (No. 136) and its briefer Latin
version (No. 180) is a fair copy with a number of emendations
which (from its handwriting) dates from about 1876. It may have
been composed much earlier. The *Apocryphal New Testament*,
high on Hopkins's list of 'Books to be read' early in 1865, contains
the 'Acts of Thecla and Paul', a legendary account of the Iconium
maiden's conversion through St Paul, and her miraculous
deliverance from fiery death at the stake, from wild beasts in the
arena and from ruffian assailants in her mountain cave. The
leisurely pace of Hopkins's heroic couplets, however, had not even
reached her conversion after thirty-four lines.

'Moonrise' to 'Epithalamion'
(Nos 137–59)

In the last of his completed poems 'To R.B.' (No. 76), Hopkins lamented the infrequency with which the *Sweet fire* of poetic inspiration flashed into his mind, and how briefly it burned when it did come. This final section contains, for the most part, pieces which were left unfinished or unpolished: the inspiring flame was quenched before it had engendered *immortal song*. Yet passages of striking beauty are frequent among them, and No. 149, '(Ashboughs)', is a Curtal Sonnet which deserves to rank with his best work, even though the poet had not decided between alternative endings.

No. 137 Moonrise, June 19 1876 Seven trisyllabic feet to the line, with overreaving. The moon in her last crescent is rising over the hill (Maenefa) behind St Beuno's College in the early morning near midsummer (when night brings no true darkness in higher latitudes). The poet, glimpsing her, quickly becomes fully awake as he watches the mountain (the *him* of l. 5) apparently still hooked (*fanged*) by one cusp of the rising moon. The 'paring of paradisaïcal fruit' (l. 3) to which the moon is whimsically compared is a longitudinal slice of plantain (*Musa Paradisiaca*)! The poem remained unfinished.

No. 138 The Woodlark July 5 [1876]. Sprung Rhythm, four stresses to the line. The text has been skilfully edited by Father Geoffrey Bliss, S.J. The woodlark (*Lullula arborea*), much less common and harder to spot than the skylark, sings more beautifully, often for an hour on end while soaring in wide circles. See *Journals*, p.

138. Lines 19–30 give a bird's eye view of a wheat-field still unripe – 'The ear in milk', i.e. yielding a milky liquid when squeezed. Poppies are interspersed, their bud-cases splitting open to reveal the blood-red silken petals. The poem makes an interesting contrast with 'The Caged Skylark' (No. 39) written the following year.

No. 139 On St Winefred A cheerful poem on a favourite saint, for whom see notes on No. 152. It was probably written (along with a Latin version, No. 175) about November 1875 at St Beuno's.

No. 140 'To him who ever thought with love of me' A verse paraphrase of a passage in *The Life and Revelations of St Gertrude* (see notes to st. 20 of the 'Wreck'). The date (discussed *Poems*, pp. xlv–vi) seems about April 1877.

No. 141 'What being in rank-old nature' Dated about June/July 1878 by Norman White from notes of a Royal Academy exhibition pencilled on the MS. (*Review of English Studies*, Vol. 20, No. 79, August 1969, pp. 319–20). Inspired by a piece of music, perhaps Purcell or Handel played on some great organ. Cf. Nos 45, 62.

No. 142 Cheery Beggar Written about July 1879. After the delayed spring and wet summer of 1879, the poem's effervescent rhythm reflects lighthearted relief at a spell of sunshine. The Plain is an open 'place' where the Oxford High meets four other streets, on the edge of the poorer district of St Clement's. This cheerful grateful beggar contrasts with the grasping ones, never satisfied, whom he mentioned in preaching, August 31, 1879 (*Sermons*, p. 20).

No. 143 'Denis, whose motionable, alert, most vaulting wit' A fragment written on the back of a version of 'Binsey Poplars', No. 43, an Oxford poem of March 1879.

No. 144 'The furl of fresh-leaved dogrose' Written like No. 143 on the back of a draft of 'Binsey Poplars' (March 1879), it may record a lad seen during a previous more sunny spring (see note to No. 142). The young boy's cheeks have patches of fresh briar-rose red, the paler skin around them being tanned by the strong spring sunshine to a lion-brown colour.

No. 145 (Margaret Clitheroe) The MS, undated, may belong to 1876–7. It contains only disordered fragments of a poem. Hopkins later planned to create a tragedy from the story of Margaret Clithero's martyrdom (*Letters*, p. 92). Living in the city of York under the Protestant Queen Elizabeth, she became a convert to the Catholic faith after her marriage. For sheltering priests and permitting mass in her home she was first imprisoned and at last in 1586 condemned to be crushed to death (*peine forte et dure*), the punishment decreed for those who refused to plead guilty or not guilty. She was declared Blessed in 1929 and a Saint in 1970.

No. 146 'Repeat that, repeat' A fragmentary description of cuckoo song, probably written in Oxford in 1879. Cf. the effect of hollow ground on its fluty call described in *Journals*, p. 232.

No. 147 'The Child is Father to the Man' One of three triolets by Hopkins published in *The Stonyhurst Magazine*, March 1883. The other two are printed in the Fourth Edition notes, pp. 312–3: '"No news in the *Times* today"', and 'Cockle's Antibilious Pills'. All three are discussed by Dr Alfred Thomas, *Modern Language Review*, Vol. 61, No. 2, April 1966, pp. 183–7. Cockle quoted the testimony of a Dr G. F. Collier that his was the 'best made pill in the kingdom' (e.g. *The Nation*, Dublin, 2.2.1884, p. 15).

No. 148 (On a Piece of Music) Though these stanzas from a draft were left in random order and undated, half were jotted down on a letter of 20 May [1879] from Walter Pater accepting Hopkins's invitation to dine with him. The title supplied by editors is misleading. The poem in fact consists of reflections upon the difference between aesthetic and moral judgments, and sprang from admiration of a building as beautifully proportioned as a musical composition.

No. 149 (Ashboughs) A Curtal Sonnet (see Reference Section), with two alternative endings. Undated. It could belong to May 1886 or a neighbouring December: both months figure in this deeply felt and moving comparison between the tender beauty of ashtrees with young buds seen against the grey smoky embers of a winter sky, and the more cheering fringes of green leaf at last breaking from those buds in May, with a blue spring sky behind them scattered with snow-white clouds.

No. 150 'The times are nightfall' An unfinished sonnet: for the *c c* rhymes of lines 9, 10 cf. Nos 53, 58, 70 and 73. The opening imagery recalls 'Spelt from Sibyl's Leaves' (No. 61). Undated: handwriting suggests 1886.

No. 151 'Hope holds to Christ the mind's own mirror out' This undated fragment is written on a scrap of paper which may have been torn from the *Dublin Note-book* of 1884–5. The idea is found in 2 Cor. 3: 18, 'It is given to us, all alike, to catch the glory of the Lord as in a mirror . . . and so we become transfigured into the same likeness, borrowing glory from that glory' (Knox).

No. 152 St Winefred's Well Mostly in Sprung alexandrines. Fragments of a play begun in 1879, added to in the 80s, but left unfinished. No. 59, 'The Leaden Echo and the Golden Echo', was to be a (final?) chorus in it. Winefred was the devout only daughter of Thewith, a noble Welsh landowner of Holywell, and niece of St Beuno (who is said to have lived about AD 640). She dedicated her maidenhead to God, but a local prince, Carádoc, became enflamed by her beauty. Her refusal of his advances after he had found her alone enraged him. When he struck off her head with his sword, a miraculous spring (St Winefred's Well) gushed from the bank on which her head came to rest. Some legends relate that St Beuno restored her to life and that his curse killed Carádoc instantly.

Hopkins's fascination with the legend is shown by some twenty-five references in his journals and correspondence from 1867–88: see especially *Letters*, pp. 40, 92, *Journals*, p. 261. The well is at Holywell, about eight miles from St Beuno's College, where he studied 1874–7. Pilgrimages to it have been made for over a thousand years, and numerous cures have been reported. See also No. 139, 'On St Winefred'.

No. 153 To his Watch Uncompleted sonnet, probably of 1885–6. Norman White in line 3 reads 'fail at our forge', suggesting that the beat of his heart and his watch are heard as rapid hammer strokes on an anvil (see *Poems*, pp. lxviii–ix),

No. 154 'Strike, churl' Undated fragment. The mention of a May hail-storm and the handwriting both point to May 1885 (see *Further Letters*, p. 171).

No. 155 'Thee, God, I come from' This beautiful hymn is found along with a draft of No. 62, and may therefore also date from 1885.

No. 156 'What shall I do for the land that bred me' A patriotic song, sent to Bridges September 1888 (see *Letters*, pp. 283–4 and 292, *Journals*, pp. 491–2 where the tune he composed for it is reproduced; also pp. 289, 301).

No. 157 On the Portrait of Two Beautiful Young People Begun at Monasterevan, Co. Kildare, Ireland, Christmas 1886, but never completed. Hopkins told Dixon (27 January 1887) that he had seen the portrait there: the brother and sister of the poem lived in that neighbourhood. The painting is reproduced in Fathers Milward and Schoder's *Landscape and Inscape* (following p. 80). It is described by Father A. Bischoff as a delicate painting 'on yellowing white velvet', showing a boy gazing tenderly at his sister, their faces 'set off by a wreath of leaves, bluebells and vines'. Norman White identifies them as Ursula and Leo Wheble, *English Language Notes*, Vol. 8, No. 3, March 1971, pp. 206–8. See *Letters*, pp. 248, 250, 253, 305–6. The stanza form is from Gray's 'Elegy'.

No. 158 'The sea took pity' A pencilled fragment, possibly of autumn 1886.

No. 159 Epithalamion An uncompleted wedding poem on his brother Everard's marriage, April 1888. His memory of boys bathing in the rock-pools of the Hodder, its deep bed overhung by 'rafts and rafts of flake leaves light', ran away with the epithalamion; when he came to apply it figuratively and spiritually to the occasion, his inspiration failed. The poem collapsed as he tried to work the names of Everard and his bride Amy into the wedding ode, and to transmute his parents and their children into fairy trees and decorative fernery. But see Winifred Nowottny, *Fourth Annual Lecture*, Hopkins Society (London, 1973), pp. 8–10.

Reference Section

Baillie, A. W. Mowbray (1843–1921). A brilliant friend and correspondent of Hopkins; he was his contemporary at Balliol, Oxford, where he obtained Firsts in Moderations and Greats (1862–6). He then joined the Inner Temple and was called to the Bar, but after a few years (1874) had to abandon his conveyancing owing to tuberculosis. In Egypt he added a knowledge of Arabic to his classical and modern languages. Returning to England cured, he resumed a correspondence with Hopkins which had begun in 1863 and which continued till 1888 (see *Further Letters*, pp. 199–294). They shared an interest in art and music, but Hopkins did not feel free to send him his mature poems for comment or often discuss spiritual matters with him (pp. 226–7). Their most animated exchange of letters was over the extent of Egyptian influence upon Greek civilization and the names of her deities, on which Hopkins was full of incautious but fascinating conjectures (pp. 258ff). Baillie's replies to his ebullient and amusing correspondence have unfortunately vanished.

Bridges, Robert (1844–1930). The friend and fellow-poet to whose provocative stimulus and lifelong interest in safeguarding and commenting upon his poetry Hopkins owed an incalculable debt, in spite of Bridges's periodic failures of sympathy and anti-Catholic sentiment. Hopkins practised the same sort of bracing and therapeutic criticism upon Bridges's poems, though probably with more diplomacy. Born the same year as Hopkins, and entering Oxford a term after him in 1863, Bridges at first shared with him an earnest Anglican High Church outlook, and soon became one of his friends. When Hopkins decided to enter the

Jesuit novitiate he asked Bridges to preserve corrected versions of certain of his poems, and later he regularly sent him autograph poems for safe-keeping and criticism. Though only Hopkins's side of their correspondence has been preserved (in *Letters*), we can glimpse the part Bridges played in keeping within bounds the Jesuit's tendency towards eccentricity and obscurity, and in making him develop his prosodic and other theories more systematically. After Hopkins's death (June 1889) Bridges wrote to C. H. Daniel, who had privately printed his own early poems, to arrange for many of Hopkins's poems to be so printed. Owing to causes not yet fully understood this project was shelved, and a few selected poems were published in anthologies between 1889 and 1918, when Bridges edited the First Edition. But even after the lapse of thirty years since his death, Hopkins's poetry was still bolder in its innovations than the public could readily enjoy. The Second Edition, published the year Bridges died was more warmly received.*

Bridges, who had gone up to Oxford originally with the intention of taking holy orders, later decided to practice medicine until he was forty in order to acquire enough knowledge of human nature to enrich his poetry. When Hopkins sent him his 'Wreck of the Deutschland' in 1877 Bridges was a seriously overworked physician in the casualty department of St Bartholomew's Hospital, London, faced with the diagnosis and treatment of some 31,000 patients a year. A few years later (1881) an almost fatal illness forced him to retire from medicine. He had already printed privately several anonymous collections of his verse, and thereafter published in his own name volumes of poetry and verse drama, benefiting from Hopkins's criticism. In 1913 he was made Poet Laureate. His last poetic work, *The Testament of Beauty* (1929) brought him the Order of Merit. His poetry is at present undervalued, but thanks to the work of Professor Donald Stanford among others a revival of interest in it is taking place. (See his *In the Classic Mode: the Achievement of Robert Bridges*, Newark and London, 1978).

---

* On the relationship between the two poets, see Elisabeth Schneider, *Dragon in the Gate*, pp. 126–43, my own article on 'Hopkins, Bridges and the Modern Editor', in *Editing British and American Literature*, 1880–1920, ed. Eric Domville (N.Y.: Garland, 1976), pp. 9–30, and Professor J.-G. Ritz's excellent book, *Robert Bridges and Gerard Hopkins: a Literary Friendship*, Oxford University Press, 1960.

Counterpoint. A cross-rhythm, usually set up in common metre by the introduction of one, two or three trochaic feet into a basically iambic line. See *Poems*, pp. xlv, 263, 265, 270, 274, for instances (marked by a figure-of-eight on its side ∞ or by the double-hooked signs ∽ ∾ used in music for turns), such as 'The world is charged with the grandeur of God' (p. 263). Thus in No. 47, 'The Handsome Heart', lines 9–10, though seventy percent of the feet are rising and the sonnet is predominantly iambic, we receive the impression of falling rhythm because of three counterpointed feet (here italicized):

> *Manner*ly-hearted! more than handsome face —
> *Beauty's bearing* or muse of mounting vein . . .

Single feet are often marked as counterpointed (reversed), though Hopkins said that such ordinary inversions did not set up a true counterpoint rhythm (*Poems*, p. 46; *Correspondence*, p. 78). See *Correspondence* p. 15 for Miltonic prototypes, and p. 43 for Dixon's mistaken example from Tennyson. Counterpoint can be frequently felt in Sprung Rhythm, but its presence there is obscured by the conventional rule of always starting (or always ending) a foot with a stress. In No. 41, 'The Loss of the Eurydice', line 13 'She had come from a crúise, tráining séamen', a reversal of rhythm from rising to falling can be sensed after *cruise*, and in common rhythm the line would be treated as two anapaests, followed by two trochees in counterpoint. But as this is a Sprung Rhythm poem, scanned in rising rhythm, *train* becomes a mono-syllabic foot, followed by an iamb and an extra slack syllable, so that the whole line is still thought of as rising and no counterpoint sign is used (*Correspondence*, p. 40). But in 'Brothers', though this was in Sprung Rhythm, he specified 'reversed or counterpointed rhythm allowed in the first foot' (*Poems*, p. 279).

Curtal Sonnets. 'Pied Beauty' (No. 37), 'Peace' (No. 51), and '(Ashboughs)' (No. 149). The name, given them by Hopkins himself (*Poems*, p. 269), makes them analogous to a smaller breed of horse, not merely to animals with docked tails: they are compressed, not simply cut short. In his 'Author's Preface' (*Poems*, p. 49) Hopkins intended to show that he had reduced to three-quarters both the normal octave (the two quatrains become two tercets, rhyming *abc*, *abc*) and the sestet (cut to four lines and a tailpiece). But his exercise in proportion went astray: he shows us only a clumsy way of adding 6 and 4½, now enshrined in the *OED*, *Supplement A–G*. The tail in 'Pied Beauty', accented in the MSS *Práise hím*, makes two full monosyllabic feet; in the other Curtal Sonnets the final half-lines are each three feet (six syllables). See the commentary on the three poems.

Cynghanedd or **consonant-chime.** The name given by Welsh poets to various complicated patterns of alliteration and internal rhyme on which their type of verse called the *cywydd* is constructed: these were imitated or adapted by Hopkins for his English verse (see e.g. *Letters*, p. 163, *Correspondence*, p. 15). The finest investigation of his use of these Welsh devices is by the German scholar, Dr Christoph Küper, *Walisische Traditionen in der Dichtung von G. M. Hopkins* (Bonn, 1973), though by insisting upon the syllabification of English words according to Germanic rules Dr Küper rejects as imperfect some Hopkins copies which satisfy my ear. Küper lists some three hundred examples in Hopkins. In the simplest form, *cynghanedd lusg* ('trailing'), the penultimate syllable in the line rhymes with a syllable anywhere earlier in it. Hopkins matches this in the first two lines of 'Felix Randal' (No. 53), 'O is he dead *then*? my duty all *end*ed,/. . . mould of *man*, . . . hardy-*hand*some'. In *cynghanedd groes* ('cross'), all the consonants in one part of the line (with specified exceptions) must alliterate in the same sequence with all the consonants in the other part. As the Welsh *cywdd* has only seven syllables per line and our pentameters ten or more, rules difficult enough in Welsh become very burdensome indeed in English sonnets. Hopkins obtains something of the effect in 'Of the Yore-flood, of the year's fall' ('Wreck', st. 32). An easier variety, *cynghanedd draws* ('traverse'), allows a middle portion to be excluded from the alliterative scheme. Hopkins gets the general effect in his 'Warm-laid grave [of a] womb-life grey' (Wreck', st. 7): here the *r* of *warm*, being silent in Standard English, is omitted from the scheme, as is the *b* in *womb*; *of a* is the middle portion legitimately traversed. But strictly speaking both consonants of *laid* should alliterate with *life*.

In *cynghanedd sain* ('sound'), Hopkins's favourite model, the line is split in three; the last portions of the first and second parts rhyme, while the second and third parts are linked by *cynghanedd draws* or *groes*. Küper quotes over forty more or less regular examples from Hopkins, including 'The down-dugged   ground-hugged   grey' ('Wreck', st. 26).

Dr Küper has carried out a fascinating analysis of the proportion of vowel and consonantal sounds worked into patterns of *cynghanedd* or less involved echoes of alliteration and assonance in sample pieces by the Welsh poet Dafydd ap Gwilym, Hopkins ('The Sea and the Skylark', and 'The Windhover'), and other melodious Victorian poets. He finds that the Welsh poet linked about eighty percent of his, Hopkins fifty-seven percent, Swinburne (who is often thought to have sacrified sense to sound), under thirty-five percent, Tennyson and Christina Rossetti thirty-two percent and her brother Dante Gabriel about half of Hopkins's figure at twenty-seven percent. (A fuller analysis of *cynghanedd* is in Gardner's *Study*, ii. pp. 143–58.)

Dixon, Richard Watson (Canon) (1833–1900). Poet, friend and correspondent. As an undergraduate at Oxford (1852–6) Dixon wrote poetry, but under the influence of the Pre-Raphaelite painters Burne-Jones and Dante Gabriel Rossetti turned for a time to art. He was ordained in 1858, and during an interlude as schoolmaster in 1861 he taught Hopkins briefly in Highgate School, deepening his love for Keats. Hopkins came to admire Dixon's poetry; the Bodleian has a manuscript volume of his poems transcribed by Hopkins just before he entered the Jesuit order so that he could carry them round with him in his various moves. Dixon became minor canon of Carlisle Cathedral in 1868. His correspondence with Hopkins runs from 1878–88, during which they encouraged each other's poetry and exchanged helpful comments (see *Correspondence*). Hopkins summarized his career and provided an acute critique of his poetry for the 1885 revised edition of Thomas Arnold's *Manual of English Literature* (reprinted *Correspondence*, p. 177). Bridges edited a selection of his poems (1909) with a Memoir, and he is included in the *Dictionary of National Biography*. There is a good modern biography by James Sambrook, *A Poet Hidden* (University of London, 1962). A tiny book edited by Dixon, *The Bible Birthday Book* (London, 1887), contains a version of 'Morning, Midday, and Evening Sacrifice' (No. 49), but since the British Library copy has disappeared Hopkins scholars have been searching the world in vain for another one. Its discovery would be welcome news.

Duns Scotus, Joannes (1265–1308). This great Franciscan philosopher and theologian, who became known as the Subtle Doctor because of his complexity, gave lectures at Oxford on the *Sentences* of Peter Lombard between 1300 and 1304 (*Opus Oxoniense*). Later in the University of Paris he advanced ideas which during the 14th and 15th centuries were more influential than those which he opposed in St Thomas Aquinas. Though Aquinas's doctrines later prevailed, and (as he was interpreted by Suarez) became the basis of nineteenth-century Jesuit theology, Hopkins preferred Scotus. Scotus differed from other scholastic thinkers in teaching e.g. that the Incarnation was not simply due to the Fall of man, but had been planned from the beginning as the culmination of the creation (cf. *Sermons*, pp. 111ff, 170, 275, 296); also that God's infinite attributes, the prototypes of qualities He gave to created things and living beings, are capable of formal differentiation from each other. His belief that beings contained a principle of individuation or *haecceitas* seems to have encouraged Hopkins in his recognition of *inscape* (q.v.), but the two concepts are not the same. At a time when there were perhaps only two Scotists in England (*Journals*, p. 249), Hopkins discovered Scotus for himself while he was a philosopher at Stonyhurst through studying a valuable volume they had recently acquired with the Badeley Library, Scotus's *Opus Oxoniense*, printed in Venice in 1514. Despite its formidable black-letter Latin text, bristling with abbreviations, Hopkins not merely understood it, but became 'flush with a new stroke of enthusiasm' (*Journals*, p. 221). Thomas, in *Hopkins the Jesuit*, p. 99, n. 2, lists important discussions of the influence of Scotus upon Hopkins; to this we can add Devlin's notes in *Sermons* (see its index). Pick (*Gerard Manley Hopkins*, pp. 156–9) cautions against exaggerating Scotus's distinctiveness and influence. Hopkins, in 'Duns Scotus's Oxford' (No. 44, q.v.) praises Scotus for his championship of *realty* (the reality of essences) and of the Immaculate Conception of the Virgin Mary. Hopkins's clarification of Scotus is singled out in the *Catholic Dictionary of Theology* (1967, ii. 201).

Falling Feet/Rhythm. This prosodic term is applied to a foot (or rhythms made out of such feet) in which the ictus or stress comes first, as in the trochee [/x], dactyl [/xx], and first paeon [/xxx]. Hopkins uses and defines the terms in his Preface (*Poems*, p. 45) but did not invent them. Although the earliest prosodic use in *OED* is 1844, Thomas Campion employed *falling accent* and *rising accent* in 1602 to distinguish such words as *spírit* from *desíre* (*Observations in the Art of English Poesie*). See also **Sprung Rhythm**, and cf. *Journals*, pp. 274–5.

Free-ended. Lines not *overrove* into each other (e.g. 'Brothers', *Poems*, p. 279). See **Overreaving**.

Hangers. See **Outrides**.

Inscape. This, the most famous of Hopkins's coinages, was used from 1868 onwards either as noun or verb, in his *Journals*, spiritual writings and letters, but never in his poetry. It has now been embodied in the *OED*, *Supplement H–N* (1976), and defined thus: 'The individual or essential quality of a thing; the uniqueness of an observed object, scene, event, etc.'. Hopkins used the word in many contexts and with varying degrees of philosophical seriousness. 'All the world is full of inscape', he wrote (*Journals*, p. 230). His best known glosses concern its application to poetic style. Defending himself against Bridges's complaint that his verse erred 'on the side of oddness' he replied that just as he recognized each (good) composer by his distinctive melodies and each painter by his own characteristic designs, so 'design, pattern or what I am in the habit of calling "inscape" is what I above all aim at in poetry' (*Letters*, p. 66).

As Professor of Rhetoric at Manresa he told his students that the main interest in a poem was not its meaning but its *shape*, for 'Poetry is in fact speech only employed to carry the inscape of speech for the inscape's sake – and therefore the inscape must be dwelt on' (*Journals*, p. 289). And much later in Ireland he predicted that Ferguson's verse, like much current Irish poetry in general, would not endure in spite of its virtues of feeling, thought, flow and imagery, because it lacked 'the essential and only lasting thing . . . – what I call *inscape*, that is species [*OED* 7b, 'The essential quality or specific properties *of* a thing'] or individually-distinctive beauty of style' (*Further Letters*, p. 373). The *OED* definition, applicable to the wide range of matters in which Hopkins found inscape, wisely omits any mention of *beauty*, which needs to be interpreted in a medieval scholastic sense to be valid (*Sermons*, 201, 309). Nor does it mention *pattern*, which may be purely superficial (though Hopkins optimistically sought it even in designs on a picture frame, or glimpsed it in snow swept from a broom, *Journals*, pp. 246, 230). See below, **Scaping**. From his spiritual writings we can draw a much more profound gloss, where he speaks of 'natures or essences or "inscapes" and the selves, supposits, hypostases, or, in the case of rational natures, persons/ which wear and "fetch" or instance them' (*Sermons*, p. 146). In this stricter sense, inscape is not a superficial appearance; rather it is the expression of the inner core of individuality, perceived in moments of insight by an onlooker who is in full harmony with the being he is observing. It is the distinctive character (almost a 'personality') given by the Creator to a particular species of rock or tree or animal. Each separate species (or in man's case, individual) through its inscape reflects some fractional part of God's all-inclusive perfection. See 'As kingfishers catch fire' (No. 57) for a poetic exposition of these created 'selves' as being in fact at their best partial revelations of Christ.

The etymological origins of the word can only be guessed at. Professor V. de Sola Pinto conjectured that it might be related to 'inshape' used in a translation of 1587 (see *OED*) to express a Platonic idea: that in God 'there is a certaine Inshape, which Inshape as in respect of God, is the knowledge which God hath of himselfe; and in respect of the world, is the Pattern or Mould thereof; and in respect of itself, is very essence' (*TLS*, 10.6.1955). Cotter (*Inscape*, pp. 18–20), working from Hopkins's letters to Baillie of March and April 1887, suggests that the Greek *skopos* is the root: his book offers a philosophically precise investigation of inscape impossible in a brief note – see p. 126 for one definition.

For the relationship between inscape and the *law* of an object's being (used by Ruskin and copied by Hopkins), see my 'Hopkins among the Victorians', *English Studies Today*, 3rd series, Edinburgh, 1964, pp. 155–169.

A helpful pioneer study of inscape is in Peters, *Gerard Manley Hopkins*, 1948, chaps 1, 2, though we ought not to identify Scotus's *haecceitas* ('thisness', or as Auden might say, 'eachness') with inscape but rather with *pitch*. Father Devlin's notes to

Sermons, and his 'Essay on Scotus' (*The Month*, Nov.–Dec. 1946) provide a more searching analysis of Scotus's thought in relation to Hopkins. Heuser (*The Shaping Vision*, chaps 4, 6 and index) has enlightening comments and examples.

Instress. *OED, Supplement H–N* (1976) defines this Hopkins coinage (when used as a noun) as 'The force or energy which sustains an inscape'. Though this scarcely covers all his examples, it seems impossible to find a simple definition which will. As a verb it may, first, have a merely prosodic use, to 'throw a stress on' a syllable (*Journals*, p. 271). In his meditation on the Principle and Foundation he speaks of the nature given to finite beings which enables them 'to "function" and determine, to selve and instress' (*Sermons*, p. 125) – a process illustrated in his sonnet 'As kingfishers catch fire' (No. 57). The handsome heart (in No. 47) is shown as 'wild and self-instressed', carrying out its own 'fine function', actuated by spiritual energy. But as in the case of the Windhover, each self-revelation may at its best provide a glimpse of some divine attribute, for the stress originates in the Creator. On special days a starlit night or thunderstorm or sunset may carry Christ's instress: 'tho' he is under the world's splendour and wonder,/His mystery must be instréssed, stréssed' ('Wreck', st. 5, with prosodic markings from MS *A*). Note that with the verb, Hopkins shifted the emphasis to the second syllable (cf. the noun 'ímpress' and the verb 'to impréss').

As a noun, instress may apply to the selving force within a being: 'all things are upheld by instress and are meaningless without it'; he equates the 'depth of an instress' with 'how fast the inscape holds a thing' (*Journals*, p. 127, 1868). In man instress seems equivalent to the 'main stress or energy of the whole being' (*Sermons*, p. 137). Carried by a bridge or stem of stress from objects seen or a tune heard into an intuitively receptive mind, this instress can set up a responsive energy in the observer if conditions are propitious and he is undisturbed by distracting companions. On the intellect a three-lancet window may give 'a simple direct instress of trinity', while on the emotions a comet may pulse out a 'feeling of strangeness . . . and of threatening', a less pleasant 'awe and instress' (*Journals*, pp. 228, 215, 249). The instress may 'float' into the mind, or hit the senses with double impact (pp. 231, 199). A simple thing, such as a blue sky, may have its own instress, or a group of objects (perhaps tall larches on a slope near a lake and mill) or a whole landscape may be harmonized by a unifying instress and charm (pp. 253, 258). Hopkins also distinguished 'the true and the false instress of nature', 'running instress' and 'nervous and muscular instress' (*Journals*, pp. 204, 215, 238). See **Inscape** and the analysis in Heuser (*Shaping Vision*, chaps 4 and 5) and Cotter (index under both terms). The fullest study is by Leonard Cochran, O. P., *Hopkins Quarterly*, Vol. 6, No. 4, winter 1980, pp. 143–81.

Logaoedic. A Greek prosodic term, suggesting a rhythm between that of speech (*logos*) and song (*aoidē*), used by Hopkins in his Preface to describe accentual verse in which trochaic and dactyllic feet are intermingled (*Poems*, p. 45). More generally it could apply wherever we interchange two-syllabled with three-syllabled feet (*Correspondence*, p. 21). This is a half-way step on the road to Sprung Rhythm. See Schneider, *Dragon in the Gate*, pp. 54ff, for the probable influence of Swinburne's logaoedic lines upon Hopkins.

Outrides or **hangers.** Defined in his Preface (*Poems*, p. 48) as a licence in Sprung Rhythm, 'one, two, or three slack syllables added to a foot and not counting in the nominal scanning' – though Sprung Rhythm can in theory have any number of slack syllables between stresses. Indeed Hopkins himself, returning to a poem after an interval, might place his outride signs (slurs below the line ‿) under 'hurried syllables' different from those which he had at first felt were extra-metrical (see e.g. *Poems*, pp. 278–9, for changes between MSS *A* and *B* in 'Felix Randal'). The outrides in 'skate's heel' and 'wind-walks' (*Poems*, pp. 266, 269) demand a medium stress. At first Hopkins intended the outride only for common metre (*Letters,* p. 45) and referred to it as an 'outriding foot' – though the fact that an outride normally has no stress and may have only one syllable makes its description as a foot confusing. Elsewhere he calls them 'half feet' (*Poems*, p. 48). He enlarges on the subtlety of its contribution: an outride is, 'by a sort of contradiction, a recognized extra-metrical effect; it is and it is not part of the metre; not part of it, not being counted, but part of it by producing a calculated effect which tells in the general success' (*Letters*, p. 45). It was designed to lend sonnets in English some of the extra length they needed to

match sonnets in Italian (*Correspondence*, pp. 86–7). Examples from
the MSS are quoted in *Poems*, pp. 269, 272–3, 276, 287, etc., all in
Sprung Rhythm. 'Tom's Garland', though in common rhythm, has
'hurried feet', marked with slurs above the line. The two signs
overlap elsewhere, to the natural confusion of critics (e.g. Gardner,
Study, i. pp. 84, 284) because Hopkins at first utilized slurs below
the line as though they were elision signs above it (see facsimile of
'God's Grandeur' and 'The Starlight Night' in *Further Letters*, p.
144); there they simply blend together two syllables into an integral
part of the metre and are therefore not outride marks. True outrides
and another definition are shown in the facsimile of 'Harry
Ploughman' (*Letters*, p. 262) – the sign 'under one or more syllables
makes them extrametrical: a slight pause follows as if the voice were
silently making its way back to the highroad of the verse'.

Overreaving. The practice of organizing a poem in Sprung Rhythm
by stanzas rather than separate lines; e.g. he explained that in 'The
Loss of the Eurydice' 'The scanning runs on without break to the
end of the stanza, so that each stanza is rather one long line
rhymed in passage than 4 lines with rhymes at the ends' (*Poems*, p.
270). In practice this required subtle adjustments to the rhythm,
discussed in *Letters*, pp. 86, 120, but not always satisfactorily
achieved or consistently indicated by metrical markings in the
manuscripts. The term *overrove* frequently occurs in his metrical
descriptions; e.g. 'The Bugler's First Communion' is overrove, but
'Brothers', though also in Sprung Rhythm, is described as having
'lines free-ended and not overrove' (*Poems*, pp. 275, 279). See
also **Rove-over Rhymes**.

Patmore, Coventry (1823–96). Poet, friend of Tennyson, Ruskin
and the Pre-Raphaelites. He first met Hopkins in July 1883 when
visiting Stonyhurst for the 'Great Academy' (Speech Day), and
exchanged letters with him from then until 1888 (*Further Letters*,
pp. 295–393). Bridges transcribed many important poems by
Hopkins into MS *B* for Patmore's benefit in the first place, but
though Patmore was a Catholic, sympathetic to his themes, he was
overwhelmed by the Jesuit's simultaneous innovations in metre,
diction and syntax; he told him so in a letter which emphatically
stated his absolute conviction that Hopkins would 'never
conciliate' the reviewers (*Further Letters*, pp. 352–4). While

Patmore thus contributed to Hopkins's melancholy, he was repaid by time-consuming and deeply helpful suggestions from Hopkins on the revision of his own poems. Among Patmore's special interests was prosody. Some prosodists have regretted that Hopkins did not discover his work on English Metrical Law (1857), with its emphasis upon isochronous and dipodic feet (i.e. units of double feet), until he had developed his own prosodic analysis (see J. C. Reid, *The Mind and Art of Coventry Patmore*, 1957, pp. 230ff). For their discussion of metre see especially *Further Letters*, pp. 326–35. Patmore's theory of isochronous feet is mentioned in the article on Sprung Rhythm below. Bridges's efforts to reconcile Patmore to Sprung Rhythm are shown in Derek Patmore's 'Three Poets Discuss New Verse Forms' (*The Month*, August 1951, pp. 69–78), but Patmore's verdict was that Hopkins's 'poetry has the effect of veins of pure gold imbedded in masses of unpracticable quartz'. Patmore's own volumes of poetry include *The Angel in the House* (1854–6, 6th edn 1885), *The Unknown Eros* (1877), *Amelia* (1878). Among his prose works are *Principle in Art* (1889) and *Religio Poetae* (1893). His *Essay on English Metrical Law* was edited in a critical edition by M. A. Roth (Washington, 1961).

Rising Feet/Rhythm. Feet or rhythm in which the principal stress or ictus comes at the end, as in the iamb (x/), anapest (xx/), and fourth paeon (xxx/). See **Falling Feet**.

Rove-over or **Run-over Rhymes.** (See **Overreaving** for overrove lines.) This type of rhyme, probably derived from *odl gudd* in Welsh, places part of the rhyme at the end of a line, and the consonant to complete it at the beginning of the next. Examples from the 'Wreck' are *drew her/D*[ead] rhyming with *endured* (st. 14); *unconfessed of them* rhyming with *breast of the/M*[aiden] (st. 31); *Providence* rhyming with *of it, and/S*[tartle]. On the run-over lines in 'The Loss of the Eurydice' (No. 41, ll. 23, 67, 91) see above, p. 103. See also 'Hurrahing in Harvest' (No. 38, l. 7) and 'The Bugler's First Communion' (No. 48, l. 3). Father Bischoff has traced an example in St Thomas Aquinas's Corpus Christi hymn, 'Sacris solemniis', in which *Deitas* rhymes with *visita/S*[icut]. Hopkins mentions run-over rhymes in his *Letters* (pp. 48, 250), *Correspondence* (p. 15), *Poems*, p. 48.

Running Rhythm. Common metrical verse, distinguished from springing or **Sprung Rhythm** (q.v.) in his Preface (*Poems*, p. 45).

Scaping. Sometimes contrasted with **inscape** (q.v.), standing for surface pattern which does not spring from an inner force, as when he describes an artist as a 'master of scaping rather than of inscape' (*Journals*, p. 245). Elsewhere scaping is used in contexts somewhat ambiguously worded, but where he seems to be equating it with 'real inscape' or 'deep . . . inscape' (pp. 175, 204–5). Scaping and inscape seem clearly identified in his description of Holman Hunt's *Shadow of Death*, since 'feet not inscaped' is paralleled with 'veined too, which further breaks their scaping' (p. 248).

Slack. The light part of the foot, the unaccented syllable(s) as opposed to the ictus or stress. See *Poems*, p. 45; *Further Letters*, p. 333.

Sprung Rhythm. Writing to his brother Everard, 5 November 1885, Hopkins claimed that 'Sprung rhythm gives back to poetry its true soul and self. As poetry is emphatically speech, speech purged of dross like gold in the furnace, so it must have emphatically the essential elements of speech. Now emphasis itself, stress, is one of these: sprung rhythm makes verse stressy; it purges it to an emphasis as much brighter, livelier, more lustrous than the regular but commonplace emphasis of common rhythm as poetry in general is brighter than common speech. But this it does by a return from that regular emphasis towards, not up to [,] the more picturesque irregular emphasis of talk – without however becoming itself lawlessly irregular.' (*Hopkins Research Bulletin*, No. 4, 1973, p. 10).

Hopkins thus differentiated common or *running rhythm*, in which the feet tend to be regular, from *Sprung* [springing?] *Rhythm*, where the feet may vary from a stressed monosyllable to a four-syllabled paeon, or an even longer foot. The name suggests the natural grace of a deer springing down a mountainside, adjusting the length of each leap according to the ground it is covering. (Hopkins seems to have partly shared Patmore's theory that the beats should recur at roughly equal or isochronous intervals, but he accepted equality in strength as an alternative to equality in time – see *Letters*, pp. 81–2, 157.) In theory he anticipated modern prosodists in prescribing that each foot must have one main stress – thus debarring the *pyrrhic* [xx] and *tribrach* [xxx] – but no more than one main stress – so that a *spondee* [//] must be regarded as two separate feet, or else have one of its two equal stresses demoted to a medium stress. In scanning Sprung Rhythm Hopkins at first ended each foot after the stress, making every foot (except of course a monosyllable) rising, i.e. climbing from the unstressed to the stressed. In Sprung verse **Rising Rhythm** (q.v.) consists of iambs [x/], anapaests [xx/], fourth paeons [xxx/], etc., in any sequence, with monosyllabic feet [/] wherever desired. But later Hopkins preferred to follow the conventions of music: just as each bar normally opens with a beat so he began measuring the foot from the stress, creating *Falling Rhythm*. A *Sprung Rhythm* line, scanned as a musician would divide a melody into bars, would consist of trochees [/x], dactyls [/xx], first paeons [/xxx], etc., with monosyllabic feet [/] interspersed where necessary.

Contrary to popular belief, a Sprung Rhythm line cannot be recognized simply by the juxtaposition of two stresses, since ordinary iambic metre may have neighbouring stresses where it substitutes a trochee (e.g. in 'The world is *chárged wíth* the grandeur of God' [x/|x/|/x|/x|x/|]), and *vice versa*, or appear to have them because of an accentual spondee (see *Letters*, p. 215; *Correspondence*, p. 129). Sprung Rhythm brings two or even three stresses together by means of monosyllabic feet (e.g. in 'Spelt from Sibyl's Leaves', l. 2: 'tíme's vást, wómb-of-all' – two monosyllabic feet, each to be given the time of a whole foot, followed by a dactyl).

A stanza in Sprung Rhythm differs from a Free Verse paragraph in having a predetermined number of stresses in each first line, each second line, etc., to form a pattern, as with Part 1 of 'The Wreck of the Deutschland'. Free verse varies its stresses at will. In practice, Hopkins frequently incorporates in Sprung Rhythm verse some lines which the normal reader unconsciously treats as Free Verse intrusions because they clearly have more candidates for stresses than Hopkins's avowed pattern allows (e.g. 'The Wreck', st. 1, ll. 1, 2; st. 35, ll. 7, 8; 'Hurrahing in Harvest', l. 1; 'Brothers', see notes on its metre above, p. 141). Hopkins would no doubt have justified these lines by declaring that some of the stresses were secondary ones, emphasized in recitation but treated as without stress in metrical analysis (cf. *Poems*, p. 285 for his application of this argument to a poem in common rhythm).

Hopkins advances his theories of Sprung Rhythm in two prefaces (Poems, pp. 45–9, 255–6), in *Correspondence*, pp. 21–3, 39–42, etc. Sister Marcella Holloway gathers and discusses all the poet's own statements about Sprung Rhythm in *The Prosodic Theory of Gerard Manley Hopkins*, Catholic University of America Press, 1947, reprint 1964. For my analyses of poems in Sprung Rhythm see Index; and for a fuller discussion of its origins and subtleties see my *Hopkins*, chap. v; Gardner's *Study* ii, pp. 98–178; The Kenyon Critics chap. 3; and Father Weyand's *Immortal Diamond*, chaps iii, iv. The most thorough study of the rhythm of Hopkins's sonnets is in German, Hans Werner Ludwig's *Barbarous in Beauty*, Munich, 1972. Harvey Gross (*Sound and Form in Modern Poetry*, Ann Arbor, 1964, p. 93) remarks that Hopkins should have distinguished between metrical Sprung Rhythm and the nonmetrical type in 'The Leaden Echo' (No. 59). As a linguist he complains that 'Hopkins confuses the speaking of verse with meter, rhetorical stressing with basic structure'.

Underthought. Explained in a letter to Baillie (*Further Letters*, pp. 252–3): 'in any lyric passage of the tragic poets . . . there are – usually . . . – two strains of thought running together and like counterpointed; the overthought that which everybody, editors, see . . . ; the other, the underthought, conveyed chiefly in the choice of metaphors etc. used and often only half realised by the poet himself, not necessarily having any connection with the subject in hand but usually having a connection and suggested by some circumstance of the scene or of the story'. This idea has since then been demonstrated in the case of Shakespeare by Caroline Spurgeon, *Shakespeare's Imagery*, Cambridge, 1935, and by many others.

Select Bibliography of Books

Note For selected articles, see Index under authors' names. Exhaustive lists of books and articles will be found in the bibliographies listed below.

A BIBLIOGRAPHIES

Cohen, Edward H., *Works and Criticism of Gerard Manley Hopkins: a Comprehensive Bibliography*, Washington, D.C., Catholic University of America Press, 1969
Dunne, Tom, *Gerard Manley Hopkins: A Comprehensive Bibliography*, Oxford, Clarendon Press, 1976

B WORKS BY HOPKINS

i   For the full, standard editions, and the abbreviated titles under which they are quoted, see p. 12 above
ii   *Selections*
Gardner, W. H. (ed.), *Poems and Prose of Gerard Manley Hopkins*, London, Penguin Books, 1953; rev. 1969
MacKenzie, Norman H (ed.), *Poems by Gerard Manley Hopkins*, London, Folio Society, 1974
Pick, John (ed.), *A Hopkins Reader*, London, Oxford University Press, 1953; rev. and enlarged, Garden City, N.Y., Image Books, 1966
Reeves, James (ed.), *Selected Poems of Gerard Manley Hopkins*, London, Heinemann, 1953; paperback edn 1967
Storey, Graham (ed.), *Hopkins: Selections*, London, Oxford University Press, 1967

C BOOKS ON HOPKINS

Ball, Patricia M., *The Science of Aspects: The Changing Role of Fact in the Work of Coleridge, Ruskin and Hopkins*, London, Athlone Press, 1971

Bender, Todd K., *Gerard Manley Hopkins: The Classical Background and Critical Reception of his Work*, Baltimore, Johns Hopkins Press, 1966

Bergonzi, Bernard, *Gerard Manley Hopkins* (Masters of World Literature), New York, Macmillan, 1977

Bottrall, Margaret (ed.), *Gerard Manley Hopkins: Poems – A Casebook,* London, Macmillan, 1975

Boyle, Robert (S.J.), *Metaphor in Hopkins*, Chapel Hill, University of North Carolina Press, 1961

Cotter, James Finn, *Inscape: the Christology and Poetry of Gerard Manley Hopkins*, Pittsburg, University of Pittsburg Press, 1972

Downes, David A., *Gerard Manley Hopkins: a Study of his Ignatian Spirit*, London, Vision Press, 1960

—, *Victorian Portraits: Hopkins and Pater*, New York, Bookman Associates, 1965

Fulweiler, Howard W., *Letters from the Darkling Plain: Language and the Grounds of Knowledge in the Poetry of Arnold and Hopkins*, Columbia, University of Missouri Press, 1972

Gardner, W. H., *Gerard Manley Hopkins, 1844–89: a Study of Poetic Idiosyncracy in Relation to Poetic Tradition* (2 vols), [London, Secker and Warburg, 1944–9]; rev. Oxford University Press, 1966 (cited as *Study*)

Grigson, Geoffrey, *Gerard Manley Hopkins*, London, British Council, 1955

Hartman, Geoffrey H., *The Unmediated Vision: an Interpretation of Wordsworth, Hopkins, Rilke, and Valery*, New Haven, Yale University Press, 1954; repr. New York, Harcourt, Brace, 1966

— (ed.), *Hopkins: A Collection of Critical Essays,* Englewood Cliffs, N.J., Prentice-Hall, 1966

Heuser, Alan, *The Shaping Vision of Gerard Manley Hopkins*, London, Oxford University Press, 1958, repr. New York, Archon Books, 1968

Holloway, Marcella M., Sister, *The Prosodic Theory of Gerard Manley Hopkins*, Washington, D.C. 1947; repr. 1964

Johnson, Wendell Stacy, *Gerard Manley Hopkins: the Poet as Victorian*, Ithaca, Cornell University Press, 1968

Keating, John E. [S.J.], *'The Wreck of the Deutschland': an Essay and Commentary*, Kent, Ohio, Kent State University Press, 1963

Kenyon Critics, The, *Gerard Manley Hopkins*, [Norfolk, Conn., New Directions, 1945]; London, Dennis Dobson, 1949, repr. 1975

Lees, Francis Noel, *Gerard Manley Hopkins*, New York, Columbia University Press, 1966

MacKenzie, Norman H., *Hopkins* (Writers and Critics series), Edinburgh, Oliver and Boyd, 1968

Mariani, Paul, *Commentary on the Complete Poems of Gerard Manley Hopkins*, Ithaca, Cornell University Press, 1970

Milroy, James, *The Language of Gerard Manley Hopkins*, London, Andre Deutsch, 1977

Milward, Peter (S.J.), *Commentary on G. M. Hopkins' 'The Wreck of the Deutschland'*, Tokyo, Hokuseido Press, 1968

—, *A Commentary on the Sonnets of G. M. Hopkins*, Tokyo, Hokuseido Press, 1969

— and Raymond V. Schoder (S.J.), *Landscape and Inscape: Vision and Inspiration in Hopkins's Poetry*, London, Paul Elek, 1975

— and Schoder (eds), *Readings of 'The Wreck': Essays in Commemoration of the Centenary of G. M. Hopkins' 'The Wreck of the Deutschland'*, Chicago, Loyola University Press, 1976

Peters, W. A. M. (S.J.), *Gerard Manley Hopkins: a Critical Essay towards the Understanding of his Poetry*, London, Oxford University Press, 1948; repr. Oxford, Blackwell, 1970

Pick, John, *Gerard Manley Hopkins: Priest and Poet*, London, Oxford University Press, 1942; 2nd edn, Oxford Paperbacks, 1966

— (ed.), *Gerard Manley Hopkins: 'The Windhover'*, Columbus, Ohio, Merrill, 1969

Ritz, Jean-Georges, *Robert Bridges and Gerard Hopkins,*

1863–1889: a Literary Friendship, London, Oxford University Press, 1960

—, *Le Poète Gérard Manley Hopkins, S.J.: L'homme et l'oeuvre*, Paris, Didier, 1963

Ruggles, Eleanor, *Gerard Manley Hopkins: A Life*, London, John Lane, 1947

Schneider, Elisabeth, *The Dragon in the Gate: Studies in the Poetry of G. M. Hopkins*, Berkeley and Los Angeles, University of California Press, 1968

Sulloway, Alison G., *Gerard Manley Hopkins and the Victorian Temper*, London, Routledge and Kegan Paul, 1972

Thomas, Alfred (S.J.), *Hopkins the Jesuit: the Years of Training*, London, Oxford University Press, 1969

Thornton, R. K. R. (ed.), *All My Eyes See: the Visual World of Gerard Manley Hopkins*, Sunderland, Ceolfrith, 1975

Weyand, Norman (S.J.), and Raymond V. Schoder (S.J.), (eds), *Immortal Diamond: Studies in Gerard Manley Hopkins*, London, Sheed and Ward, 1949

Index I: Selected Names and Topics

(Main entries in *italics*. Hopkins abbreviated as H)

Index II: Short Titles or First Lines